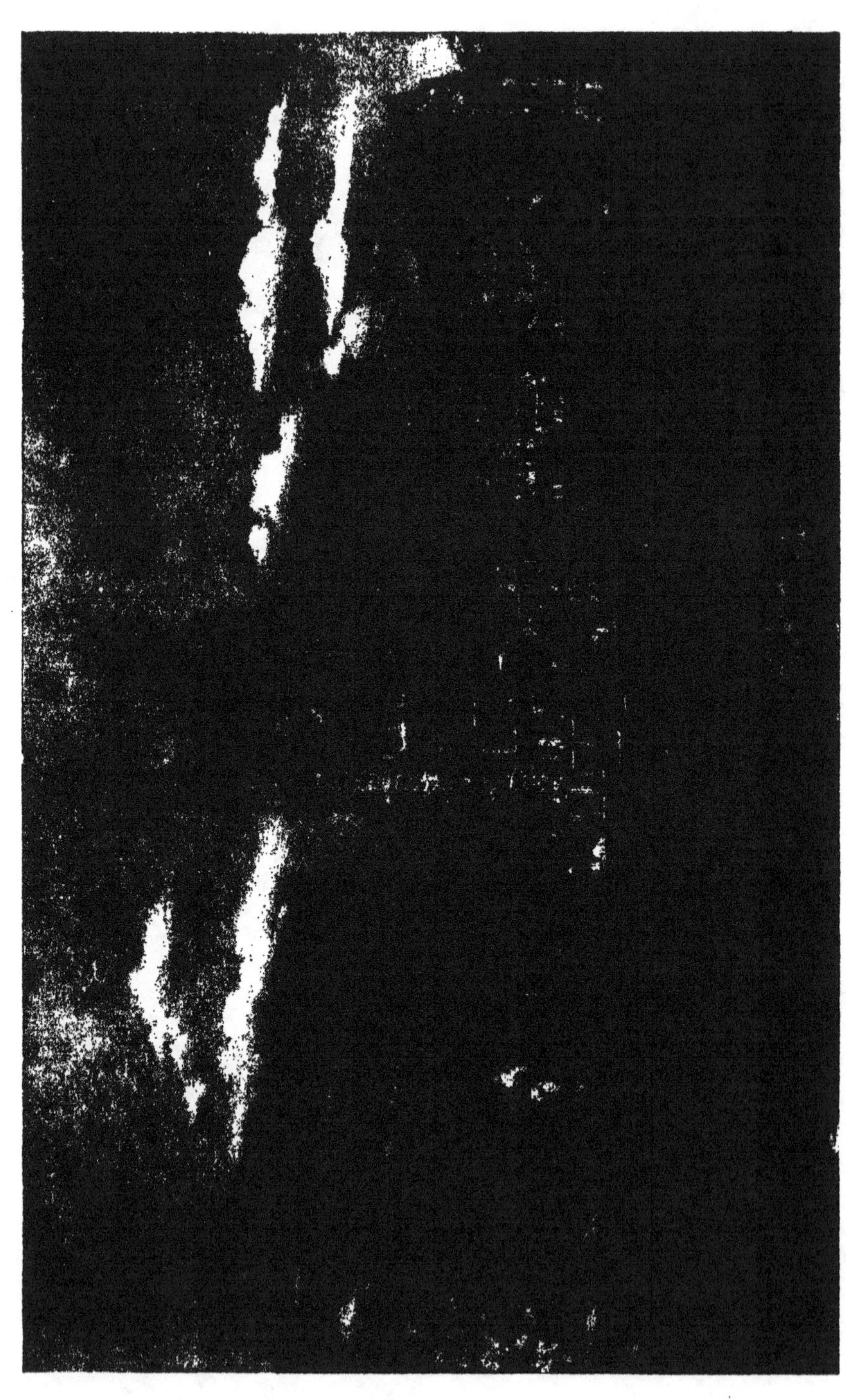

The New College

From the design by the Architect, George B. Post

The City College

Memories of Sixty Years

Edited for the

Associate Alumni

of

The College of the City of New York

By

Philip J. Mosenthal, M.S., '83

and

Charles F. Horne, Ph.D., '89

G. P. Putnam's Sons
New York and London
The Knickerbocker Press
1907

The Knickerbocker Press, New York

At the annual business meeting of the Associate Alumni of the College of the City of New York, held October 20, 1905, it was determined by resolution to publish a memorial volume to record the life and history of the old College at the time of the change to new conditions in the new buildings on St. Nicholas Heights. To carry on this work, a committee was appointed consisting of the members of the Alumni below mentioned. Messrs. Mosenthal and Horne of the committee were designated as editors.

PHILIP J. MOSENTHAL, '83, *Chairman.*
RICHARD R. BOWKER, '68,
FERDINAND SHACK, '74,
CHARLES F. HORNE, '89.

Contents

Adspice

Prospice

Illustrations

The Spirit of the College

Philip J. Mosenthal, '83

Proem

THIS book has come to be because it seems right that we make a record of the spirit of the old College before it become merged into the larger spirit of the new. A larger spirit, yes, but not a deeper one. You of generations now beginning will have wider opportunities; perhaps you will learn more things; you must learn them differently, you cannot help doing so. Since the day of many of us, and not of the oldest, men have learnt how to apply electricity and to teach psychology with a yard-stick.

The economic and the social world must change or stagnate. The world of the spirit endures and still strives for the ideals descended from the marble halls of Athens and the stable of Bethlehem.

These ideals were given us by the mothers of our bodies; they were fostered by the Benign Mother who gave us intellectual life. Our strength and our loyal service are theirs!

With this feeling of thankfulness I would try to interpret the spirit of our College. There are many who would see differently and write better; the errors will be those of love and gratitude.

The spirit of the old College will live on deep in the lives and achievements of some thousands of hard-working, clear-thinking, and straight-living citizens of this mother of cities. They have worked hard because that is what the College taught them if it never taught anything else. They have thought clearly because they were trained by a body of the best, pure *teachers* a lot of boys ever had the good luck to learn from—teachers who had no other mission but to *teach*. They have lived straight because the inspiration of their early manhood came from men to whom right living was a religion.

This republic was founded by men who worked and were free and by the work of freemen it must endure. By teaching us to toil for success and that success for the individual and the commonwealth comes through toil, we were fitted to be citizens.

As the boys, or most of them, came to work, so the teachers stayed to teach. Did we ever realize or understand the sacrifice of achievement, the loss of the chance of fame as the world counts it that lay in that persistent, painstaking teaching? Rarely less than four hours of actual instruction each day and hours more of preparation and incidental work—no teachers in any college in the land have done more. Fortunately, few have to do as much. What books are unwritten, what scientific research is unfinished because the brain grew weary, and time was not left after the hard pounding hour after hour to make boys understand! This is the debt we owe them, this is what they gave for us. Our lives, our characters, our successes are the product. Was it worth while? They must judge from the heights of duty done, from the deeps of unfulfilled ambition. We can but thank them.

They say that the men of to-day are to have a better chance. So be it. Whatever you do, you of the new College, give your men time to do their work!

But we played too. Curious, is it not? We did not come to College for a good time but we managed to have it. We did not come because it was the thing our world demanded of us so that we might prove our respectability, and nevertheless, perhaps we have proved it.

We never had a paid coach, but we played football, we boated, we did the things that boys with healthy bodies must do. We rarely won matches, indeed we did not often have the chance to try. But we played the game, whatever it was, for the game's sake. Some important institutions are just beginning to remember that that is what the game is for. Did the boys who ran races on the new avenues to the northward—they are now in the heart of town—or who played football in a vacant lot get less health and less of the keen joy of living because no stadium full of cheering thousands spurred them on to win? They played with tense muscles and full, deep breathing and with a great joy. And they won when they could.

I think that we have always had less trouble in keeping together our literary societies than our Athletic Association. Has it been said that we were weaklings?

The victories of an earlier generation of our athletes are worth recording. In the 'seventies, we held the intercollegiate records, I believe, in the mile walk and the pole vault and perhaps in other games. I have an idea that this was before the days of the higher training and when a fraction of a second taken from or an inch added to the last great effort was not a matter of newspaper extras or national pride. Since then our friendly rivals have bought with lavishness, urged by the desire to win and advertise, coaches and training systems beyond the dreams of simpler days. Our poor little records are separated by minutes and yards from the scores now remembered by college youth.

They say that we are again to become winners in intercollegiate contests. We hear that the College is to have all that heart can desire to help us do it. None will cheer louder than those who ran and played in the vacant lots. May they not then have the hope, too, that the sound bodies of the many will be developed before the records of the few?—that all may join in the game, that there may be no subventioned gladiators?

Cheering the contestants is a good, whole-souled custom, but joining the fray is better sport.

May the conquerors of the newer day remember the vanquished of the old—and may they play as hard and as fair!

We were certainly the heirs of West Point tradition. It made for work and endurance, for discipline and for standing up to face the fight of the world more than it made for the more elegant learning. We have produced few dilettanti and no idlers. But the spirit of the finer culture was not lacking. If we had the military discipline of Webster and Webb, we had the literary influence of Anthon and Barton. The base of the college work was its rigid, strenuous course in mathematics. But we were perhaps the first college in the land to have a chair in English and among the first to give equal importance to modern as to ancient languages. Since the earliest days we have taught the practice and appreciation of the fine arts. We have had an ethical and a political ideal. It is suggestive that the professor of moral and intellectual philosophy taught also economics and constitutional and international law.

The military spirit did not create in its out-working an ideal collegiate atmosphere. It made us stand upright; it gave us discipline of mind and habits; it made us more or less respecters of established authority and, within limits, law-abiding. It gave us too a sense of responsibility. As an officer is charged with the care of his men, the men of the upper classes were held to maintain the tone of the College. I think that President Webb trusted us and made us feel his trust.

But the military spirit did not tend to beauty of environment, it gave us no feeling of the holiness that makes of some college halls shrines for pilgrimage. The old College is not beautiful, however sanctified it be to many of us by association and friendship. It has never become a place of worship to which men in their age return as they must to the gray towers of Oxford or the elms of the Harvard yard.

The College was founded and given its limits before the day that the nation realized that beauty as a part of education tends to beauty as a part of life. Soul, mind, and body, all three must be trained for universal harmony.

Again, from that stern discipline came the loss to us of personal association with our teachers. Far too few of those who could have made us loyal to our College tried to do so. Far too few cared or perhaps had time to care for the human being within the pupil. This is written with a deep hope that it be not misunderstood by the men who in the hard grind of their teaching still made time to be friends with their boys. May coming generations be blessed with such friendship as was ours though from but a few. The city is full of those whose earliest inspiration came from two men, still of the College, ever laboring and ever young—and you all know who they are.

The new College is a thing of beauty and if we outside read the signs aright, the new spirit will find many men who will feel the responsibility of building up character as well as giving knowledge. They will be inspired by the noble men who thus saw their duty during fifty years. May one, high in the new order of things, forgive the indiscretion if I quote his saying to me when he was new to his task. Said he: "They want discipline—what I care about is those boys!" This was the spirit of the old College as it came to those of us who were greatly privileged. This is to be the spirit of the new College as it must come to all who have the power to feel it. Others will tell of it in the years to come.

Men from sixty college generations have joined in the writing of this book that those who are to share in the new order may not forget the older days which were good days too. They have written of what they remember as the best things in the best time of their lives. They have written of the College for the men of the College in words of a common language. Read the record in the spirit of the writing. It is not intended to be history. It may furnish the material from which some day history will be written. Whatever else it is, it is human. If it err in being personal, forgive! As men stir the embers of the fires of other years it is personality that burns with the brightest flame of fair memories.

It would be a pleasant task to thank by name those who have helped to make this book. But their names are many and the help was finely given. So be it said.

When the time of moving to the new buildings seemed to be coming near, the Associate Alumni resolved to preserve the memory of the old buildings and the life within their walls in photographs of every detail that could be taken by the camera. These pictures will be mounted in frames prepared by the architect and placed on a suitable background at the new College. From many Alumni came requests for copies. It was then decided to publish most of them in a book with suitable reading matter. The hearty co-operation of the Messrs. Putnam has made this possible. May they accept this word of appreciation.

The writer speaks in his own person that he may have the privilege of saying for the men of his College that they owe a debt of thanks to the last man who would ask for thanks. By the labor and devotion of his working fellow-editor, this record was accomplished of the life of the Benign Mother whom we would praise as we love her.

Respice

The College of the Past

The College of the Past

Richard R. Bowker, '68

"LOOK forward and not backward" is a wholesome counsel in the conduct of life. But an institution must be judged somewhat in the light of its past, from which its present has developed and which emphasizes to some extent its future. "*Respice—Adspice—Prospice*," the motto suggested by Prof. Charles E. Anthon for the College of the City of New York, tells the whole story, and in the critical change in the affairs of the College of which this volume is a memorial, it is peculiarly fitting that there should be first of all a retrospect of what the College has been as we look forward to what the College is to be.

The story of public education in New York City is almost an epitome of the history of its general development in this country. Public education was first a matter of private enterprise, and it is interesting to note that the earliest provisions for it had to do with the higher education. This was especially true in New York. King's College was in fact a child of the State, and when, in 1784, after the Revolution, "the Colledge of the Province of New York," as it was also called, was revived as Columbia College, under which name it is to-day making New York the seat of a great university, it was at first proposed to call it definitively the State College, and eight State and city officials were included in its governing body. Its munificent endowment of 24,000 acres was a gift of the province, made in 1767, and when, in the early part of the nineteenth century, after the cession of those lands to Vermont, this was replaced by the magnificent estate in the upper part of the city which is the foundation of its present fortune, the State added also a money donation of ten thousand dollars. In recognition of its origin, Columbia has always made provision for free scholarships for boys from the public schools; but it was, and still is, under certain restrictions of a particular religious denomination, and the time soon came when public opinion demanded that the city of New York should include, in its system of public education, a collegiate institution free in every sense of the word.

Public education on the elementary side received its first development in New York at the hands of a voluntary association of citizens, the old Public School Society, whose noble work was really the foundation of the magnificent system of grammar school instruction which exists in New York to-day. That Society was started in 1804, and it was not until 1853 that its "public-schools" and the ward schools were united into one system, under the control of the Board of

The Old College

The Students, just dismissed, are issuing from the Twenty-third Street Entrance. The Old Campus extended well out in front of the building, but has been twice reduced in size and the sidewalk broadened. The Ivy is a growth of the last thirty years.

Education, organized on lines not dissimilar from those of the present Board. The schools of the Society, intended originally as charity-schools for the poor, had proved so excellent that the children of the rich also knocked at their doors, until at last the people were glad to undertake the responsibility of providing for their support by public taxation, and making them a place where the rich and the poor should indeed meet together. In the meantime, from as early as 1826, there had been proposals for a Latin school, a high school, a normal school—the movement assuming different phases with different years. It was after the organization of the Board of Education, however, that definite steps were taken for the foundation of that institution for the higher education which has since become the College of the City of New York. Townsend Harris, whose name is interestingly associated with the earliest American relations with Japan, has been properly regarded as the real founder of the College, as is acknowledged in the naming in his honor of the first of the new college buildings to be finished. It was on his motion that a committee was appointed July 27, 1846, to report upon a plan which took final shape when, under a legislative act of May 7, 1847, the people of New York, in the school and judicial election of June, 1847, decided, by a vote of 19,455 to 3409, that they would establish the New York Free Academy. In November, 1847, the building for the Free Academy was commenced, and on the 15th of January, 1849, one hundred and forty-three boys, picked representatives of the public and ward schools of New York, assembled in the chapel of the completed building as the first class of the Free Academy. The original building still stands, with its curious buttresses and corner turrets, at the corner of Lexington Avenue and Twenty-third Street, a monument to New Yorkers of a city frugality which has not been the rule in later years. The building should be doubly famous from the fact that it cost actually two thousand dollars less than the appropriation of fifty thousand dollars, and that its cost per cubic foot, nine cents, was less than that of any building for public purposes ever erected in New York City. The cost of the ground was but twenty-five thousand dollars, making the total investment, including furnishing, considerably less than one hundred thousand dollars. Except that the stucco and paint, which gave it a make-believe effect of stone, have of late years been removed, and the brick construction honestly shown at the surface, the building is to-day what it was sixty years ago; and, although the attendance at the College has doubled several times, as college generations have passed, it still serves for the main work of the institution, with the additions only of a laboratory building to the east, and a class-room building with a Natural History hall, which takes up some of the space originally the "yard." But it is no longer above the centre of population as once it was, nor can its professors and students look across green fields

Lexington Avenue Façade.
Showing on the right the house in which President Webb resided for many years.

southward, over Gramercy Park; westward, beyond Madison Square; northward, to Rose Hill, now Twenty-seventh Street, with its few houses; and eastward clear to the East River. Nor can the boys go home "across lots," at the venture of a fracas with the roughs frequenting Stuyvesant Square, nor steal away for a half hour for a swim in the unfrequented river. The city long ago outgrew its bounds of those days, and has moved northward beyond the imagination of any man of the '40's, and soon the College will no longer be "cribb'd, cabined, and confined," on its old site in narrow quarters.

From the beginning, the school officers who proposed the Academy, the legislature which authorized it, the people who established it, had held firmly to two ideas which were clearly set forth in the report of the first Executive Committee for the government of the Academy. They meant to establish an institution which, on the one hand, "in the character, kind, and value of the education imparted, should be inferior to none of our colleges," and on the other, "should be so organized that the course of studies to be pursued would tend to educate the pupils practically, and particularly qualify them to apply their learning to advance and perfect the operations of the various trades and occupations in which they may engage, and to furnish peculiar facilities for instruction of the highest order in the various branches of knowledge omitted altogether, or not practically taught, in our colleges." These two ideas are developed in the original course of studies. "This institution," said those who drew the curriculum, "unlike other academies, is intended to be a substitute for both the academy and the college, offering to its pupils the means of general education now furnished by both these institutions together. Its course of studies, therefore, should be liberal, and embrace those both of the ordinary academy and the college." These purposes were furthered by prefixing to the usual four college classes a fifth class, known originally as the Introductory class, and later as the sub-Freshman, which was really a connecting link between the schools and the college proper. Throughout its development the College has not only held fast to these ideas, but it has been saved by them from aping a university, and from running riot in elective studies as so many of its sister colleges have done. It has held to the belief that during the academic and early collegiate years the student's work should be planned for him by those competent to survey the general field of education, as the student himself is not. Only in the Junior and Senior years are "electives" permitted. But from the start the College has ingeniously met the diverse needs of students of diverse aims by providing, in place of optional studies, alternative curricula, each assuring a broad acquaintance with general knowledge, but specializing in the specific direction of the choice of the student or his parents. From the beginning, therefore, there were a classical course and a scientific course, to

Lexington Avenue Front

A closer view, with a group of "sub-freshmen," the raw material upon which the College works.

which later was added a mechanical course. The original distinction was that the ancient languages (with one optional modern language) included in the classical course were replaced in the scientific course by three modern languages. The students of the respective courses were commonly known as the "ancients" and the "moderns," which was indeed a more correct nomenclature. In later years the two courses developed on more distinctive lines. A mechanical course was established, which, while omitting a few of the studies in the other courses, embraced actual shop practice in the use of tools, as well as studies in mechanical theory.

The course of studies originally outlined included in the first year elementary Latin, which elsewhere was a part of the academic preparation for college, the elements of a modern language, book-keeping, phonography, and drawing—certainly an unusual combination of studies for that day.

In another sense, the College was the child of West Point, and it adopted West Point traditions of strict discipline and the importance of higher mathematics, of drawing, and of thorough training in English. Its first president, Horace Webster, was a graduate of West Point in the class of '18, and its first professor of mathematics, Ross, was also a West Pointer. The organizers of the College were indeed fortunate in gathering, as the first faculty, a remarkable body of men. In those days class instruction was given almost entirely by the professors, and their personal influence was therefore direct and efficient. The first president, who ruled with a rod of iron for twenty years, is remembered by his students for his distinguished bearing, his high faith in the future of the College and his earnest devotion to its interests, his strict, indeed dogmatic, views of discipline, his wholesome intolerance of laziness and carelessness.

"Ye students think how great a man is he
Who can at once Horace and Webster be,"

was the amusing tribute of the college poet; but "the Doctor" was rather a combination of Cato and Andrew Jackson. He stamped his mark indelibly on the College and upon the students of his time, as a man who looms up in memory as the years go by.

The first president was succeeded by General Alexander S. Webb, another graduate of West Point and a veteran of the Civil War, and these two men, Webster and Webb, in the presidential chair, span the whole history of the College up to 1902. In that year General Webb retired, and Professor Alfred G. Compton, an alumnus of the first class to graduate from the College, served as acting president of the institution for a year. In September, 1903, Dr. John H. Finley, formerly president of Knox College and later professor of politics at Princeton, was inaugurated as president on the same day with the laying of the corner-stone of the College of the future on St. Nicholas Heights.

The faculty, consisting originally of ten men, has

THE LEXINGTON AVENUE ENTRANCE

This entrance has for sixty years been held sacred for visitors and the instructing corps. The diamond-shaped window immediately over the door sheds light into "Cana's den," the tiny office of the sore-tried Registrar.

been enlarged again and again with the growing needs of the institution, until to-day it includes twelve professors who are heads of departments, fifteen associate professors, and ten assistant professors. These, moreover, are assisted by a staff of instructors numbering over a hundred and forty.

The relation of the College to New York life is thorough and vital. Its fifty-seven classes have given more or less training to about thirty thousand students, and though its 2659 living alumni (out of 2911 in all) are found from Maine to California, and in such distant centres as London, Beirut, Foochow, Sidney, and Hawaii, over two thousand are recorded as remaining in New York City, and probably a thirtieth of the entire male population of the city, above the age of fifteen, have been students in the College. Nearly every family in New York, except among the latest immigrants, has had directly or indirectly some knowledge of the advantages of the College, and it is therefore not surprising that one of the several attacks made upon it was met by a memorial in its favor signed by fifty-five thousand citizens. Many of its students come from the poorest classes, the fathers working harder that their boys may have a "better chance" than themselves, and of these many are the children of foreign parents who speak little if any English, for whom the public schools and the College are the living link between the bright future which they seek for their children, and the dark past from which they have escaped. Of late years foreign names have been more and more predominant on the roll and among the honor men—direct proof of the assimilating influence of our public school and college training, and of the peculiar value of the chair of English in the City College. The students lack dormitory life, but as an offset they are constant centres of unconscious development in their own homes, when they belong to the less developed part of the community; and the continued association in the schools, in the College, and in business life has developed friendships which knit together usefully a great many of New York's most effective citizens as the men of no other college are knit together.

The same influence has been exerted usefully upon and through the public school system, although the College has not even yet developed its full powers as a guiding force in our system of public education. The City College has been virtually a normal college for men, and in this way has also greatly influenced the public school system. Three members of the Board of Education (and numerous ex-members) beside many of the superintendents, principals, and male teachers in the city schools, and professors and instructors in the College, are City College men. More than twenty per cent of its graduates have returned to be teachers in the public schools which educated them, and the College has also sent professors to Yale, Columbia, Princeton, Johns Hopkins, Pennsylvania, California University, the Stevens Institute, Roberts College (Constanti-

Basement Hall from Lexington Avenue

Showing the inside of the Professorial Entrance, with letter-boxes, janitor's chair, and entrance to janitor's apartments on side.

nople), the Anglo-Chinese College (Foochow), and other universities and educational institutions.

For many years the entrance examinations at the College offered annually an opportunity of test and of contest which aided in keeping the several public schools well up to the highest standards. The masters of the upper classes made personal reputations through the boys whom they sent up to college, a fact which proved usefully stimulating throughout the public school service. For many years admission could be obtained only through the public schools, a premium on these city schools which since 1882 has no longer been felt necessary, and the writer is one of many who passed a year in public schools for the express purpose of entering the College. Many boys came up for examination simply to obtain the credentials which the certificate of admission afforded, and many others, unable to take time for the full course, have had a year or more of college training to their permanent benefit. The large number of boys who have had this partial advantage, in comparison with those who have achieved their degrees, is one of the best proofs of the usefulness of the College. The entrance examinations, at first oral, were soon made written, as the throng became too large to be handled orally; and of recent years the ancient custom has been perforce abandoned entirely and students are admitted on presentation of a public school certificate of graduation. All applicants, however, must still survive one of the former tests. They are given a probationary trial of eight weeks, during which those who would be absolutely in the way of their fellow-students are definitely weeded out. The written examinations, which demand good spelling and good form in writing as part of their requirements, have done much to safeguard the College against the deficiencies in the elementary branches as to which there has been so much recent complaint from our more famous colleges. An applicant was formerly required to be fourteen years of age, and a resident of the city of New York; he must "pass" in writing, spelling, the English language, arithmetic, geography, the history of the United States, and industrial drawing. These are all "common sense" studies. At the entrance examinations which were held in June, the applicants often exceeded twelve hundred; no one was permitted to be present save instructors and Trustees, and the examiners were permitted to know the candidates and their papers only by numbers.

As soon as the student entered, he was in past years subjected to a discipline unusually strict. The first president had military ideas as to certain routine virtues, such as punctuality and application, which have remained fundamental principles in the College. Every student must be punctually in his seat at "chapel," so called; no "cuts" were allowed, and if a student were absent for whatever cause for more than one day in a term, he was obliged to make up his lost work by examination. In fact the whole theory of the College

THE JANITOR'S OFFICE
The Second Generation of Bonney's.

centres on what a man *does*, not on what he ***might*** do if he had not been late or absent or at other disadvantage—a faithful premonition of the hard tests of life. A two weeks' oral and written examination, in January, reviews the work of the first term; a similar examination, in June, extends over ten days and is mostly in writing.

The system of demerit marks long in force, somewhat childish in one sense, had a certain advantage in keeping before men the fact that conduct and punctuality, as well as scholarship, are to count in after life. One hundred demerit marks in a term, or 175 within the year, caused a student to be dropped from the rolls. Recently Dr. Finley has done away with the demerit system and established a reliance upon student honor, a harmony between instructor and instructed, which is more in consonance with modern educational ideas.

Through the early years the college day always opened with the "chapel exercises," over which the first president presided with an iron will for twenty years. Beyond a reading of a chapter in the Bible, which gave opportunity for mischievous Freshmen to replace "the Doctor's" bookmark, so that for days at a time he read over the chapter on Shadrach, Meshach, and Abednego, there has been no distinctively religious feature. But punctually at 8.40, on pain of "five demerits" if late, each student was required to be in his place, duly noted by the "head of the section," and listen to "senior oration," "junior oration," and "sophomore declamation." The Doctor's "Time's up!" was the awful conclusion to the unhappy student who took more than his allotted five minutes for stammering speech or too prolific rhetoric, and his "That will do" imposed a still more awful penalty on the unfortunates who forgot their "orations," which had always to be delivered *memoriter*. The chapel, which occupies the entire top of the building, remains to-day almost as it was at the beginning, except that then but a portion of it was occupied by the students, whereas in later years only a portion of them could be crowded into its space and some of the sub-Freshmen assembled elsewhere. It has been the scene of a good part of the college pranks. A dog or a goat would occasionally appear among the subjects for instruction and the coat-rooms ranged under its eves were a place of refuge from wrath to come. One of the corner-rooms communicating with the turrets, which reach from bottom to top of the building, was the scene of the college legend of "the striped trousers." The chapel was used in early days for the "study-hour" of the students who had no recitation specified for the time, and once an enterprising group let one of their number down by a rope through the turret, to the astonishment of a professor and his class, as a pair of striped trousers kicked their way vigorously through the little window placed in the turrets for purposes of ventilation. The professor immediately aroused "the Doctor," and both together started on a search for the culprit. By the

Janitor's Apartments
The Third Generation of Bonney's.

time they had reached the corner cloak-room and obtained entrance through the barricaded door, the wearer of the striped trousers had found time to exchange with some other of the party and the man who was promptly identified by the professor as promptly swore out an alibi.

When in 1861 the war swept over the country and carried away on its crimson flood the flower of our youth, the College had graduated but eight classes, and had perhaps two hundred alumni. Of these two hundred, some forty went to war, and the class of '61 and succeeding classes gave up their best men. A modest tablet in the College commemorates the sacrifice of Grey, Wightman, Crosby, Van Buren, Young, Keith, and Elliott, the last the valedictorian of his class, *facile princeps* among the men who had up to that time graduated. When Elliott fell on Lookout Mountain, the most brilliant man the College had yet produced sacrificed a life full of promise. The name of Weed, who fell on the second day at Gettysburg, is not on the tablet, because he was credited to West Point and is commemorated in its chapel. Others, like Tremain, Van Buren and McKibbin, won their stars as brevet brigadier-generals, and as commanders of military districts aided to restore order to the country they had aided in saving for the Union. While these men were in the field those remaining did their duty at home, Professor Wolcott Gibbs in especial being one of the foremost men on the Sanitary Commission. The war had also its effect on the college course. West Point textbooks on military engineering and on ordnance and gunnery were introduced, and these studies remained in the curriculum for some years after the war.

In 1866 the original title of the New York Free Academy was changed by the Legislature to the College of the City of New York. The change recognized the real standing of the institution, but happily it did not affect its combination of high school with college. The Introductory class remained as the sub-Freshman, affording to boys who otherwise would be in schools of an academic grade the considerable advantage of direct intercourse with and oversight from the college faculty. The professor of chemistry and physics, for instance, delivered two lectures a week throughout the year to the boys of the sub-Freshman class, and thus interested them directly in science; and other professors had also more or less direct relations of the same nature. The course of studies has developed somewhat from time to time, but the wisdom of the founders has been shown by the fact that it has required so little change to keep the College "up to the times." The most important change during many years was the development of a mechanical course with work-shop practice under the charge of Professor Compton.

Long since the College has outgrown its shell, but the old building was admirably arranged for its original purpose—the whole top floor the "chapel," an impressive, pillared room, with nave and aisles and great

TWENTY-THIRD STREET ENTRANCE.

Through this doorway have passed over sixty successive classes of students. More than once delinquents of a little learning have scrawled across its yawning front: "All hope abandon ye who enter here."

dows at either end; the other stories divided by a main hall lengthwise and a stairway hall crosswise, into four divisions, each containing two or three spacious lecture-rooms. On the first floor these four sections are given respectively to the president's and faculty rooms, the library, the chemistry lecture-room, and the laboratory. The basement floor gives janitor's rooms, store-rooms, and workshops for the mechanical course. Curiously enough, "Room No. 1," in which for his entire term President Webster, as professor of philosophy, delivered his lectures to the Senior class, was in these depths, occupying the space now devoted to the workshops. But the spacious class-rooms had soon to be cut up, one after another, into smaller rooms to accommodate the increasing throng of students. In 1870 an additional building, including, besides recitation-rooms, a gathering-place for the lower classes, and a good natural history hall, was erected, and an extension to the main building has also afforded opportunity for a better laboratory in which students can do individual work. But with all these makeshifts the College has been cramped at every turn. The excellent library, containing above 37,000 volumes, became almost useless by lack of space, and the collections, containing 75,000 specimens, have been housed here and there about the buildings to the very last corner, while valuable physical apparatus suffered equally for want of room. With the new provision for the city's great educational institution, it should be possible to put these several collections at the service of the public as well as of the students proper, and it is to be hoped, also, that the college buildings may become a centre of university extension, and thus increase the vital relations of the College with the population of the metropolis.

When the College opened, its site was more than a mile above the city's centre of population, and in 1851, two years later, only 57 out of its 382 students lived north of Twenty-third Street. At the turn of the century the old site was more than a mile below the city's centre of population, and that population was several times what it was in 1848. Forty years ago it was proposed to move the College uptown, to where the Seventh Regiment Armory now stands, or to Reservoir Square. Both of those sites were already too far downtown, and the movement for removal took final shape in a plan for a site well to the north, about where the centre of population will be in the early part of the present century. The old college site, which even with the addition of the Twenty-second Street plot, cost only $37,000, is now valued at a dozen times that amount. It was "manifest destiny" that the College should take part in the northward movement of all our educational institutions.

One by one the alumni of the College and then other citizens of our metropolis began to recognize the pressing needs of this their favorite educational institution. Their united efforts resulted finally in 1895 in the passage of a bill by the State Legislature which

Inside View of Students' Entrance.

In this hallway, whose gloom doubtless first suggested the association of the entrance with Dante's gate, the students gather between hours. To the right are the various bulletin boards, and posted notices; to the left the professorial entrance and the drinking place.

authorized the erection of the new college buildings now standing on St. Nicholas Heights. A thousand obstacles, some foreseen, others unforeseen, delayed the acquirement of the site and the construction of the buildings. Meanwhile the crowded conditions in Twenty-third Street became unbearable. Rooms were partitioned off by curtains in the chapel; classes recited in the old "faculty room," once reserved solely for the deliberations of that august body. Finally even the library, already overflowing, was pressed into service, and a class-room partitioned off among its shelves.

The first definite move toward relieving this congestion took place in 1899, when the authorities leased for the College the upper floor of the two-story addition to the Metropolitan Life Building on Twenty-third Street between Fourth and Madison avenues. To this temporary annex were transferred ten "sections" of students, and the groaning floors of the main building found some slight relief.

The respite was but brief. Other changes were impending about the College, sufficient to make the year 1900 an epoch in its growth, a year as important as that which brought to it the name and dignity of a college.

In 1900 was passed the law which removed the College from under the supervision of the New York Board of Education and placed it under trustees of its own. These trustees were made ten in number, nine to be appointed by the mayor of the city, the other to be the president of the Board of Education. This was dreaded by some as holding within it a possibility of the weakening of the associations connecting the College with the public school system, a danger which fortunately has proved illusory. On the other hand, it withdrew the College from the care of a large group of overworked gentlemen not always in sympathy with its needs, and placed its guidance in the hands of a compact body of select men, several of them its own alumni, and all devoted to its welfare.

The advantages of this more concentrated control have been made most happily manifest not only in the construction of the new college, but in the government of the old. Modern education had made such advances that a change notable and far reaching was being forced upon the College from without. High schools had been established by the city and, their four-year course of study being only a single year shorter than that at the College, the older institution was brought into obvious competition with the new ones. Moreover, colleges everywhere throughout the country were being sharply separated from the so-called "secondary schools" and were demanding four years of high school study as a preliminary to "college" work. The extra pressure put upon students at the City College, and the more numerous hours of recitation, had long been held to make the course equivalent to a more extended one elsewhere, but the discrepancy was growing too great. Finally the New York State Board of Regents warned the college

BASEMENT CORRIDOR, LOOKING SOUTH.

This view, the reverse of the preceding, shows the passage out to the rear yard, and also the stairway by which the students ascend.

authorities that unless the course was enlarged they would refuse to recognize the college degrees. Under this urgency changes were made. The old plea of heavier work was still admitted, and in consequence the Regents did not ask that the course be extended to eight years, but agreed that seven were sufficient. They also approved of the change being made gradually. It began its operation in 1900. The students entering in June, 1899, and graduating in 1904 formed the last five-year class. The practice was begun of admitting the public school graduates twice a year, in February as well as in June. A class was thus begun in February, 1900, and graduated in June, 1905, after five and a half years. The class of 1906 spent six years in the institution; that of 1907 entered in February, 1901. Not until 1908 will the graduating students have had the full seven years' tuition. And after that the College, since it has continued the policy of welcoming students in February, must face the problem of graduating them in that month also and possibly having two "Commencements" each year.

This change has of course greatly altered the old system at the College. The former "sub-Freshman class" has been extended over three years and is known as the "academic department." Its entering class is known as lower C, then, after six months, as upper C, then come lower and upper B, and lower and upper A. From A there are regular graduation exercises and a formula of admission into the four-year course of the College proper. Professor John R. Sim has been made "professor in charge" of the academic department.

This increase in the number of the lower grades has resulted in a temporary displacement of the centre of gravity in the College. There are many lower-class students; while in the upper classes, spread apart to cover the gap between five years and seven, the men are comparatively less numerous. But this disproportion will balance itself in another two years, and the classes resume a more normal relation as to size.

Turning again to the practical conditions which the College faced in 1900, one can readily imagine how the increasing number of classes accentuated the crowded condition of affairs. The annex in the Metropolitan building soon proved too small, and in February, 1901, the building was abandoned and a larger one was leased. This new annex, known as the Cass building, was situated on the north side of Twenty-third Street (No. 209) between Third and Second avenues. During the period of shifting, afternoon sessions were held in the old buildings; and then the Cass building was put hurriedly into use with temporary paper muslin partitions marking off the rooms, and with instructors' voices ringing from end to end of the crowded floors. The new annex, when arrangements were completed, had space for over a thousand students; yet within a year it was overcrowded and still further room required. A second building, the Beach, was therefore leased (Feb., 1902)

A Snap-Shot of the Third President.

Here in the basement hall the President is discussing with a group of students their lateness and the unwisdom thereof.

on Twenty-third Street between Lexington Avenue and Fourth.

With these two annexes the College continued until 1905. But the two thousand students of 1901 had increased to three thousand and beyond. One night the Beach building was gutted by fire, and the expedient of afternoon sessions was perforce resorted to again. After that there was no escaping them, and the Cass building had regular afternoon classes from one o'clock till five.

Fortunately the uptown structures were approaching completion. The Beach building was abandoned in the spring of 1905. Townsend Harris Hall was made ready for some portion of the academic department, and in September, 1905, began the gradual transference of the students to their new home. Only the academic A's and B's were sent there at first; and students and instructors worked amid the clang of hammers, without doors to their rooms, often without glass in the window openings. On cold days everybody was sent home.

In September, 1906, the buildings were so far advanced that it was possible for them to accommodate the entire academic department. All of those students were established there and the Cass building, last of the downtown annexes, became, so far as the College is concerned, a tradition of the past.

The alteration in the length of the college course made necessarily an alteration in its course of study. After careful deliberation and consultation with the faculty, the trustees separated the old three courses into five. These were established in September, 1901. Three led to the degree of B. A. and are known as the Language Course, Classical; the Language Course, Latin and French; and the Language Course, Modern. The other two, leading to the degree of B. S., are the Scientific Course, and the Scientific Course, Mechanical. Of these the first, third, and fifth may be regarded as enlargements of the old Classical, Scientific, and Mechanical Courses. Still another scientific course has recently been added.

With such training and with the thoroughness which has always been insisted on in every branch, it is no wonder that the City College man is distinctively a worker. The strict discipline and effective scholarship of the College are well shown in the after-record of its men, particularly in the professional schools of New York. Not many of its graduates have become ministers, but the other professions have taken a good number, and these men have won a large share of the prizes in the New York professional schools. Of the college graduates studying in the School of Mines, in the years for which records are at hand, City College men numbered sixteen per cent. and took forty-three per cent. of the prizes. Perhaps the Civil Service examinations at the New York Custom House prove the most interesting test. A report of 1882 stated that "applicants educated at the New York Free Academy have been so signally successful that they have been

The Engine Room.

A portion of the basement seldom revealed to students. Herein the fires of the institution are kept aglow.

placed in a distinct class." Out of 377 applicants up to 1880, fourteen were educated at the College; the general average of all applicants was 64 per cent., against which the City College men had reached the average of 82 per cent., the men of special technological education coming next with 80 per cent., those of other colleges following with 69 per cent., those of academic education with 68 per cent., those with free-school education with 61 per cent., and those educated in business colleges with 59 per cent. Here is the best of evidence both that education tells in practical life and that the College of the City of New York has held its own in general education.

The excellent mathematical and scientific training of the College was not only serviceable during the war, but has given its men an advantage in the army, and in engineering life and scientific work generally. Major Michaelis, of '62, who enlisted as a private in the first month of the war, was the first civilian to pass examination for admission into the Ordnance Corps, one of the two blue ribbon divisions of the army, in which the honor men of West Point find place. Many of the students of the College after a partial course there have won their way by competitive examination to West Point or Annapolis, and thus, though lost to the College records, have taken its training into those fields of life. Cleveland Abbe, at Washington; Ira Remsen at Baltimore; Edward W. Scripture at Yale; J. Bach McMaster at Princeton; Bashford Dean and Charles L.

Poor at Columbia; Robert F. Weir at the College of Physicians and Surgeons; Charles Derleth at the University of California; Frank Schlesinger at the Meadville Observatory, and W. E. Geyer at the Stevens Institute, are among the men who stand in science as its representatives.

The College has no dormitory life, but it has strong society spirit. In the early days the "Amphilogian" set the example which was followed by the "Clionian" and "Phrenocosmian," the two literary societies of to-day, which semi-annually meet in joint debate in the college chapel in contention for a prize. The Amphilogian limited its membership to the first class, but its men for several years kept up the memory of the past by a rowboat excursion to Riker's Island, where they "celebrated" under the shade of cedar groves which are now no more. The first Greek letter society, the Sigma Xi, was also a '53 society, but later came Alpha Delta Phi, Delta Kappa Epsilon, Phi Gamma Delta, Theta Delta Chi, and others of more recent date, in which fraternities the New York chapters have taken a prominent part. In opposition to these the Manhattan League, one of the anti-secret societies, was early established, and later a chapter of the Delta Upsilon. For the present the secret societies have no opposition societies, but the one evil which is associated with them, the domination of college politics, has never been marked in the City College. The most distinctive student organization,

The Engineer's Apartments.
Mr. Reid, the Chief Engineer.

perhaps, was the so-called "Senate," which was an endeavor by the present writer with others to establish, in 1866, a form of self-government among the students, which afterwards took root and grew to success at Amherst, Michigan, and other colleges. This was probably the first attempt of the kind; but it was vigorously repressed by the first president, whose military methods permitted of no democratic independence. Among Dr. Finley's recent progressive efforts has been the re-establishment of this old idea in the shape of a "students' council." This is composed of representatives from all the college classes, and already it takes no small part in the control and guidance of the student body. The Gamma chapter of New York of the Phi Beta Kappa was established at the College in 1868, only Union College and the University having at that time chapters of this venerable but not very secret society. Soon afterwards the Delta chapter was established at Columbia and now a number of the leading colleges of the State have charters from that honored fraternity of scholars.

In athletics the City College has not made a great name for itself. Forty years since, before baseball had become professionalized, its nine held the championship among the college clubs with which it had come in contact, and the Harlem and Passaic rivers afforded opportunity for very amateurish boat-clubs and "excursions." Twenty years ago its lacrosse team stood deservedly prominent among college teams; and to-day its basket-ball players are achieving a temporary glory. But the fact that the College recruits itself largely from the poorer classes has perhaps made impossible the development of a set of men who could give themselves chiefly or largely to athletics. Clubs of many kinds, for music, chess, cross-country running, natural history, etc., have flourished more or less.

The City College, though it has never attempted a "school of journalism" has always been more or less a school for journalists, and several of its men have gone into that profession, partly as a result of their training as editors of college publications. The "Cosmopolitan" and the "Free Academy Monthly," published so long ago as 1861, were among the earliest college magazines, and "The Collegian" of 1866, conducted by the present writer, was one of the earliest examples of modern college journalism proper. Another paper of the same name was started in 1875, and in 1876 "The College Echo" was issued. None of these papers survived the college life of their first editors, if so long; but in March, 1880, appeared the first issue of "The College Mercury," which is still in existence and which has been one of the most creditable of college journals. The early "Collegian" and the later "Mercury" both showed so much independence that their editors were more or less subject to criticism and discipline of the authorities. But the "Mercury" has now outlived seven college generations and is so organized

First Floor Corridor, Looking South.

This shows the heads of the two stairways rising from the basement. To the right is the Trophy Case and the entrance to the library and offices. Along the southward corridor are the frames in which students' marks were formerly posted. Above these are portraits of former professors. Overhead is the ancient bell, to ring which was once the highest ambition of disorder.

as to insure a safe prospect of continuity. Besides these papers the College has had an unusual number of skits and burlesque papers, under various names, and its student literature also includes an annual devoted to the various societies, known as "The Microcosm," and a considerable supply of song-books, burlesque programmes, and the like. It is a pity that a full collection of the earlier among these student publications was not preserved in the college library, for a first aim of a college librarian should be to provide the most complete collection possible of the student as well as the official publications of the college. In 1904 was started the "City College Quarterly," an alumni publication of which Professor Lewis F. Mott, head of the department of English, is now the editor. The solid nature of the Quarterly, and of the alumni support behind it, gives promise of its permanence.

The College is very large in numbers, having at the fall opening in 1906 over 3,900 students. The lower classes have always been the largest, for the severity of the course soon results in the "survival of the fittest" only. It takes a really able man to complete the work. Moreover, this decrease in numbers is, in another sense, an essential feature of the relations of the College to the community, and suggests how many boys come to it for such collegiate education as they can get, and drop out necessarily to take their places in the work-a-day world. The College gives them plenty of work while they are there, for one of its statisticians has computed that the total hours of actual college work, namely 2960 hours in the four collegiate classes, is larger in the College of the City of New York than in any other American institution. Yet many of the students earn their education by the hardest kinds of work. A number, of course, pursue a frequent plan of college students, in giving lessons of one sort or another, but others among past or present students have really lived two lives, one of study, one of work. One student earned his living by a milk wagon round before the college day opened; another sold morning papers; another notable example acted as night watchman in a store in which he lodged, and gave private lessons to earn food and clothes; another worked half the night in the post-office and yet maintained a high standing in his class. Other students, as waiters in summer hotels or telegraph operators during the summer, have made it possible for them to become college graduates. The Associate Alumni as an organization early founded a Students' Aid Fund, which is in the hands of five trustees, Professor Compton, Professor Sim, John Hardy, Everett P. Wheeler, and Ferdinand Shack. From this fund loans are made to students, to be repaid in later life.

The college year runs on steadily, with a break for the first term review examinations, until it culminates of course in the high festival of Commencement Week. This is enlivened by the prize debate between representatives of the college literary societies, by the prize

First Floor Corridor, Looking toward the Library.

Pictures of many graduating classes are grouped along the walls. Professor Draper's portrait is on the left. At the extreme end is the ancient registrar's "den."

speaking, by the social meeting of the Associate Alumni, and by Commencement itself, when the extraordinary number of prizes and medals which have been showered upon the College by would-be benefactors are distributed from the stage to the heroes of the hour. These prizes include gold and silver Pell medals, for general proficiency; gold and silver Cromwell medals, for history and belles-lettres; the twenty bronze Ward medals; the two gold Riggs medals, for English essays; the two gold and silver Claflin medals, for proficiency in the classics; the Ketchum prizes, for excellence in philosophy; the Devoe prizes, for handicraft; the Mason Carnes prizes, for translations from modern dramatic literature, and other prizes almost beyond number. The six honor men who represent the college training as orators of the night usually show to the large audiences which crowd Carnegie Hall good common-sense results of their course, and as a matter of fact few citizens of New York, who either in this way or by more careful observation learn what the College of the City of New York really is, would fail to desire that this institution should have the means for growth and progress which will keep it at the forefront in the work which it has been organized to do.

The First President

Horace Webster—the First President

Everett P. Wheeler, '56

HORACE WEBSTER was the first president of the College of the City of New York, which in his time was known as the New York Free Academy. Its original name was suggested by that of the Military Academy at West Point, and it was very natural that its first president should be a West Point man.

Dr. Webster was born in Hartford, Vermont, on the 21st of September, 1794. This little village stands in the beautiful Connecticut valley. In the New England States at that time Vermont filled the place which was afterwards taken by the far West, and enterprising emigrants, especially from Connecticut, Massachusetts, and New Hampshire, found their way into the fertile valleys of what afterwards became the Green Mountain State. Webster's parents were of this hardy and courageous stock. When he was born the Constitution of the United States had just been adopted. Into the more perfect Union thus effected Vermont was admitted in 1791. The boy grew up amidst a proud, high-spirited race of mountaineers. He knew the men who had fought at Bennington and Saratoga and he learned to feel, as they felt, the blessings of the Union and the necessity of a strong central government which should ensure to the people domestic tranquillity and efficient administration.

He had his first lessons in the free district schools of Vermont. He received an appointment as cadet at West Point about the close of the war of 1812. He graduated in 1818 at the head of his class and was appointed assistant professor of mathematics in the Military Academy, which post he filled until 1826. There he imbibed those lessons "of work done squarely and unwasted days" which he inculcated in the Free Academy, and which have been its unbroken tradition from that time to this.

His success as an instructor at West Point was so signal that in 1826 he was appointed the first professor of mathematics and intellectual philosophy at Hobart, then Geneva, College, which place he filled from 1826 to 1848. He was always a strict disciplinarian, and could not tolerate any neglect or indolence in his students. In his sharp, quick, military manner he would snap up the man who came to the class-room without preparation, except that derived from his inner consciousness. On the other hand, he loved the faithful student, encouraged him in every way, and was always ready after graduation by every means in his power to aid the graduate to achieve success.

When in 1848 the Free Academy was about to begin its work, the Board of Education selected Horace

Horace Webster

Webster to be its first president. He served the city faithfully in this capacity for twenty-one years. In 1849 he received from Columbia College the degree of Doctor of Laws. He was made Professor of Moral and Intellectual Philosophy in 1851 and was the instructor of the Senior class in those subjects, as well as in the Constitution of the United States. Moral Philosophy he taught from Wayland, Intellectual Philosophy from Mahan. The latter was a West Point man, the father of Captain Mahan of the Navy, and he put into his book a clearness of statement and vigor of thought that were bracing to the mind of the student and harmonized well with Webster's precision and thoroughness. Instruction in these subjects was, however, but a small part of the activity of Dr. Webster. In co-operation with his faculty he established an organization and system of discipline, the object of which was to bring into harmonious activity the boys who came from the public schools, and to set before them such a standard of excellence, both moral and intellectual, as should develop their characters and make them fit for the conflict of life. In this he certainly succeeded.

He was the soul of honor and integrity, and he taught his students to feel that their aim should be "to maintain the honor of the flag"; to scorn everything that was mean, and to do their duty as good citizens and true men.

The curriculum of the City College has always been exacting. To a degree unusual in colleges, it has combined instruction in the sciences, with classical and literary training. This combination has in practice proved most useful. No college has produced a larger proportion of manly and efficient citizens. Much of the honor is due to the skill with which Webster planned the course and the fidelity with which he administered his office.

His faults were the defects of his qualities. He was sometimes too much of a martinet, too precise in little things, but he was always just, would always listen to what the student had to say, and did aim to stir up all that was manly in the breast of the young man. The ground of his character was his religious spirit. He was unobtrusive in this, but loyal and sincere. He was for twenty years a communicant in St. George's Episcopal Church, and for several of those years was a Vestryman and Superintendent of the Sunday School. The distinctive principles of the Gospel of Christ were dear to him and he strove to embody them in his life.

In 1869 he gave up his active participation in the college work and retired to Geneva, where he died July 12, 1871.

Dr. Webster married Sarah M. Fowler of Albany, March 28, 1827. They had three children who grew to maturity: Horace, who was born in 1832 and died in China in 1865; Margaret Stevenson, who was born in 1840 and died in 1903; and Edward Bayard, born in 1842, who is still living in Geneva.

THE LIBRARY CORRIDOR, LOOKING EAST.
A reverse view of the earlier picture. The entrance to the library is in the fore-ground to the right and the president's office to the left.

The resolutions adopted by the class of 1872, November 17, 1871, are worth preserving:

We, members of the class of '72, now the last in college who have enjoyed the benefits of Dr. Webster's administration, would express our sorrow for his death, and our appreciation of his many admirable qualities.

In the course of twenty-one years of generous labor, he had so identified himself with the College, that his loss is sincerely regretted, and it is in recognition of his worth and of our regard, that, in this memorial, we would recall the career of one whose memory we cherish, and whose influence, wherever exerted, has left its indelible impression.

Recognizing in his devotion to the interests of education, in his fidelity to his trust, and in his sterling excellence, a life well spent, we would reverence his memory and "be of good cheer; for he hath prevailed."

In behalf of the class, H. D. Cooper,
H. van Kleek,
S. J. Strauss,
J. B. McMaster,
R. van Santvoord.

A public meeting in commemoration of his services in the cause of education was held in St. George's Church, November 17, 1871. Addresses were made by the pastor, who was familiarly known to many of the men of his time as "Old Dr. Tyng," and also by the Chancellor of the University, Dr. Howard Crosby.

Perhaps there is no better statement of his character than that given by another West Point professor, Davies:

Few men have left behind them a nobler record. He had a great work assigned him, and he lived long enough to perfect it. He will be long remembered as an able educator. His academic life was marked by a love of knowledge, which grew and strengthened with his years; by habits of study, early formed and long continued; by a firm and gentle manner, which commanded obedience and won regard; by a sense of justice never weakened by fickleness or passion; and by a punctuality in the discharge of every duty which was an admonition to the heedless, an encouragement to the orderly, and a beautiful example to all.

This notice would be incomplete without reprinting from the "Hobart Herald" an amusing incident of Webster's professorship there:

In the morning, both summer and winter, all the students were rung up to prayers in the chapel and for a recitation before breakfast. But there was an occasion when the morning prayer was made to suffer. It was a bright summer morning when the sleepyheads appeared in the chapel in their usual hasty toilet of the early hour. But the sleepyheads were suddenly waked up and the eyes were opened quick and wide at the spectacle which saluted them. For behind the breastwork on the platform stood tied as in a stall, an old street horse. Outside and in front of him sat the faculty, Prof. Webster in their midst. He looked with his thought-reading eyes at the students as they came in, one by one, and wholly ignored the presence of the quadruped behind him. As for the students, they looked only at the horse. Prof. Webster was a West Point disciplinarian, and as though nothing was more agreeable to him than to have a horse there, he proceeded with the morning devotions. The recitation followed the prayers, every man carefully and innocently in his place. After breakfast, it was felt that something must be done.

THE LIBRARY, WEST END.

The main part of the library, choked with books and cases, lies to the left. The distributing desk and shelves of the deputy librarian, Mr. Bliss, are in the background. It is there that everybody applies for information of every kind.

Strengthened by the matutinal meal, all gathered together in the chapel to do it. And so the poor animal was led by the halter to the hall and fairly, but with difficulty, "graduated" hind end foremost down the stairs and into the open. The feat was accomplished with hearty cheers for the only horse among the many of a longer-eared race that had gone through college.

It seems also appropriate to add to this notice a characteristic letter from Geneva which he wrote to James R. Doolittle, who afterwards became United States Senator from Wisconsin:

My dear young Friend:

I have just had the pleasure of receiving your letter of the 19th inst., requesting my assistance in getting you a situation in New York, etc. I will write to Mr. Foot, as you desire, immediately, and communicate you the result when received.

There are a great variety of openings in New York, yet if they are desirable and such as a young man of talents and acquirement would desire to occupy, they are almost immediately filled by young men in the city, or in the neighboring vicinity; besides the influx of foreigners is so great at this time that even those who are well educated solicit places temporarily for a bare subsistence and submit to impositions which one who has breathed the independent country atmosphere could never do. I mention this to you lest you be too sanguine in your expectations and finally fail. I shall give Mr. F. such a recommendation of your capacity and integrity that no doubt he will exert himself much for you; perhaps he may desire a clerk in his own office. Would it not be best for you to spend two years in the country in a law office and the last year in the city? I am by no means decided in my own mind, whether I would advise a young man to go to the city for employment; quite half that go there from the country are ruined. A young man of industry and correct habits will succeed anywhere and be distinguished, yet it is true the field is rather more extensive in the city than in the country, still the chances for failure are greater in the former than in the latter.

Be moderate in your expectations, yet severe in your attention to duty in whatever situation you may be placed, and success must attend you.

We have thirty scholars in the College at present; ten in the Freshman class. Our medical school goes into operation in February. With this I send you a catalogue of officers, etc. I shall be very glad to hear from you frequently and be useful to you in any manner in my power.

Please circulate our course of studies.

Your friend, etc.,
HORACE WEBSTER.

As I close this memorial I seem to see our old "Prex," standing on the platform of the Gothic chapel, at the top of the Dutch stadthaus, that was the first home of the Free Academy, and which we soon are to leave. He was tall, broad-shouldered, with erect, military figure. His voice was clear and not unmelodious. He read the selection from Scripture (often from the book of Proverbs) with a decisive intonation that showed he felt it to be the very word of command. We dispersed to our recitation-rooms, which then were commodious. The total number of students in my time was less than five hundred, and there was room for all. The old Doctor's minute requirements were often irksome. But all were proud to have such a fine looking

SECRETARY'S OFFICE.

This was once a mere anteroom to the president's sanctum, but many years ago it was partitioned into two. Beyond the partition one peeps at the secretary's desk and other paraphernalia, the position of which changes yearly. Through the open doors are visible the president's room and desk.

gentleman to preside on public occasions. We attached to him the mot that first was applied to Lord Thurlow—No one was ever so wise as the Doctor looked. Even those who most were irked by his discipline could not, in their hearts, but respect his integrity and simplicity of character. Blessed be his memory.

The First Faculty

The First Faculty

Alfred G. Compton, '53

ON the 27th of January, 1849, the New York Free Academy was opened to the people of the City of New York with public exercises in the chapel of its recently finished building. On this occasion Mr. Robert Kelly, the President of the Board of Education, introduced to the audience the first Faculty of the Free Academy, consisting of the following gentlemen:

Horace Webster, LL.D., Principal.

Edward C. Ross, Professor of Mathematics and Natural Philosophy.

Gerardus B. Docharty, Assistant Professor of Mathematics and Natural Philosophy.

Theodore Irving, Professor of History and Belles-Lettres.

John J. Owen, D.D., Professor of the Latin and Greek Languages and Literature.

Oliver W. Gibbs, Professor of Chemistry.

Jean Roemer, Professor of the French Language.

Agustin J. Morales, Professor of the Spanish Language.

Theodore Glaubensklee, Professor of the German Language and Literature.

Paul P. Duggan, Professor of Drawing.

These are the men who are always in mind when any student of the first three or four classes speaks of the Faculty, and the addition of Professors Nichols, Benedict, Barton, Anthon, Koerner, and Doremus and their successors extends the old Faculty down to the mid-way Faculty, and so on continuously down to the Faculty of thirty-one members of the present day. Of this first Faculty, at whose feet I sat for four years and whose friendship I enjoyed till the days of their deaths, I have been asked to give such account as I can.

Horace Webster was a man of strong and imposing aspect, with thin lips, lofty forehead, piercing eye, and erect carriage, wearing the air of a master. And a master he was, at least of the students, for many years from that winter of 1849. He was not a great orator; his speech was crisp, exclamatory, blunt in figures, devoid of ornament. But as a giver of laws he was respected and obeyed. It must not be imagined that the boys never outwitted him. They did sometimes—but they often thought they did, when he knew very well what they were about. When he walked one day into the drawing-room and found the assembled plaster gods and heroes, from Ulysses down to Dante, each with a clay pipe in his mouth, his turning out of the room without a word was not because he did not note the undignified demeanor of the gods, but partly, I think, because he did not choose to enter on a hopeless inquiry, and still more because he was almost exploding with

PROF. ROSS IN '50.
PROF. ROEMER IN '58.
PROF. GIBBS IN '63.

PROF. GLAUBENSKEE IN '58.
VICE. PRES. OWEN IN '58.
PROF. DOCHARTY IN '58.

PROF. IRVING IN '52.
PROF. MORALES IN '58.
PROF. DUGGAN IN '60.

mirth which he wished to conceal. This tact was, I believe, as important a factor in his discipline, especially during the earlier years of his government, as his firmness, and many instances might be cited in which the just balance of these two traits was shown.

Dr. Owen, I think, was not famous like his president, for strenuous government. I speak here, not from my own observation, for this is the one member of the old Faculty in whose class I never sat. He governed by concession. I never heard that he gave "demerits," though I suppose he did, for that was the established mode of government in those early days. I imagine that he looked at an offending boy, and brought him to order by a few serious words, accompanied and emphasized by the ominous waving of his long index finger. For that finger certainly did wave, at times, in an impressive manner. Often have I heard one or another of his pupils quote:

> "Honor and fame from no condition rise;
> Act well your part, 't is there the honor lies,"

swaying his index finger in imitation of his master and fashioning his voice in supposed likeness of the master's orotund speech. But Owen was not a gay man, even by contrast with Webster, and Webster with all his apparent austerity had far more fun in his temper. Owen was a scholar and a clergyman, and he wore something of the seriousness of both.

Ross was different from both of these. Tall, a little

awkward, but erect and dignified, with a forehead like an imposing dome, and a keen eye which held you with a kindly glance, he was, during the short period of his academic life, the favorite of the students. He taught in the Academy only two years and three months, when he died, at the age of fifty-one, after only a week's illness, and in the prime of his life and strength. He was personally known only to the classes of '53 and '54 and a part of the class of '55; but his name was in the mouths of later classes than these, as if they themselves had personally known and loved him. What they used to say of him was that he made the rough places of the mathematics smooth, that the dull boy especially he led up the steep paths, trusting in the ability of the able student to get up with anybody's help, or even with none, that he kept no count of time, but was ready with effective help whenever and wherever it was asked, that he was always full of interest in his pupils, in their past achievements and in the promise of their future career; he was not only a great teacher, but he was the students' friend.

Ross was professor, not of Mathematics only, but of Natural Philosophy, which was the name in those days for what we now call Physics. He died before the teaching of Physics began, and his place was filled by another West Point man, Lieut., afterwards Gen. W. B. Franklin. He accepted the position, during a furlough from West Point, and was succeeded by John A. Nichols, after having filled the chair only a few

THE PRESIDENT'S OFFICE, LOOKING NORTH

The judgment-seat stood facing the door in General Webb's day and the General sat underneath where his portrait now hangs. In the anteroom we see to the left the remarkable electric clock, which is fabled to move slower than any other in the city. To the right is the most used telephone in New York.

months; but this short time was long enough for him to inspire the Senior class with a deep respect. His manner was quick, sharp, decisive, his questions were rapid and searching, and his tolerance for dullness and slowness was small. He returned to his work at West Point leaving a name spoken of with admiration by the few who knew him.

Nichols, who followed him, though not from West Point, was appointed on the recommendation of Professor Davies, and continued the West Point influence on our mathematical teaching. He was a perennial spring of kindness and good temper, yet he could lose patience once in a while under adequate provocation. He would spend any amount of time on the difficulties of Bartlett's "Analytical Mechanics," a tough volume just introduced from West Point where it was born, and he had plentiful sympathy with those who could not see through all its puzzles at the first trial, though very little with those who made no trial. The pleasant influence of his sweet temper and kindly voice were with us till the fall of '68, when he died, after a long struggle with consumption, and he bridged over the space from the Old Faculty to the New.

"The pirate Gibbs," as the much admired Professor of Chemistry was approvingly called by his pupils, was perhaps the strongest man in the Old Faculty, and he is the only one who still lives. Black-haired, black bearded, black eye-browed and moustached, tall, erect, quiet, firm, he was known to us all as a man devoted to scientific research, not very fond of teaching, but teaching clearly and well, marking severely but fairly, looking on the lecture-room demonstrations which used to be called "experiments" with mildly tolerant impatience and not infrequently apologizing for their failure after they had been carefully prepared. From his chemical lecture-room, which was the identical lecture-room of to-day, he retreated to his little laboratory under it on the basement floor, where all metallic things rusted,—even aluminium and gold ones I believe, —and we wondered where and how he brought forth those chemical laws enunciated in his papers on the "Cobalt bases" and so on, whose titles mystified us, his pupils, but inspired the respect of his scientific colleagues throughout the land. When invited to Harvard he exchanged the teaching of the rudiments of chemistry for the investigation of its laws, and has since been living the life he dreamed of in his youth.

Gerardus B. Docharty was not the solemn and formidable mathematician his first name might suggest, but rather more the joking, hilarious Irish gentleman prefigured in the second. In his eye was always a mischievous smile, on his tongue a joke or a "sell." He was always ready to help inquiring students over rough places in their Latin, or their French, and they, on the other hand, often carried to their Latin teachers such puzzles as "Gallus tuus ego et nunquam animam," which after brief inspection were declared to be "some of Docharty's nonsense." He was a good though not

PRESIDENT'S OFFICE—THE JUDGMENT-SEAT.

perhaps a great teacher; but the boys loved him for his geniality and good nature and his patience with their blunderings, and cheerfully pardoned the rude treatment the skin of their faces sometimes received when he took a head between his hands and scoured a tender cheek with his scrubby gray beard.

What a contrast to Docharty was Theodore Irving, nephew of the classical Washington Irving. A clergyman, with the manners of a well-bred and well-trained rector of the Church of England, a well-dressed, courteous, well-spoken gentleman, never hurried, never impatient, never, I think, very enthusiastic, he neither over-stimulated nor discouraged his pupils, and I do not remember ever to have heard of or seen any disorder, however slight, in his room,—a trait however, that he shared with almost every other member of the Faculty.

I think we all felt that our Professor of Drawing, the lightly built Irish artist with graceful figure and movements, sharply but not cruelly biting critical tongue, and clear incisive speech, was most conspicuously, of all this Council of Ten, the man of his profession. He developed, we men who could not draw used to think, most astonishingly the skill which seemed natural to some. Their large highly finished drawings, often from the flat, but also often from the heroic casts on our walls, and still more the white chalk figures of the same on the blackboards, sometimes the full height of the board, used to fill us poor bunglers with wonder and envy; but we never thought of blaming him for that our bungling still went on. He gave us some hints on architecture which we always remembered, pointed out some buildings that we always admired, and he made himself in art our master, as Ross did in mathematics, and Roemer in French.

Our three masters in modern languages were as unlike as it was possible for three teachers to be. Roemer was really a "master" in all senses, a strong, firm, self-reliant man, never harboring any fears or misgivings—or perhaps rather, never showing any, for I have a notion that the strongest men have fits of timidity sometimes,—a man of the world, who impressed us with the feeling that he had seen all things, and done all things, and that he knew all things. We felt that he was a leader of men, that he had the art of impressing his opinions on them, and of taking up and supporting their opinions in such a way as to assist in making them effective—and when we afterwards became acquainted with him as a colleague, our estimate of him was confirmed; we recognized him as a leader in the Faculty, a power in the government of the College.

Such was not his mild little colleague Professor Morales. A timid, polite, yielding man, he was essentially a follower, as Roemer was a leader. He was the very soul of kindness and goodness of heart, to students as well as to colleagues. His rebukes to imperfect students were mild expostulations rather than harsh censures, and almost any kind of recitation would

Corridor, First Floor, Looking North.
Showing portraits of former Professors Docherty, Scott, and Draper.

command a passing mark. And yet it was always possible to learn Spanish from him if one would, and many graduates of the College have profited greatly by his instruction. He was a man of the gentlest and politest manners, a musician of considerable skill, even in composition, a writer who produced small plays for his pupils to perform and text-books from which they might learn, and a teacher who was beloved, not only by his best pupils, but even by the mischievous ones who played tricks on him.

Glaubensklee, the Professor of German, was cast in a heavier and rougher mould. Like Gibbs, he never was fooled or imposed on by students. His mastery was differently based however. When Gibbs came into a large study-room where three or four sections of students were ready for fun with any one who was afraid of them, with a scientific periodical or volume in his hand, he sat down and worked as if there were no boys there; but if student Smith began to talk to student Jones, Gibbs never failed to note it, and to bring both, and all other whisperers, to sudden order by the cry, almost without raising his eye from his book, "Stop talking there, Smith." The boys were convinced that he had some inscrutable means of detecting disorder, and very soon gave up venturing to try it. Glaubensklee commanded order just as easily, but more I think by the friendly bonhomie with which he was always ready to chat with them when off duty, either in the recitation-room, or wherever he chanced to meet them.

On the whole, this Faculty of the old College was a strong body of men. There were among them substantial scholars, great teachers, polished gentlemen, men of the world, strict disciplinarians who never allowed the least disorder, kindly governors with whom no student ever thought of disorder. The students respected them, in general loved them, studied for them, learned of them. Their departments were not so widely expanded as they have since become, their course of studies was not so broadly laid out, but they gave a broad general training with but little election, which was recognized in those days as preparing young men to do their duty in whatever career they might be called to follow. The Old Faculty left its permanent mark on the reputation and the traditions of the College.

The Second President

The Second President

Charles E. Lydecker, '71

ALEXANDER STEWART WEBB, second president of the College of the City of New York, was born in New York City, February 15, 1835. His father was James Watson Webb, editor for many years of the *Courier and Enquirer;* a man of striking appearance, who bore out some of the so-called fire-eating traditions of the fifties, in his newspaper career. He was an officer in the U. S. Army, serving in the infantry and artillery over nine years, was U. S. Minister to Brazil from 1861 to 1869, and author of the famous flag order, then promulgated. His grandfather was Samuel Blatchley Webb, an aide-de-camp on the staff of General Washington, who served from Lexington until he was captured, and remained a prisoner of war from 1777 to 1780, when he was released and commissioned Brigadier-General. His house in Connecticut was the meeting place of many distinguished men.

Our president was educated at private schools, and

entered West Point in 1851, from which he was graduated in the class of 1855, along with Gen. George D. Ruggles, Gen. A. T. A. Torbert, Gen. Wm. B. Hazen, and other able soldiers.

Within a few weeks after graduation, he was engaged in putting down the Seminole Indians in Florida, as an officer of artillery, and had some of the most exciting experiences of his life.

After service in Minnesota, he became assistant professor of mathematics at the U. S. Military Academy at West Point, and junior officer in Griffin's West Point Battery. Assigned by his regimental commander to Light Battery "A," 2d U. S. Artillery, April 1, 1861, he proceeded under orders from the War Department with the battery, Capt. W. F. Barry commanding, to Fort Pickens, Santa Rosa Island, Florida. He was present at the first battle of Bull Run, and later accepted the appointment of Captain in the 11th U. S. Infantry. In August he was ordered to report for duty in the Artillery Department of the army afterwards designated the "Army of the Potomac." Later in the same year, he was mustered into the U. S. service as Major, 1st Rhode Island Light Artillery, and remained on duty at headquarters, Army of the Potomac, as assistant to the Chief of Artillery, until appointed by the President, Assistant Inspector-General of the 5th Corps, with the rank of Lieutenant-Colonel, August 30, 1862.

He was Assistant Inspector-General and Chief of

Alex. S. Webb, LL.D

Staff of 5th Corps, to November, 1862, when he was assigned to duty with Brigadier-General W. F. Barry, Inspector of Artillery. He remained on duty in the City of Washington, as Inspector of the Artillery Camp of Instruction, Camp Barry, D. C., until January 18, 1863, when he rejoined the 5th Corps as Assistant Inspector-General, reporting to Major-General George G. Meade.

On June 21, 1863, he was appointed a Brigadier-General of Volunteers, and was assigned to duty with the 2d Brigade, 2d Division, 2d Army Corps, assuming command of that brigade the same evening.

He was in command of the 2d Brigade until August 11th; he then became temporary commander of the Division, which command he held until September 5th, when he became its commander permanently, and so continued after its consolidation until incapacitated.

Severely wounded in the terrible conflict at Spottsylvania, May 12, 1864, he was absent sick to June 21, 1864, when he was detailed to recruiting and court-martial duty to January, 1865. He then served as Chief of Staff to General G. G. Meade, Army of the Potomac, to June 28, 1865, and then as Acting Inspector-General, Division of the Atlantic, to February 21, 1866.

He returned to West Point as assistant professor, July 1, 1866, and remained there until October 21, 1868, as instructor in Constitutional and International Law.

From March 4, 1861, he was present at the following battles and engagements:

"Yorktown," as Assistant to Chief of Artillery, Army of the Potomac.

"Mechanicsville" (first), Acting Aide-de-Camp to General Stoneman.

"Hanover C. H.," assigned to duty on Staff of General Porter, temporarily, by order of Major-General McClellan.

"Gaines Mill," General Staff, assigned to General Porter's Staff, Army of the Potomac.

"Seven Days," General Staff, assigned to General Porter's Staff, Army of the Potomac.

"Antietam," Chief of Staff, 5th Corps.

"Shepherdstown" affair, Chief of Staff, 5th Army Corps.

"Snickers' Gap" affair, Chief of Staff, 5th Army Corps.

"Chancellorsville," Inspector-General, 5th Corps.

"Gettysburg," Brigadier-General commanding 2d Brigade, 2d Division, 2d Army Corps.

"Bristow Station," commanding 2d Division, 2d Corps.

"Robinson's Tavern" and "Mine Run," commanding 2d Division, 2d Army Corps.

"Morton's Ford" affair, February 6th and 7th, commanding 2d Division, 2d Army Corps.

"Wilderness," commanding 2d Division.

"Spottsylvania," commanding the consolidated 2d Division, 2d Corps.

A Fraternity Corner in the Main Hall.

"Siege of Petersburg," Chief of Staff, Army of the Potomac.

"Hatcher's Run," Chief of Staff, Army of Potomac.

His leaves of absence before Gettysburg amounted to thirty-one days total.

General Webb's letters from the field, written to his father, and other members of the family, are an index to the energy and patriotic zeal which infused him in the performance of his official duty.

A letter from General William F. Barry, Colonel 2d Artillery, and Brevet Brigadier-General U. S. A., deserves to be quoted in full, as testimony of the time. He says:

> In the first week of April, 1861, he was assigned by the War Department to duty in my Battery [A, 2d Regt. U. S. Arty.], and with it he embarked at New York for the relief of Fort Pickens, Pensacola, which at that time was closely besieged by the rebel forces under Bragg, as was Fort Sumter by those under Beauregard. The expedition, as you are aware, was successful, and this most important military and naval depot was secured to the United States. In the labors of a hurried embarkation of guns and horses, in the care and preservation of the horses, during an unusually stormy sea-voyage, and in their difficult debarkation through the surf upon the open sea-beach of Santa Rosa Island, the Transport being anchored a mile from shore, he rendered me that intelligent, faithful, and energetic assistance that gave promise of the still greater soldierly qualities that distinguished him later in the War.
>
> He remained with my Battery as a lieutenant until Sept., 1861, rendering good service at the first Battle of Bull Run,

and during the annoying and hazardous outpost duty which succeeded. Having been myself appointed in Aug., 1861, by Maj.-Gen. McClellan to the duty of organizing and equipping the immense force of Artillery, which was deemed requisite for his Army, I selected him as my assistant, and assigned him to the duty of inspecting and instructing the volunteer batteries prior to their assignment to duty in the field with the Infantry Divisions. He entirely justified my selection, for in this laborious duty—running through a period of more than six months—he exhibited his characteristic energy, industry, and intelligence. To this he added so accurate a knowledge of the tactics, care, and uses of Artillery in campaign, as well as in camps of instruction, and so thorough and judicious a manner of imparting his information to others, that I consider him the best inspector and military instructor I have ever seen.

When I took the field with the Army of the Potomac in March, 1862, he accompanied me as Inspector-General on my Staff. During the siege of Yorktown—a period of thirty days—he was employed night and day and most of the time under the fire of the enemy's position guns and sharpshooters. In the duty of disembarking our heavy siege guns (100 and 200 pounds Parrotts, and 13-inch sea-coast Mortars), and conducting them over boggy roads to their various positions, he labored assiduously, and in the special instance of running the heavy Mortars into the mouth of Wormley Creek, under a concentrated fire of the enemy's artillery, he exhibited not only energy and high intelligence, but also very great coolness and gallantry.

Throughout the remainder of McClellan's Peninsular Campaign, and especially at the Battles of Hanover Court House and Gaines Mill, he rendered efficient and gallant service.

During the movement from the front of Richmond to James River—commonly called "The seven days' Battle"—he was everywhere conspicuous, and with such incessant industry did

CORRIDOR, FIRST FLOOR, LOOKING NORTH.

Showing Fraternity Corners and the Old Clock, also Portraits of Professors Anthon and Nichols. On the right is the Memorial Tablet.

he labor, that on the sixth day he fell fainting and exhausted from his horse. On the day before the Battle of Malvern Hill, at the critical time when the right flank of our entire retreating column, with its long train of artillery and baggage, was exposed to the attack of the rapidly advancing enemy, he discovered and personally reconnoitred a hitherto unknown road into which the larger portion of the train was turned, thus saving it, and leaving the main road unincumbered for the manœuvres and concentration of our troops when attacked by the enemy a few hours afterwards.

In Sept., 1862, when I was assigned to other duties, he preferred to remain with the Army of the Potomac, serving successively as Inspector-General, 5th Corps, Commander of a Brigade, and afterwards of a Division in the 2d Corps. Not being an eye-witness of his services in these capacities, it is better that they should be described by those under whose immediate command they were rendered.

In conclusion, I beg to assure you that in all the soldierly attributes of subordination, intelligence, energy, physical endurrance, and the highest possible courage, I consider him to be without his superior among the younger officers of the Army. I also consider that both aptitude and experience fit him to command —and to command well—anything from a Regiment to a Division.

When General Webb received his brigade and his division, he fought them well. To quote from the Report of the Committee on Military Affairs of the U. S. Senate, concerning one incident:

General Webb's conduct at Gettysburg, July 3, 1863, is particularly worthy of mention. He was in command of the Second Brigade of the Second Division of the Second Corps, and had been with the color guard of the Seventy-second Pennsylvania Volunteers, of whom every man was wounded or killed. General Webb left the color guard and went across the front of the companies to the right of the Sixty-ninth Pennsylvania all the way between the lines in order to direct the fire of the latter regiment upon a company of rebels who had rushed across the lower stone wall, led by the rebel general, Armistead. Thus General Armistead and General Webb were both between the lines of troops and both were wounded, but by this act of gallantry General Webb kept his men up to their work until more than one half were killed or wounded. In this action he was wounded by a bullet which struck him near the groin. General Meade, in his letter presenting a medal to General Webb, mentions this act as one not surpassed by any general on the field.

In presenting to General Webb a medal, which the Union League Club of Philadelphia caused to be struck, one of a few replicas of the elegant gold medal presented to him, General George G. Meade, in November, 1866, wrote these strong words in an autograph letter:

> In selecting those to whom I should distribute these medals. I know no one General who has more claims than yourself, either for "distinguished personal gallantry on that ever memorable field," or for the the cordial, warm, and generous sympathy and support so grateful for a Commanding General to receive from his subordinates. Accept, therefore, the accompanying medal, not only as commemorative of the conspicuous part you bore in the Great Battle, but as an evidence on my part of reciprocation of the kindly feelings that have always characterized our intercourse both official and social.

The brevets which General Webb received are an indication of the intensity of his army life. He was brevetted for "gallant and meritorious services" as

CIVIL WAR MEMORIAL TABLET.

Erected in 1875 by the Associate Alumni to the graduated who perished in the Civil War. Overhead is President Webster's portrait.

follows: Major in the battle of Gettysburg, Lieutenant-Colonel at Bristow Station, Colonel at Spottsylvania, Brigadier-General for services and gallantry in the campaign terminating in the surrender of General R. E. Lee, and later Major-General for gallant and distinguished services during the war; he was also the recipient of the Medal of Honor from Congress.

After the war, General Webb served in various capacities in the work of restoring order, and was the Military Governor of Virginia, commanding the 1st Military District, in 1866.

On the retirement of Horace Webster, LL.D., from the Presidency of the College of the City of New York, in 1869, General Webb was sought, and upon the highest testimonials was given the office by its Board of Trustees. The Governor of the State of New York, John T. Hoffman wrote:

"Your appointment to the presidency of the College of New York gives me much satisfaction."

This was one of many expressions of feeling, shared by some of the most prominent of the citizens of the city. The College had always been moulded after the U. S. Military Academy, in its courses of study, particularly in science and the mathematics, and a graduate of that institute seemed to be a logical successor of Dr. Webster.

It may fairly be said that in the fourteen years from 1855 to 1869, General Webb had had an experience of men, of vital problems, and of political agitation, which few can parallel, and when he came to the task of presiding over a college faculty, and of guiding the destinies of the College, he was a man of very different mould and temper from the average instructor and trustee. Those who remember his first appearance recall a fairly slight, dark-haired, young-looking man, rather swarthy bronzed face, handsomely moulded head, erect upon a compact but nervous and active frame, displaying, possibly, an element of assertion, as of one who had assumed a command and was taking it up with vigor. His address indicated rapid and energetic action and the desire of an eager gentleman to give encouragement to success.

The following, written in 1902, is a summary of General Webb's work as President:

> He promptly set about acquiring a grasp of the situation, and his report to the Board of Trustees in October, 1869, shows how early in his new position the path of the College was made thorny.
>
> The Board of Trustees had resolved in substance October 4, 1869:
>
> 1. To consolidate the chairs of English and of History.
>
> 2. To consolidate the chairs of Mathematics and Mixed Mathematics.
>
> 3. To require the President to teach all the Philosophy taught.
>
> 4. To abolish all tutorships except one.
>
> 5. To give professors $5000 per annum "in view of their increased duties."

A FRATERNITY CORNER.

Northern corner of the main hall with portraits of Professors Nichols and Ross.

It must have astonished the new President to see how many ways there were of criticising and balking the work of the institution. Of course the Trustees listened to reason and the arguments of General Webb, and did not do any of the things threatened. But they put a firm limitation on the broadening views of the professors and President, and every one settled back to the old work.

The following statements appear fairly to be sustained by the records of the Board of Trustees:

General Webb at once suggested changes in the course of studies, some of which were made in 1870. He recommended that German be put upon an equal footing with the French and Spanish languages, and that those in the lower classes be given an opportunity to study that language. Theretofore the study of German had been limited to the comparatively few who became Juniors and Seniors.

He advised that the students of the Introductory class be on probation the first eight weeks, and that those who clearly showed their lack of preparation, or their indisposition to enter upon the College work, be dropped. This effective change was made and relieved the College greatly; it also improved the tone of the sections.

He early advocated the enlargement of the classical schedule of studies, and this has eventually resulted in separating the classical and scientific courses very markedly, so that the graduates of the College now have no cause to regard themselves as stinted in their collegiate training in the ancient languages.

In 1873, the Commercial Course was added to the College, but this was never regarded as of a character to warrant its association with the regular courses, and after a few years it was abandoned.

In 1875, through the advocacy of Professor Compton, a post-graduate course in Civil Engineering was created, but no degree was ever favored by the President. General Webb had early founded a manual instruction course by which students were given an opportunity after hours to perfect themselves in the use of tools. Ultimately the Mechanical Course was incorporated in the College schedule in 1881. Originally this was a three years' course, but in 1889 it was enlarged to a five years' course, and became a regular Collegiate course, yielding to graduates the degree of B. S.

General Webb has always opposed those who considered young men in the Sophomore class ready to enter upon a proposed course of pedagogy. He was consistently opposed to the establishment of the Commercial Course, and his aim has always been to steady the work of the institution along the lines of its original foundation. He never believed that the average student attending College should be given early in the course too much indulgence in electives.

When in 1897 the High Schools were established and inaugurated as a part of the public education of the City by those whose aims appeared to be hostile to the College, the foresight of the President forced the establishment of a College High School by the subdivision of the entrance classes, and an extension of their courses, so as to maintain the supply necessary to keep the College alive.

During the years 1895 and 1897, when the earnest and successful efforts of the friends of the College, led by its Alumni Association, were made to procure the legislation for a new site, there was no one who gave more continuous and intelligent application to the accomplishment of the work than the President of the College, never thwarting but always aiding that movement, and when finally in 1898 the supplementary act had to be passed to provide the additional sum of $200,000, General Webb's personal aid on the floor of the Senate was instrumental in having the

Chemical Lecture Room.

Where joint debates were formerly held and Professor Doremus lectured to over fifty successive classes.

bill taken up out of its course on the last day of the session, thus insuring its successful passage.

It was an exciting moment, when, in the hurry and struggle and bustle of the last hours of the legislature, Mr. Ellsworth, the leader of the Senate, taking the distinguished President of the College on the floor of the Senate, and introducing him as the hero of Gettysburg, asked unanimous consent to pass out of its order the bill which had come from the Assembly after over a week's careful watching and urging, and in a few minutes the work of its adoption was done.

General Webb was a conspicuous defender of the College from what he regarded as the injurious attacks of Universities—so-called "Universities in distress," whose aim and purpose was to invade the college classes, and get recruits from them for their institutions. Educators the world over have come to know of the existence of those alleged benefactors, whose purpose is apparently more to benefit teachers and professors than the youth in search of education.

In one of his papers, which was earnestly approved by Chancellor Anson J. Upson, of New York, and which embodies the argument he so long urged, he said:

Colleges will differ according to their especial objects and location, but not in the essential lines of instruction. Every college graduate is to-day as good a man as any other college graduate, or he is, in his own estimation, a little better than any other college graduate. The term is a well known one and we must respect the title, and see to it that no reputable college reduces its course, or changes its general course in a way to bring contempt on the Bachelor's degree. But the advocate of the elective course comes in and tells us that we are all wrong. Parts of our course studied in excess are better for this man and that man than the whole course.

One cannot conceive how the plan proposed could tend to produce harmony amid all these conflicting interests. We sincerely deplore that we must differ conscientiously from high authorities in matters which refer to the policy to be adopted by our institutions of higher education, but, at this time, it is especially necessary to be plain spoken against invasions of the present college course as arranged by the best minds of the country, and to express determined hostility to the abuse of the elective system, leading as it does to these discussions, when this system is applied to students not of the university grade.

It would have been gratifying to General Webb and to his students if he could have conducted them to the new City College on the Heights, but a wave of opposition was felt to beat against the progress of affairs under the new régime in 1902, which indicated a contest from which the gentlemanly instincts of this high-minded officer shrank, and he laid down the office to retire to private life. No less, however, do the great body of students who knew him during his thirty-three years of leadership respect the ideal which he embodied, of truth, loyalty, steadfastness, honorable ambition, and manliness, coupled with genuine collegiate scholarship, and faith in the usefulness of the first City College of the land, as a people's college.

He found the College with 768 students, and left it with 1969. The language of the students' tribute to him was:

And we who have known the General so well, will ever remem-

A CHEMISTRY LECTURE.
Delivered by Professor Baskerville in the old hall.

ber that noble, gentle face and kindly eye, reflecting as it does a heart "as big as the man himself." In him we have always found a staunch friend, a wise counsellor, a merciful judge. Slow to anger, steadfast in the right, dignified, courteous, noble, generous, in fact an ideal man whom we all might well follow as a precept and example, for it can truly be said of him, "He was a man the like of whom we shall not soon see again."

These words at the end of his career as president may be placed beside the language of a distinguished graduate of the College, who wrote in November, 1870, as follows:

If the right man getting into the right place ever fitted better, I am much mistaken. I believe most thoroughly in the need of the Doctor Arnold kind of man at the head of our great schools; a man *integer vitæ*, who shall be a model as well as an instructor or mere disciplinarian, and it has always been my regret, that the sons of our Alma Mater have been without such an one to pattern by; one whom it was easier to love than to fear, to reverence than to dread, a thorough man and universal gentleman. I think my ideal has been found.

In conclusion, the College of the City of New York may always feel proud that its second president was so true and earnest a man, one incapable by birth and youthful training of ignoble or improper impulses, a man so fearless and successful in showing by deeds his character, and so upright an example to the many thousand students who came under his control.

College presidents may be said each to represent some dominant trait,—Eliphalet Nott, the learned preceptor of youth; Dr. McCosh, the sturdy Presbyterian moralist; Dr. Barnard, a leader of education; and our President Webb was a manly example of heroic, patriotic, and straightforward worthy actions. There was no "God of War" thought in his personality at the College, but his presence brought to youth a suggestion of consecrated greatness.

The Later Faculty

The Later Faculty

Adolph Werner, '57

ONE evening in July, 1852, five new professors delivered inaugural addresses to an audience of old professors, students, and citizens in the great hall (which was not then called chapel). The speakers were Charles Edward Anthon, Professor of History and Belles Lettres; John Graeff Barton, Professor of the English Language and Literature; Joel Tyler Benedict, Professor of Civil Engineering; Robert Ogden Doremus, Professor of Natural History, Anatomy, Physiology, and Hygiene; John Augustus Nichols, Professor of Natural Philosophy. And they began to lecture and teach on the ninth of September following. Professor Barton was thirty-eight years old, the others in the neighborhood of thirty. They have all passed away: Nichols in 1868, Barton in 1877, Anthon in 1883, Benedict in 1892, Doremus in 1906.

How they looked, at least how they looked each on some one day of his life, the crayon portraits on the walls of the old college building will have shown to the readers of this book. And how shall we portray in words what they were, their characters and their successes? Everybody remembers vividly what Professor Doremus was during the forty years of his occupancy of the chair of chemistry, to which on the resignation of its first occupant, Gibbs, he was transferred in 1863: an ardent devotee of science, a brilliant experimenter, an eloquent lecturer, an impressive teacher, a lover of art, poetry, and all learning, a man of the world. In his first professorship, he delivered annually courses of lectures on human physiology and hygiene, on physical geography, and on geology. Though these courses were brief, some consisting only of weekly lectures during one term, they were impressive, giving the students an adequate notion of these sciences, or, let us say, a notion considered sufficient in those remote days, when, as all college men know, the ideal and nature of a college course were not what they are now.

Professor Anthon also was a scholar of more interests and accomplishments than one. He was as deeply interested and as much at home in literature, classical and modern, as in history, and his scholarship in both was thorough, extensive, and brilliant. For many years he taught the Sophomore class personally in modern European history and the Senior class in literature, giving usually, with the aid of Mrs. Botta's handbook, a survey of two literatures in the year.

Professor Barton was, as the students saw him (and, no doubt, when they did not see him), a serious man. He was considered a strict man, not severe, but strict, kind, and kindly. While he delivered few lectures, he

Prof. Nichols in '58.
Prof. Roemer in '89.
Prof. Anthon in '58.

Prof. Koerner in '63.
President Webb in '70.
Prof. Doremus in '70.

Prof. Benedict in '66.
Prof. Morales in '76.
Prof. Barton in '69.

was a fluent and interesting talker, and, drawing upon a fund of information, supplemented the text-book generously. The student could count upon the professor's speaking a large fraction of the time; but he must also expect a searching examination of his own knowledge. Always, the professor held the attention of the class, and he always secured careful preparation of assigned lessons and performance of assigned work.

Professor Benedict was, like Professor Barton, serious and strict, and in addition, frequently austere. He taught half a dozen Senior classes civil engineering; not those who elected it, but the whole class. But while the early Boards of Education laid stress on the practical, meaning, presumably, preparation for such professions as the engineer's, the students were looking forward to law, medicine, the ministry, teaching, and business.

After some time the department was discontinued and Professor Benedict was made Adjunct Professor of Mathematics, in which position he remained until 1866. The next dozen years he assisted his wife in the management of a school; after her death he lived in retirement, with his books, his memories, and his thoughts. Mathematical brains are, at all events they were forty or fifty years ago, scarcer than, say, grammatical; and a serious, strict, and occasionally austere teacher would not be adored by all his pupils, nor indeed by all his classes. But Professor Benedict was a fine mathematician and an excellent teacher—his Algebra was by many teachers and students called the best of its day—and there were classes that swore by him.

Professor Nichols—there is hardly any shading yet in the picture of the group exposed on that 1852 July evening—and yet how could any one speak of Professor Nichols but with admiration and love? His genuine devotion to science and knowledge, his unwavering belief in education, his optimistic faith in the capability of the student mind, not everybody might share, but everybody must admire. Professor Nichols was an assiduous student all his life, while he was in health and when his health failed. Though cheerful—cheerfulness is lovable—and ambitious to the close, he was sadly hampered during the last two or three years of his life by the disease to which he succumbed at the age of forty-six. He did a noble piece of work in a span in which only men above mediocrity accomplish anything memorable.

The first president of the College was, as all American college presidents used to be, Professor of Philosophy. Soon, in 1855, the institution had grown so large that he needed an assistant, and George Washington Huntsman was appointed Assistant Professor of Philosophy. He taught the Sophomores logic and political economy, and later the Juniors intellectual philosophy or mental science, which comprised portions of what are now called psychology and metaphysics.

Faculty Room.

This room, still known by its ancient title, has long been pre-empted as an annex to the Library and as a classroom for the Professor of Oratory. The Faculty usually meets in the "Greek" room.

When President Webb succeeded President Webster, in 1869, the president was relieved of the work of teaching, and Professor Huntsman became Professor of Philosophy. He occupied the chair for ten years, when he retired.

Dr. Hermann Koerner was in 1851 appointed substitute for Professor Duggan, who was away on account of sickness. On Duggan's return a year later, a new department, Descriptive Geometry and Industrial Drawing, was created, evidently because Dr. Koerner was too valuable a man to lose and too venerable a man for the rank of tutor. Venerable? He was not yet fifty years old, but his hair was white, having turned so in a night during the Revolution of '48. Dr. Koerner was a political exile. He was, as every German of his generation was, a philosopher, and he preached idealism fifty years before Prince Henry of Prussia. He never acquired an English tongue, but made himself understood, and when, after the death of Professor Duggan, the two departments became one again, Professor Koerner even delivered lectures on esthetics, "Art and its division into Arts" he entitled the course. He was the first and for many years the only professor in the College who had the foreign degree Ph.D., as he was the first and for many years the only professor in the College who used the not yet naturalized word Pedagogy. Professor Koerner added strength to the Faculty and was in many ways an interesting man, nor without a picturesque trait, not inappropriate in an exponent of art. To the younger students he seemed queer; the older students came to recognize the depth of his character and thought and to sympathize with his sentiments. Professor Koerner retired in 1877.

Dr. John Christopher Draper followed Professor Doremus as Professor of Natural History. More hours were assigned to the department; physiology could be treated more fully, the study of botany and zoölogy was added, and—what is perhaps most interesting, seeing that it was done over forty years ago—blowpipe analysis, the experimental study of minerals by the students themselves in a rudimentary laboratory, was introduced.

Professor Draper was not apt to overrate the young men and their performances; yet he did not fail to discover ability and merit and to recognize them cheerfully. Two weeks before his death, in the spring of 1885,—though he had no premonition and was evidently talking without ulterior purpose,—he spoke to a colleague of his experience in the College and of his relations with the students. "They have been good to me, they have always treated me well." Let the students' estimate of the professor implied in his praise of them stand in place of other opinion; it seems sufficient.

When in 1869 Professor Owen died the professorship of Latin and Greek was divided, and Jesse Ames Spencer, S. T. D., the well-known clas-

Prof. Huntsman in '70.

Prof. Scott in '80.

Prof. Draper in '70.
Prof. Fabregon in 1902.
Prof. Spencer in '86.

Prof. Sturgis in '81.

Prof. Hardy in '94.

sical scholar, was elected Professor of the Greek Language and Literature. He occupied the chair ten years.

David Burnet Scott was principal of the grammar school which had been sending the second largest classes to the College when in 1871 he was appointed Principal of the Introductory (sub-Freshman) Department. Then the first attempt at the separation of the academic department was made.

The building on Twenty-second Street had, in these first years of President Webb's administration, been erected and arranged for the accommodation of the sub-Freshmen. The top floor, later known as Natural History Hall, was the assembly room and portions of it were recitation-rooms during the day. The young boys did not disturb the scholastic calm of the main building; they never entered it except when they came, under supervision, to the first floor to listen to Professor Doremus and behold his magnificent experiments. When Professor Barton died, in 1877, Professor Scott was elected his successor—and no new principal was appointed.

Professor Scott had long been a student of English literature and had lectured thereon with marked success to the teachers' classes instituted by the Board of Education before the establishment of the Normal College. He continued to evince during the seventeen years of his professorate—he died in 1894—the same traits of intellectual keenness and force, the same individuality and personal strength which had characterized him as a principal. He made himself felt among men, and he exerted a strong influence on boys and young men.

George Benton Newcomb succeeded Professor Huntsman in the chair of philosophy in 1879 and served the College until his death in the fall of 1895. Professor Newcomb was a native of New York and a graduate of Williams College. For some years after graduation he was a journalist; then, for a series of years, a clergyman, the pastor of a church in a Connecticut town. He taught the Junior and Senior classes personally, the former in economics and law, the latter in psychology and the history of philosophy. He was a scholarly man, endeavored to get his students both to think and to read, and generally succeeded. In addition to delivering lectures and appointing and hearing lessons in text-books, he set individual students individual tasks and gave them individual opportunities according to their abilities and needs. He was seldom seen on his way to and from college without his satchel, in which he carried the books and pamphlets for this individualized instruction and the papers which the students wrote—indeed, were proud to write—at the periodical examinations or tests scattered through the term, which he held to a greater extent than had been customary in his department or was customary in most departments.

James Weir Mason was Professor of Mathematics from 1879 to 1902. He was a graduate of our own Col-

THE CHEMICAL LIBRARY.

Private room and library of the Chemical Department, for fifty years the sanctum of Professor Doremus.

lege in the class of 1855. The twenty-four years between his graduation and his return, he spent partly as a teacher, partly as a mathematician, having been Principal of the old Albany Academy and Actuary of the Massachusetts and the Penn Life Insurance Companies. As a young man, as a man, as an old man, he was serious, faithful, earnest with the Kingsley earnestness, a lover of literature, at home in romance and history and poetry, seldom at fault as to the authorship of a verse and generally able to complete the stanza. At the start and during the first twenty-five years of the college, mathematics was, in a sense, the leading study; it was obligatory to the same extent on all students. Then came a change. The classical course was differentiated from the scientific, the natural and experimental sciences, here as elsewhere, assumed greater proportions. And when Professor Mason came, he hoped to accomplish and he found that many expected him to accomplish under the new conditions what tradition said had been accomplished under the old. He himself adhered to the high standard of his own student days; he upheld it so far as it could be upheld in a modern faculty and a modern college not yet committed to electives (in which only the mathematically minded take mathematics beyond the elements, and a larger portion succeed). Anxious, like other good and loyal teachers, to save those of the weaker students who were not past redemption, he formed—for years, if not to the end—special volunteer classes to whom for a month before examination he gave supplementary instruction and drill several times a week, outside the regular college hours (and, of course, without fee). He labored in a transition period, but his true mind never lost its temper, and his incisive, earnest teaching bore (if, in speaking of a man of pure literary taste, the metaphor may be changed) good fruit.

The Life of the College

The Beginnings

James R. Steers, '53

HAVING been requested to give some reminiscences of my school-days and my impressions of the Free Academy, now the City College, I shall begin with some few instances of early childhood showing the condition of public schools at that time.

My earliest school-days were in a little school kept by a lady friend of my parents, who had, perhaps, eight or ten other pupils. When I was about six my mother took me to the Public School in Fifth Street, between Avenue C and Avenue D, the principal of which was Mr. Abraham Van Vleck, a thin sandy-haired man, who to my childish mind seemed the incarnation of severity and dignity. My mother led me up to the platform, and to test my acquirements, to see whether I was a fit subject to be admitted, I was required to read several verses from the Bible, which I accomplished to the satisfaction of Mr. Van Vleck, and I was duly enrolled as a member of the Junior Sixth class, the lowest of the school.

I remained at this school about five years and, in spite of strong efforts on my part to be promoted, I never rose above the Junior Seventh. The classes were Junior Sixth and Senior Sixth, Junior Seventh and Senior Seventh, Junior Eighth and Senior Eighth, Junior Ninth and Senior Ninth.

Those were the days of flogging and the more serious misdemeanors that schoolboys are prone to were visited by a punishment with the rattan. Mr. Van Vleck had a unique and varied assortment of rattans, shaved to different degrees of thinness, which seemed to me to be adjusted to the age of the misdemeanants. After I had been in the school for a year or more, there grew upon my mind a feeling of resentment against what I thought was the injustice with which I was treated. I saw boys who were, I knew, not as well qualified for promotion as myself, advanced, and strive as I would and work as hard as I could, I never seemed to be able to get along. I do not recollect that I was punished very much with the rattan. I enjoyed a more ingenious form of punishment. Boys who had been guilty of unnecessary talking, or some such trifling thing, were made to stand holding out at arm's length heavy slates for an hour or so at a time.

All our writing of the lower classes was done on these slates, and when I was about eight, steel pens were first introduced into the school. Up to that time, the upper class boys had used quills, which were prepared for them by Mr. Van Vleck or some of his assistants.

RESEARCH LABORATORY.

Workroom of the Chemical Department with Professor Friedburg and assistants.

The boys were required to buy their own steel pens, a factory for which was started across the street from the school. My great ambition at that time was to be promoted from slate writing to copy-book writing, but this I was not able to accomplish so long as I remained in the school. The boys would write on their slates sentences ordinarily quoted, like "Evil communications corrupt good manners," and submit them to Mr. Van Vleck and ask to be promoted to the dignity of a copy-book. I did that a number of times, but my application was invariably rejected, although the boys around me said that my writing was better than that of a great many of the others who had been promoted. There was one boy among us who helped other boys to the much-desired copy-book by writing their task for them and these were invariably successful. Despairing of getting the desired promotion in any other way, I got him to write some copies for me on my slate. I took them to Mr. Van Vleck, feeling I was sure of promotion this time, but to my dismay he rejected my application again.

This school was one of the original Public Schools, so-called, established and supported by the Public School Society. When I was about eleven years old the city began to build its own Common Schools. About this time Common School No. 5 had just been finished and stood at the corner of Stanton and Sheriff streets, in a delectable neighborhood of rag pickers, drinking saloons, and breweries. As soon as the building was ready for occupancy I was transferred there, and upon examination by the Principal, Mr. Seneca Durand, to my astonishment I was immediately put into the highest class in the school and then I received my first realizing sense of what good teaching was. Mr. Durand himself was a good teacher, though not a highly educated man. For arithmetic we went to a New Englander by the name of Hall, whose method was clearness itself and under whom it was a great pleasure to sit. I use his method with vulgar fractions to this day. In this school I remained between four and five years. I had finished the whole course of studies in 1847, in fact a year before, but I stayed as a sort of occupation, my parents thinking I was too young to go to work.

In the summer of 1848 I would have left the school, but my parents learning of the proposed establishment of the Free Academy, now the College of the City of New York, it was suggested that I should not leave school until the new academy was ready to receive my application for admission.

The interior arrangement of Mr. Durand's school was somewhat similar to that of the old public school, that is to say, it had a large assembly room with a gallery in the rear, with class-rooms under it and at either side of the platform. This platform stood in the middle of the assembly room at the other end and opposite the gallery. There was a broad aisle down the middle of the large room and two broad side aisles. The desks were arranged on both sides between the

AT WORK IN THE RESEARCH LABORATORY.

Taken while the members of the Chemical Department were engaged on some important investigations for the City Government.

middle and side aisles. Boys did not have separate desks. There were long desks, each arranged for twelve pupils. At the end toward the side aisles of each was a raised desk at which a boy, usually one of a higher class, sat on a tall stool, so that he could overlook all the boys sitting on the lower seats. These seats were small oval stools, without backs, the legs of which were set in a board on the floor. There were six seats fastened to one board, and six to another, making twelve to each long desk. Each boy had a little open drawer in front of him where he put his books, or his luncheon or what not, and in winter he jammed his hat in there and also his overcoat if he had one.

There were no janitors in those days and the good boys were allowed, as a matter of favor, to stay in after school and sweep and dust the schoolroom, in which sweeping and dusting I took my part with a great deal of pleasure.

In each class-room was a sort of easel, upon which was placed a large board of wood painted black. Upon this the teacher would write or explain the sums from the arithmetic, and sometimes a boy would be called up "to do a sum." The chalk was always a small irregular piece like that used by a carpenter. The rubber or wiper of the board was a more or less soiled rag.

The selection of the school-books was very largely under the control of the principal, who, as he used to say, could usually get new books for the school from publishers on condition of giving up the use of the old ones.

Our principal, Mr. Durand, was a fine singer, with a beautiful voice, and he trained the boys in singing the tenor and bass parts of many old English glees, and also taught the girls, who had the floor below ours, the soprano and alto parts. At the close of the school each summer there was a grand concert, with quartettes and duets sung by the boys and girls, accompanied on the piano by one of the teachers, and with some rousing choruses.

In December of 1848 I went up to the Free Academy with a certificate from my principal and applied for admission. Those who had applied were assembled in what was called the chemical lecture-room, and the President, Dr. Horace Webster, called one applicant after another, gave each a number, and directed him to a certain class-room to be examined. It seemed to me that he was very slow in doing this. I grew a little impatient and thought I would discover, if I could, whether there was any method in his order of selection. I soon noticed that the boys who were making a noise or talking were selected, as I then thought, to get rid of them, so I immediately began to talk and at once was called up and was given a number, 43, by which I was known in all my examinations. The first room to which I was sent was the room of Professor Ross, professor of mathematics, and I still remember the impression he made upon me. He was

STUDENT'S LABORATORY.
The large class room laboratory looking north.

tall, somewhat ungainly, with an old-fashioned turn-down collar and a sort of rambling necktie or handkerchief tied around his neck, with an unstarched shirt front; rather rambling clothes, so to speak; but he had a fine amiable countenance, bright blue eyes, a high impressive forehead, and a general air of kindness, dignity, and one might also say knowledge. He always addressed us as "men" to our great pleasure.

The room filled me with amazement. All around the room on the walls were blackboards of slate. In a little shelf at the bottom running along the base of the blackboards were sheep-wool rubbers with handles and small pencils of chalk, and I involuntarily contrasted this magnificence with the simplicity of the school from which I had just come. The sum or problem given to all those at the boards, about twenty I should think, was to extract the square root of .5. I worked this out with some difficulty and announced my answer, which, to my surprise, was pronounced correct. Thereupon my card was marked and I was dismissed from that examination. The other examinations I do not particularly recall.

Attending upon notice, full of tremors, sometime afterwards, I was informed by the venerable Doctor that I was admitted and was asked which course of study I would select, one with the ancient languages, or one with modern languages. I selected the course with ancient languages.

As most boys do, perhaps, unknown to their teachers,

I began almost involuntarily to study the characters of the principal and the teachers to whom I recited, and inasmuch as they have all passed away it may perhaps be no impropriety if I give my youthful impressions of them and of the internal arrangements of the Academy.

If my surprise at finding slate blackboards and the rubbers and chalk was great, my surprise was still greater at what were to me the luxurious appointments of the class-rooms. In these rooms each student had a revolving stool, with a back, and, so to speak, an individual desk which instead of being of pine grained to resemble oak was of cherry, or some other natural wood, and these finely furnished desks and seats gave an air to me of great luxury. The heating apparatus, the hot air system, was another great surprise. The heat in my school was from great coal stoves, one in each class-room and several large stoves in the large room. All the appointments of the Free Academy were so fine and superior in comparison with that of the school I came from that it was a long time before I came to look upon them as a matter of course.

Doctor Webster was an honorable, high-minded gentleman but, while a fine disciplinarian, was, in my opinion, a very poor teacher. As he graduated very high in his class at West Point, he was undoubtedly a well educated man, but he lacked that indefinable thing, the power of teaching, of stimulating the minds of the students to take an interest in the subject under consideration, the power of clear thinking as to the best way of

SECOND FLOOR CORRIDOR.

View to the north, showing '85's Memorial Window, side glimpse of the Ichthyosaurus, and the series of art photographs ranged along the wall.

communicating knowledge to those minds, and the power of clear, succinct expression. Our class had opportunities to study him when he taught us in his own branch, Moral Philosophy, or in other subjects in the absence of some of the other teachers.

Professor Ross was in some respects the best teacher I ever sat under. He also was a West Point graduate and stood high in his class. In fact, the whole atmosphere of the Free Academy, when I was there, was strongly suggestive of West Point. During the last year I was at school one of the teachers took up for the highest class the study of algebra. Study as I would I could make nothing of it under him. When I went up to the Free Academy I had a dread of beginning that study; but under Ross not only algebra, but geometry, descriptive geometry, analytical geometry, and plane trigonometry became to me as simple as A-B-C. When our class had reached trigonometry Professor Ross was taken ill and died soon after. Doctor Webster took our class in mathematics for a few months and it was unfortunate, perhaps, that he should follow such a teacher as Ross, for the contrast between his methods, if one may call them such, and Ross's was too striking not to make a great impression on me, at least, and apparently on the whole class. Ross's place was subsequently taken by William B. Franklin, another West Pointer, afterwards one of the prominent generals in the Civil War, on the Union side. He conducted our studies for six months, in the mathematics of mechanics, such as the inclined plane, the wheel and axle, and the pulley. We used "Bartlett's Mechanics," written in the synthetic method.

Franklin was a fine teacher, with a manner, however, quite different from Ross's, not so suave nor sympathetic, but with a method somewhat after the military style. For instance, the students would be seated in the class-room; Franklin would enter, a tall, erect, broad shouldered, handsome man, the students having their books open, cramming for the recitation. The moment he sat down would come the order, "Down your books," then he would say, "Steers, take the floor," and I would immediately march out and stand midway between him and the students in the rear of me, and he would catechize me upon the lesson. He would not limit himself always to the immediate lesson, but would ask questions collateral to, or which might be deduced from, the particulars stated in the books. While one might answer, if one had time to think, his manner was very apt to nonplus the students, especially those who did not have their lessons very well committed to memory. He was a man of clear mind, clear expression, knew what he wanted, and even if his method savored more of the driving than the enticing, he was a fine teacher.

After him in that department came Professor Nichols, a mild, gentle, amiable gentleman, not with the power of either Franklin or Ross, but with a clear and sufficient knowledge of the subject to carry the class

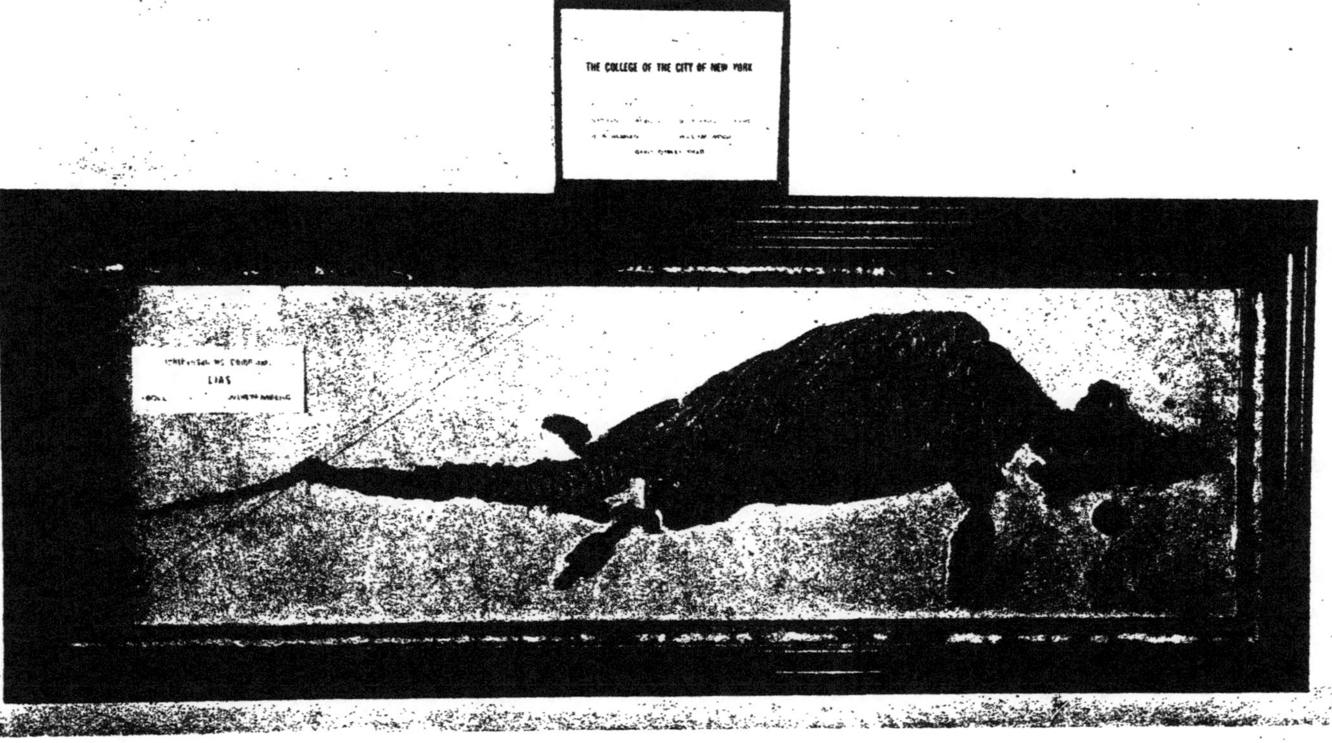

THE ICHTHYOSAURUS.

The pet of the college, adopted as a mascot by many successive classes.

into spherical geometry and trigonometry, astronomy, and the calculus.

Our Professor of English Language and Literature was the Reverend Theodore Irving, a nephew of Washington Irving, a slender man, with beautiful dark brown eyes, intellectual face, somewhat scanty dark hair, and in every way a refined and cultivated gentleman. I think the class enjoyed the sessions with Professor Irving as much if not more than with almost any other professor in the Academy. He seemed, to me at least, to have a very broad and full acquaintance with English literature, and his rhetoric and spoken English were perfect, without any trace of pedantry. When Professor Irving resigned his professorship to become the rector of Saint Ann's Church on Staten Island, Professor Barton was appointed to succeed him.

Professor Barton was another gentlemanly, cultured man, of great dignity and reserve. The recitations under him, to me, were much less interesting than they had been under Irving. They were chiefly recitations, with very little discursive criticism of the writers or their styles, which, as I remember, we had enjoyed under Irving.

Our Professor of Chemistry and Physics was Doctor Oliver Wolcott Gibbs, who came to us, I think, almost fresh from his studies under Liebig. He was a remarkably handsome man, dark, with almost black hair, finely cut features, clear complexion, blue eyes, and a certain air, one might almost call aristocratic in his general manner. He was not what seemed to me a great although he was a good teacher. His strength lay rather in scientific investigations in his department than in teaching. He was a little impatient of the time lost in preparing experiments for his class, which sometimes succeeded and at other times did not, just for lack of preliminary preparation, but at the same time he made the subjects he taught very interesting to me, and, as it seemed to me, to most of the members of the class, except one, who would persist in apparently going to sleep. He would be awakened by the cry, "——, don't go to sleep," which angered him and caused us much amusement. This gentleman has subsequently become a very prominent lawyer. I enjoyed the mathematics under Ross and the chemistry and physics under Gibbs more than any other studies. Gibbs subsequently left the Academy and became famous at Harvard University.

The Professor of Latin and Greek, Doctor John J. Owen, was undoubtedly a very learned man in his subjects, and he was what might be called a fair teacher, but his manner was dry and uninteresting, to me at least, and, so far as I remember, he rarely smiled and he seemed to be absorbed in his Greek and Latin studies, and especially in his Greek books, which we used in our studies.

Of course, it is understood that I am only giving my own impressions, which it is quite possible were wrong because of my immaturity.

I did not enjoy the lessons under Doctor Owen for

THE LATIN ROOM.
Professor Herbermann lecturing to a class.

two reasons: First, owing to a defective verbal memory, it was not easy for me to commit words literally to memory. If I could work out a result from premises or facts, I could retain the result in my memory, but a naked statement, even though expressing a fine thought, would not stick in my memory, except after great study and innumerable repetitions. The second reason was the entire absence of a feeling of sympathy between Dr. Owen and myself, the cause of which was quite possibly in myself.

There was a Professor of Drawing, Mr. Paul Peter Duggan, a slender, pale gentleman, with big, sad gray eyes, and a general air of physical feebleness, but an artist to the tips of his fingers. I enjoyed the drawing very much, perhaps because of a long line of ship-building ancestors. If I remember aright I was, much to my surprise, awarded the prize for drawing (my only prize) upon graduation.

Among other studies which I disliked was ancient history. I cannot now recall the professor or assistant professor to whom we recited, but I know the whole subject was dreary to me, because it consisted of committing to memory a large volume of stories of individuals, kings and warriors, with whom I felt no special sympathy, and this process was to me dreary drudgery. I am not sorry to say that not a trace of it, so far as I can discover, remains with me to this day.

In the second or third year, I forget which, some proportion of our class took up Spanish under Professor

Morales, a small, dignified gentleman, with the typical black hair and eyes of his nation, a man who was extremely sensitive, but a good teacher, and while I still found difficulty in committing arbitrary words and sounds to memory, yet I enjoyed studying with Professor Morales, as he was a kindly, sympathetic teacher.

About the same time our class took up the study of German under Professor Theodore Glaubensklee, a typical Teuton, who might be called, without intending disrespect, a mechanical teacher. That study I also enjoyed to a degree—not quite so much though as the study of Spanish—but it was still open to the same objections that I had to other studies which required the committing to memory of words and sounds which had no connection with any process of reasoning. The result was that while my lessons in mathematics and in chemistry and physics were a pleasure, all the other lessons were hard, and in order to get them I was obliged to study from five to six hours outside of the regular hours of the Academy.

Our hours at the Academy were from nine to three five days in the week, with an intermission of half an hour from twelve to half past twelve, and a half day on Saturday. Saturday, was I think, usually given up to oratory with an instructor, who was, if I may speak as I think, a pompous incompetent. He indulged in the flowing gestures of the arms and the old elocutionary modulation of the voice and more or less ungraceful poses of the body, which were, perhaps, considered

Clionia in Session.

Another view of the Latin Room as seen at evening with the students in possession. Clionia's president is addressing the meeting.

absolutely necessary elements of oratory in those days, but which struck me as being rather absurd.

I am afraid that I was deficient in a proper respect for some of my teachers while in the College, which sometimes led to my discomfiture. I recall one circumstance in Professor Ross's room when he, having a severe cold, called in an assistant, a Mr. Palmer, to conduct his lessons while he himself sat there, to supervise, in a way, the recitation. I had a proposition in geometry to recite, and I thought a remark or question by Palmer to be foolish. I answered him in a rather flippant manner, whereupon Ross instantly arose to his feet and, with an expression of almost wounded dignity, chided me for my lack of respect and in his deep serious manner said that I should treat Mr. Palmer with just as much respect as I treated him. Feeling that I was in the wrong, and having no defence, I said nothing. My lack of respect for my teachers unless they showed mental power or ability appeared on several occasions in my relations with Doctor Webster. It was not long after my entrance before I realized that his system of discipline consisted very largely in magnifying trifling violations of rules which it is often best not to appear to see; and his severe and almost imperious manner, developed by military training, was, to me at least, very unpleasant. While I might, and probably did, violate some of the rules, yet I would never admit that I was in a sense disobedient or disorderly, but from the first I felt an utter lack of kindly sympathy between the Doctor and myself. That lack of sympathy showed itself on several occasions in a greater or less degree, but one of the more striking examples of it which I now recall happened in this wise: The boys used to run races in the recess hour around Gramercy Park, which then had an earth walk all around it. One of the students in our class was a great favorite with the Doctor, partly because he was a very well behaved young man and partly because he studied to win the Doctor's good favor by a kind of obsequiousness which did not bring him into favor with the other students. Upon one occasion, when I was chasing a boy around Gramercy Square, and had nearly captured him, this student, who by the way wore glasses, suddenly appeared in my way. He was walking aimlessly and regardless of the racers, and I was rather vexed at losing my prey, so with my open hand I slapped his face, knocking his glasses into the Park through the railing, partly to get him out of my path and partly by way of resentment. I immediately stopped and made a long search for the glasses, but could not find them. In a short time I was summoned by the Doctor, with my victim as the complainant. The Doctor stated what the complaint was and asked me if that was correct, and I said it was. He asked me why I did it, and I told him frankly of my vexation at being interrupted. The Doctor immediately lectured me on the impropriety of my behavior and after he had finished I stated to him as mildly as I could, because I was feeling a little vexed,

GREEK ROOM.

Professor Tisdall with a class. This room is now used for the Faculty meetings.

that I did not think the authority of the college officers extended beyond the limits of the college building and grounds. His face flushed and in very angry tones he announced that we "were always under the authority of the college officers." I repeated my former statement, insisting that I only considered myself subject to their authority when I was either in the college or in the college grounds. The Doctor seemed at a loss for words for a time and then exclaimed, "How, how, you are all wrong." In a moment of diplomacy I gave my victim a dollar for a pair of glasses and the incident was closed.

On another occasion, the Doctor, being fond of encouraging military exercises among the students, approved of the formation of a military squad of about twelve or fifteen students, which was under the command of Mr. Nicholas Babcock, a student. This squad were armed with wooden guns and they used to drill in Twenty-third Street and on Lexington Avenue during part of the recess hour. Four or five members of my class, including myself, took it into our heads to test the military skill and proficiency of this squad, and forming ourselves into what used to be called the Macedonian phalanx, now called the flying wedge, with myself at the apex of the triangle, we charged the army under Captain Babcock, pierced its centre, and drove it into full retreat. Captain Babcock duly made his complaint to the Doctor and we were all haled before him, and I, as the apex of the triangle, was required to give an explanation of our disorderly conduct. Recalling to mind such military terms as I could remember, I in subtance told the Doctor that we had become interested in military manœuvres, and having in our studies learned about the Macedonian phalanx, thought it a fine opportunity to try its efficacy, and seeing what we thought was a good opportunity to put our theories in practice, we drove the phalanx against Captain Babcock's squad, resulting in the defeat of the squad. It took all the Doctor's self-possession to refrain from smiling, but I could see a twinkle in his eye, an unusual thing for him, and after a few words of reproval the Macedonian phalanx was dismissed.

Our class was named Class A, admitted in January, 1849. There was a summer examination for admission in 1849 and Class B was admitted. At admission our class numbered about one hundred and forty. I do not remember the number in Class B, but at the end of a year and a half or two years both classes had been so reduced by students failing to pass subsequent examinations and by those leaving, that the two classes were united; so that while those of A spent four and a half years in the Academy, those of B spent only four.

Among the students of Class B. was Mr. Alfred G. Compton. There was nothing remarkable in Compton's appearance except a very sandy head of hair, a very freckled face, and a somewhat short stature, but when he was called upon to recite in any of our studies, it was a very close thing between him and John Hardy,

PHRENOCOSMIA IN SESSION.

Another view of the Greek room, taken at night. The lady on the extreme left is the favorite subject for poetry and apostrophe in the Phrenocosmian magazine.

Charles L. Holt, and Benjamin S. Raynor. I think Hardy had the better verbal memory, but in no other respect was he superior to Compton or Holt. When either Hardy, Holt, or Compton, and particularly Compton, was called to the board to recite in mathematics, there arose in my mind mingled feelings of envy and pleasure; envy because I could not do the thing so well, and pleasure because the thing was so well done. Those four, Hardy, Raynor, Compton, and Holt, were our banner students, but Raynor was only a memorizer, and he was mentally far inferior to the others. The honor men of our class were in this order: Hardy, Raynor, Compton, Holt, Steers.

Our amusements consisted chiefly in races around Gramercy Square, and around the Academy building. There was an open space all around it about the width of the present dooryards on Twenty-third Street, and the boys, especially the younger ones, were very much given to shouting and racing and sometimes wrestling there. The Doctor, in pursuance of his minute system of discipline, usually stood in the middle of the walk leading from Twenty-third Street into the building, partly for the purpose of stopping the racing across the walk, and partly for the purpose of detecting the culprits and demeriting them. He was not at all a striking object as he stood there, bald-headed, with his thin gray hair blown about by the breeze, furtively watching whom he might identify, and the boys racing past him when his back was turned.

Another of our amusements was playing "knuckle all over" in Twenty-third Street, between Third and Lexington avenues. One can fancy the primitive state of things when twenty or thirty boys could play "knuckle all over" with a powerfully thrown ball through Lexington Avenue with no one to forbid, no policeman in sight, few, if any, houses, in the neighborhood. If I remember rightly the street was unpaved. Another of our amusements when we came to a holiday, generally during the May week or on Saturday after the morning session, were the boating parties on the East River to Riker's Island. The several preparations for these excursions were allotted to sub-committees. The committee of the whole generally comprised Hardy, Holt, Compton, Brant, and myself. I think Compton was the committee on *res frumentaria*, Brant the committee on liquid refreshments, Hardy was on complex apprehension, vulgarly known as a pack of cards, Holt I forget, and mine was the committee on boat and the tides.

The means of reaching the College or Academy in those days were very primitive. Some lived in Harlem and could only reach the Academy by means of omnibuses or stages, which ran, I think, every half-hour or hour. My home was in Seventh Street, near the East River, and my only means of getting to the Academy was to walk, a little less than two miles. The walks during the spring and fall were very pleasant. In the winter heavy snows and storms made it rather

THE REPOSITORY.

James Toher (late U. S. Cavalry) was for many years Assistant to the Librarian and held here under his care all books and all supplies of every kind distributed free of charge to the students.

the reverse, and innumerable days I spent in the college building with more or less cold, wet feet and wet clothes.

Several of the students lived at or near my home, and we generally went together both coming and going. There were very few buildings for most of the way and we used to make the trip across lots and in doing so we excited the attention of some of the young inhabitants of "Mackerelville," then so-called, a shanty district in the vicinity of Fourteenth Street and First Avenue. These lads took a great interest in our coming and going to the extent of stoning us regularly. By force of a bad example we naturally fell into the same habit by way of defence, stoning them, so it was that every morning and afternoon there was a running battle until we reached a more built up part of the city at either end of our journey. Of course, there were no policemen about then, except now and then one, who evidently sympathized with the attacking party. One of these occasions was made very interesting to us by the assistance of a very large student by the name of Sullivan, a name which to me has always the suggestion of pugilism. He was at least six feet tall, broad-shouldered and powerful, and a very indifferent student. The attacks on us growing more and more violent we retained Sullivan as guard, and asked him to accompany us, not to be with us, but appear as an outsider and so get close to the enemy. When the shower of stones was flying pretty thick he pounced upon the stone throwers and in a few minutes they lay scattered on the ground. This settled them for a long time.

At our graduation Hardy was valedictorian and bore off most of the prizes, which he deserved. Raynor was salutatorian and got some prizes. Holt and Compton also received prizes, while I trailed along with the prize for drawing, which I did not care for as I did not need that stimulus to make me wish to do as well as I could in my studies. I disliked the system of marking, partly because the results were so largely dependent upon the point of view of the teachers and their inevitable mistakes, and partly because of the heart burnings and charges of unfairness against the teachers made by disappointed students.

Naturally, as the last year of our stay in the Academy drew towards its close, our graduation ceremonies became of great interest to us, and we prepared our graduation orations with which to entertain our own relatives and friends, and bore the relatives and friends of our fellow-graduates. The subject I chose, "The Feudal System," was interesting to me, but it did not occur to me that it would be of very little interest to the patient audience which listened to us.

The ceremonies were held at Niblo's Garden, a large theatre in Broadway near Houston Street, and the class sat in the theatre seats in front of the stage. The stage was arranged with chairs for the president, seated behind a large table, and professors, members of the Board of Education, and invited guests.

French Room.

Long the home and council chamber of Professor Fabregou, and in earlier days sacred to the classics under Professor Owen. A section reciting to Professor Downer.

On the table were our certificates of graduation and the prizes which were to be distributed. There was music by a small orchestra alternating with the orations. All of the seventeen members of the class spoke. I forget the subjects chosen by the other orators, but I thought they all did better than I did, for right in the middle of mine I forgot the rest of it for a few minutes. The audience kindly applauded me, then I rambled on extempore awhile until the rest of the oration came back to me, and I never knew how I dovetailed the new with the old, but I did it, and retired with more applause.

The finest oration, I thought, was John Hardy's valedictory, both in matter and delivery. Then came admonitory addresses to the students, by the president and others, then the prizes were distributed, and as prize after prize was awarded to Hardy, there was most tumultuous applause. Each of the other prize men were applauded; even I with my solitary prize in drawing received a proportionate amount.

Our certificates were handed to us by the venerable Doctor and we departed to seek out our friends to receive their congratulations.

The Early Sixties

Ira Remsen, '65

THOUGH I have the honor to be a Bachelor of Arts of the College of the City of New York, I am not in the usual sense an alumnus of the College. This may sound paradoxical but nevertheless it is true. For reasons which I need not go into, I left college towards the end of the Sophomore year. If I had stayed I should have received my degree in the ordinary course of events in the year 1865. As a matter of fact I did receive it about 1890, or thirty years after entering. It took me thirty years to earn the degree, and the average student earns it in five. That is a plain statement of fact. What conclusion to draw I do not know, nor do I know that it is necessary to draw any conclusion. My only object in referring to this matter at all is to avoid sailing under false colors.

And now as an alumnus, who is only half an alumnus, I am asked to write something for the Memorial Volume. What shall it be? The circumstances naturally tempt me to an estimate of the value of the training I received at the College. How far has it been helpful

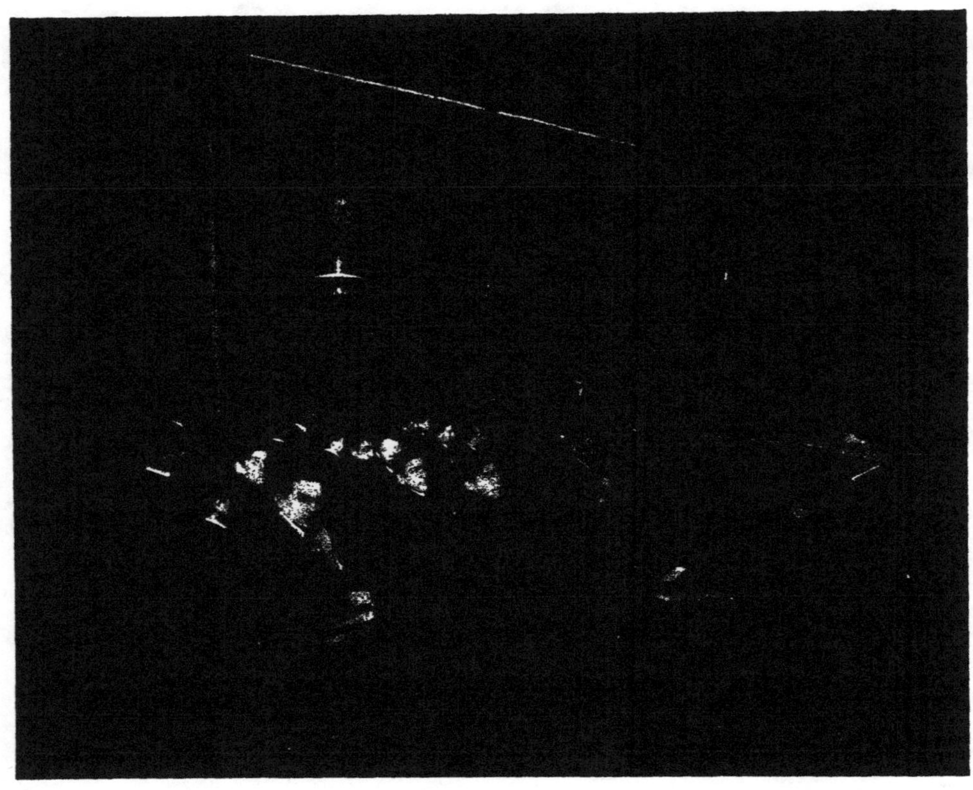

Room Five.

Recitation Room of the Physics Department, Professor Parmly explains.

to me in my life work? I wish I could tell. But I find it extremely difficult to reach definite conclusions on such subjects. My inclination was toward scientific pursuits. I did not know this when I was at the College nor was there much opportunity to find it out. We had a few lectures in chemistry by Professor Wolcott Gibbs. Now, Professor Gibbs was an excellent chemist, of whom the country is proud, but what can any one do with one lecture a week in chemistry or any other subject? I remember very little of that course of lectures except the word sesqui-oxide. That made an impression. But this can hardly be called scientific. Indeed, I am quite sure that chemistry did not appeal to me in that form.

The only other attempt at science made in those days was a course given once a week by Professor R. Ogden Doremus. He lectured in the chapel on human anatomy, physiology, geology, and astronomy. I think he also gave us a few talks on natural philosophy but I came out of this unscathed and without any feeling that I should like to devote myself to scientific pursuits. This is no reflection on Professor Doremus. He did the best he could under the circumstances. At about this time, if I remember correctly, he gave a popular course on chemistry and physics at the Cooper Institute that did interest me very much. His experiments were highly spectacular. Great crowds went to hear him. I looked forward to each lecture with longing. I cannot say that I carried away any clear ideas.

That was probably my own fault. But the exhibition pleased me and that was worth something.

Mathematics came easy to me. At the end of the Introductory year I found that one of the Ward Medals was awarded to me for "Greatest Proficiency in Algebra and Geometry." That gave me satisfaction and does even now. I was looking at the medal not long ago. I came across it in arranging my treasures. The fact that I was head of the class in mathematics without being conscious of any effort led me to think about taking up some occupation requiring the use of this branch. I talked it over with my father and we rather felt that civil engineering offered an excellent field, and for a time that idea took possession of me. The next year we took up calculus and this also seemed easy, and I could not understand why any one should find it difficult, as some assuredly did. Its significance I failed to grasp. I could do the tricks and liked to do them, but I could not see that they were of any value whatever. One day I met Professor Docharty, who was then the principal professor of mathematics. He was always pleasant to me and I felt that he was more or less sympathetic. He asked me how I liked my work. I told him truthfully that I liked the calculus but I could not see what it was for. To this he replied, "Never mind, that will all come out right in time." At this late date I do not wish to complain, but I think the professor might have done me a great service by pointing out, what appeared clear much later, that calculus is the

Room Three.

Students' Laboratory in the Physics Department.

science of growth. I lost my interest in the subject not long after that and later lost my knowledge of it, so that it became extremely difficult to acquire facility in its use. This experience has impressed me with the great difference between the plasticity of the mind in early youth and the comparative rigidity which characterizes it a few years afterward.

Latin and Greek I studied conscientiously but they did not give the pleasure that mathematics did. They caused me no special difficulty and I believe the daily drill was valuable. The interpretation of a difficult passage presents numerous problems that can be solved definitely, and the teacher can hold the pupil accurately to his work. With a good teacher there is nothing slipshod about it. We were not required to read a great deal in order that we might "imbibe the spirit of the ancients," but we were required to know a certain amount each day and to defend our knowledge at every point. That drill, I repeat, I believe was valuable, and the most valuable feature of it was, in my opinion, its accuracy. I cannot believe that we should have been nearly as much benefited if we had been obliged to skim over a lot of material and leave it with a most imperfect knowledge of its meaning. The tendency of this latter method is to develop slovenliness, while one of the chief objects of education is, it appears to me, to overcome the natural tendency to slovenliness.

History was to me the most difficult subject. I could not remember dates and the other important facts that make up a certain kind of history, such as the names of a long line of rulers, the names of generals, the number killed in battle, and the number taken prisoner. I tried hard enough, but it was no use. Before going to bed I would repeat over and over again the main points that were to come up the following day, only to find that they had not stuck, and in the morning I had to go at it again, and with very little time. The examinations in history were terrible to me. I may say that I have always felt since that this was my greatest weakness so far as power of acquiring knowledge is concerned, and I have been led to read more history than I should perhaps otherwise have done. This has given me a good deal of pleasure and also some pain, for I still find it very difficult to remember what I read in this line. Curiously enough I do not find it difficult to remember the history of chemistry. My knowledge of the literature of chemistry, which is extensive, is unusually good, and, apparently, for facts in which I have, as it were, a personal interest my memory is better than the average. I mention this because I think it is interesting from the psychological point of view.

In connection with the work in history I am reminded of an incident which I think worth recalling. My standing in my classes was high during the first year. I think I was head of the class the second half year. I am not sure of this. It may have been another half-year. At all events the next term we took up history and that, for the reason I have given, pulled

THE DRAWING ROOM.

Looking south, showing casts, and Parthenon frieze upon the wall.

me down. My recollection is that I fell to the seventh or eighth place. Well, that was a good deal of a fall. I felt badly about it, but I simply could n't help it. Now for the incident. One day one of my teachers with whom at that time I had had but little to do, came to me and said, "Remsen, I notice that you did not do as well last term as usual. What 's the matter?" I did not explain. Perhaps I was ashamed to. Perhaps I felt that the explanation was not adequate. I do not know how this may have been, but I do know that the kindly word of this teacher made a lasting impression upon me. I have since had the satisfaction of telling him so. My fellow alumni will not be surprised to learn that the teacher I am speaking of is Professor Adolph Werner. At that time he had our class in logic. I never studied German under him. I am glad to be able to say that as soon as I got through with history my standing rose again, and I believe Professor Werner rejoiced as much as I did.

Drawing played an important part in our course and I am glad it did. I believe it furnishes excellent training. At all events I have always felt since that the time spent in the drawing room was well spent. I could draw fairly well, at least outlines. I did try the Laokoön group and finished it after a fashion. This was, of course, too much for me, and I imagine the result was not very satisfactory. I afterwards had, for a time, the idea of taking up artistic work for a profession because I liked it and had some skill at drawing. But

I came to the conclusion that my skill was not sufficient. In this I was confirmed by the judgment of a friend who was a professional artist. He did, to be sure, encourage me somewhat but he did not at least insist that I should take up art. I remember the old German professor who taught us drawing. His name was Koerner. The boys used to call him "Point in space." I have no doubt that he was a good teacher, though my memory of his efforts in this line is not clear. One thing I do remember. He was unconsciously guilty of a great act of injustice to me. He never knew it. If I tell the story now it can hurt no one's feelings, and it may serve as a warning to some who may be inclined to reach conclusions too hastily. The case was this: Among other exercises in free-hand drawing we had to copy some outlines of heads. These were placed before us on the wall and we drew them as best we could. I happened to hit them pretty well. At the end of the week the professor told us that he had marked the drawings which we had handed in. The names of the class were called off in the order of the excellence of their work. To my great surprise my name was not called at all. At the close of his remarks the professor said, "There is one set of drawings that I have not marked at all because they are so accurate that I am sure they could not have been done honestly." Imagine my feelings! I did not say a word to him about it. What good could that do? I protested to my classmates, but I fear some of them were never convinced of my honesty in this matter. I

A LECTURE IN THE DRAWING ROOM.

View to the north. Professor Diehlman, President of the National Academy is lecturing on Architecture. It was here that Professor Woolf delivered his notable series of lectures on Æsthetics.

learned what it was to be a martyr in a small way. In this connection it may not be out of place to mention the fact that one of my sons had an uncontrollable desire to be an artist and that he is now following that career. My own tastes lead me to take much pleasure in his work.

There was n't much mischief among us as I remember it. Certainly nothing very bad. We used to misbehave in one class-room with great regularity. The teacher in this case simply could not keep order. If a teacher can't he can't and there 's an end on't. It was a waste of time for us to go to this room. We were wrong, of course, and yet that same thing will happen in every class-room in charge of a teacher who, as we say, "can't keep order." A teacher of this kind lacks personal force and ought not to be a teacher. His work is bound to be a failure. Nature provides that the pupils of such a man shall make it as uncomfortable for him as possible—Nature's hope being apparently that he will give it up and go into something else. Too often Nature hopes in vain.

But I have wandered on far enough—perhaps too far. I have found pleasure in recalling those old days. Sometimes I regret that I should have left college. At all events I do not regret the time spent there. My life might have been more satisfactory had I completed the course, or had I had the opportunity to go to one of the larger colleges and stay there until I was twenty-two or twenty-three years old before receiving the degree. No one can tell. As matters turned out, I spent five years at German universities not long after I left and, while devoting myself largely to a specialty, I did make some effort to make up for the defects of my earlier education. The training I received at the College was of value to me, I am sure. I have already said that I believe that the chief value lay in the daily drill in subjects the nature of which makes it possible for the teacher to follow every step of the pupil's mental processes, and to secure accuracy.

After the War

John R. Sim, '68

WHEN at some meeting of old friends and college-mates I look back through a vista of more than forty years to the days of my first entrance into the old "Free Academy," I find that the pictures then impressed upon my mind seem more vivid than those preserved by most of my companions. Perhaps this is only because I was a country boy freshly come to the city, so that everything about the metropolis struck me as strange, and my mind was in a state peculiarly alert to receive impressions. Those were the war days, when we lads talked more of battles than of books, and the old Free Academy—or young, I suppose I should call it, for its years then, as now, almost exactly matched my own—had not yet changed its name. That came in my Sophomore year, when, with its new title as the College of the City of New York, the institution assumed a formal dignity to which the depth and thoroughness of its studies well entitled it.

Looking back I can see, as plainly as if yesterday.

the great barn of the chapel, in which we assembled daily. About that time everybody was singing how they would "Hang Jeff Davis on a Sour Apple Tree," and the boys used to cut out endless effigies of the unhappy victim. A thread was placed about the figure's neck, a moist, clingy wad of paper was attached to this, and then projected violently upward against the walls or lower ceiling of the chapel. Generally these missiles returned to vex the sender, but occasionally to our unhallowed joy, one of them would stick high out of reach. When a gentle breeze swept through the hall each of these little manikins would flutter about and jerk and toss in grewsome suggestion of the gasping struggle between life and death.

Another vivid picture shows me four large, open registers, one in each quarter of the great hall. Through these, when all went well in the regions below, there arose a steady stream of hot air. Scarce a student of any originality whatever but made personal investigation of the odd experiments in which this ascending column of air could be employed. If one brought from home a carefully prepared pocketful of old paper torn up very fine, and if, in a fit of scientific enthusiasm, one tossed the whole of this over the register, the atoms did not fall, but sweeping upward with the rush of air rose grandly to the ceiling, thence to scatter and descend in what seemed a delicate snowfall over the entire hall. No other experiment proved so alluring as this—if we except the similar one of dropping a few grains of

PROFESSOR ANTHON'S HISTORICAL CABINET.
A corner in the Second-Floor Corridor.

pepper into the air column. The variety of echoing sneezes which responded throughout the chapel was a marvel and a thing of beauty, to remain in some unregulated minds a joy forever.

Then there were study hours in the chapel, when we gathered round those registers in close and merry comradeship. The back of the great room had seats and desks, but in the front were benches ranged to avoid those heated centres of temptation. These benches were easily gathered in social squares around the source of heat, while on the outskirts of the section hovered livelier students on mischief bent. A favorite prank with those desks in the back—old-fashioned desks such as many of you must remember, made for two with a hole for an inkstand in the centre—was to kindle a paper fire inside and let the flame shoot upward through the ink hole. Well do I remember the startled impression made upon my youthful mind the first time I saw this happen, and saw Fabregou—young tutor Fabregou then, beloved old Fabregou now, still happily here among us—saw him rush with vigorous expostulations to extinguish the blaze.

I could recall for you other bits like these, an endless series, as for instance, of the huge wood stoves in the lower rooms and the disorder occasioned by them; but this entire book is not for one man's reveries, and I hurry on.

Away back in the later sixties, and for years preceding and following, students in the Classical Course had the option of taking French, German, or Spanish in the Senior year. Of the Classical students in the class of '68 seven elected to study German. In alphabetical order they were: Baker, Bowker, Chambers, Crawford, Knox, Pope, and Sim. Baker, the class poet, and afterwards author of "Point Lace and Diamonds," and other popular verse, presently dropped out for reasons not now remembered, and graduated with '69. The remaining six survived the perils of the first term, and February, 1868, found them in good spirits, undoubtedly well satisfied with themselves—as is the manner of Seniors—and looking out upon the world with a sort of wonder that the world had thus far got along so well without their help.

In those days, which seem but as yesterday to the writer, the schedule of recitations was dotted here and there with "study hours," which, as I have suggested, were usually passed in the chapel under the supervision of one or more of the instructors. It fell to the lot of the Classical German squad of six to have a couple of these study hours per week assigned to them in among the recitations of the second term, Senior year; and as a special favor from President Webster they were permitted to use his recitation-room as a study-room, without supervision. This room was on the ground floor, in the northeast corner of the old college building, its end windows opening on the College yard, the Workshop-Laboratory Drawing Room extension not yet having been dreamt of; it is the same room that now

History Room.

Professor McGuckin. On the walls are copies of illuminated MSS. made by the students, also a facsimile of the original pact of freedom, made between the three Swiss cantons in 1291

contains the engine and other machinery of the electric outfit. Of course it extended then, as now, under a part of the chemistry lecture-room, and in the old days a large stove occupied a prominent position in the east centre of the room, and sent its surplus heat—when it had any—through a register into the lecture-room overhead. It may be said, by the way, that this stove engaged a large share of student attention from day to day, during cold weather especially. It was generally either red-hot or stone-cold, its condition at any time being the result usually of studied effort on the part of some student or students. From time to time it would emit the pungent odors of burning snuff, and other substances, introduced on the sly by students curious in the line of experiment; while every now and then muffled explosions would reverberate through its vast interior and up the hot-air pipe into the lecture-room, also the result of unholy student activity.

In this room, rich with memories and associations, the study of German went on apace on the part of the six Seniors, and great was the progress they all made, for the acquisitions of each were at the service of all during these conferences. And even in comparatively modern times the Professor of German has been known to refer with apparent pride to the amount and variety of German text which some classes covered in "the brave days of old."

But even to these men there came at times yearnings and longings of the soul for other, if not always better, things. And thus, now and then, a weary brother would interrupt the proceedings with a story or a joke; and presently it was suggested that a limited portion of each hour be devoted to listening to such stories, jokes, conundrums, etc., as the researchers and narrators might think worthy of being presented to such a company. At once there was manifested a variety of opinion as to the merit of many of the offerings; and it was soon determined that orderly procedure required that a vote should be taken to determine officially the merit of each story, joke, or conundrum presented; and that a majority vote should be necessary to authorize a laugh; and that any one, even the narrator himself, who ventured to laugh, before a favorable vote had been declared and a signal given, should be subject to a fine. A Master of the Revels was then appointed and the German section entered upon a new phase in its career.

The scheme worked wonderfully and with many surprises. Occasionally a really funny thing was voted down—when some unfortunate to whom the fun of it was irresistible, no longer able to contain himself, would explode and so subject himself to the reprobation of the Master, as well as to a fine. Whenever it was voted to laugh, on the signal being given, the quiet of the room would be broken, by from three to five voices, with such shouts as might fittingly accompany "bedlam broken loose." The company discovered presently, to its grief, that the old stove with its hot-air pipe lead-

THE THIRD-FLOOR CORRIDOR

Looking west. Along the walls are the cases containing models and apparatus of the Physics Department.

ing into the chemistry lecture-room acted as a speaking-tube on a large scale, and faithfully discharged the noises from the "study"-room below in full volume into the lecture-room above. When Dr. Doremus inquired into the origin of these disturbances, and learned that they resulted from the "concerted study of German" in the room below, he lodged a complaint with Dr. Webster, and the German section was forthwith dispossessed and ordered to report on study hours in the ante-room of the president's office. In after years a part of this room was partitioned off and used by Mr. Mayell as his office. In the old days it was undivided by partition, and its furniture consisted of a few chairs and a low table covered with green oil-cloth, which stood on the right hand as you passed into the President's office. It was at this table that the President usually interviewed the young men who were sent to him on account of disorder. The office proper was closed by a heavy, solid door which was long afterwards replaced by the present swinging glass doors. The solid door usually stood open when the President was in his office.

Dr. Webster kept himself posted as to the times and seasons when his German friends should report in the ante-room; he always greeted them kindly, took note of any absences, and frequently urged diligence and increased application to study—though the Doctor knew as well as any one that the little group was far above the average in scholarship, containing, as it did, four men of honor rank, one of them being the valedictorian of the class.

The Doctor found it a difficult matter to keep his wards together all the time. Very often when he stepped to the door, apparently to count them, he would find one or more missing, and he had the good sense never to presume that the one or more present had the faintest idea of where the missing ones were. He would search them out himself and bring them back to the ante-room, one by one; and very often he would restore the wanderer to his place at the table with an audible chuckle.

Time and space would fail me to tell of all the varied pranks of this joyous little "German band" of six while supposedly under the eye of the good Doctor, but two stand out in memory so distinctly that they must be referred to. On one occasion two of the party had slipped away unobserved and had descended to the ground floor and were circumspectly peeping through the door into Twenty-third Street. They presently heard the tones of a hurdy-gurdy near by in the street, and it was the work of but a moment to get into touch with the owner, lead him into the building and to the head of the first flight of stairs, and there inspire him, with a small fee, to do his utmost, while slowly advancing along the hall to the west. The two culprits had barely time to reach their places in the ante-room when the old organ began to do its loudest, with one of the popular airs of the time. There was much excitement in the immediate neighborhood for a few moments; heads appeared at

THE OLD DRINKING FOUNTAIN.
Third-Floor Corridor.

the doorways opening into the hall; the little German band, closely followed by the Doctor, was out at once to note the cause of the hubbub, the four innocent members exhibiting marked signs of astonishment, and the other two feigning to do so. The Doctor advanced on the poor organ-grinder; the latter backed slowly to the stair-head, but kept the crank of his machine going furiously the while, as if determined to earn his fee; and when he started down the steps, having understood that he was no longer wanted, he waved his hat in general farewell to the small crowd which had by this time assembled. The Doctor had him escorted to the street by the worthy janitor, Mr. Delaney, who had appeared in the rear, shortly after the concert had begun; and thus ended the episode. As the Doctor passed by on his return he looked sadly at his wards, who appeared to be hard at work with their text-books; but whether he suspected any of them of complicity in the musical outbreak they never learned.

The other incident occurred on an occasion when the Doctor passed out of his office to escort a lady visitor to the stairway, and inadvertently left the key in his office door. It was the work of but a moment for one of the group of six to close the door, lock it, and slyly drop the key into the pocket of another of the party—the valedictorian. After parting from the lady the Doctor went on a short tour through the building, and did not return to his office at once. When he did return he had forgotten that he had left the door of his office open. He searched his pockets for the key, and looked all about the ante-room for it—in vain. Then he sent for the janitor and had him call at the rooms he had just visited and make inquiry, but the key was not found in any of them. The mystery truly was great; and the man with the key in his pocket was the most sympathetic and the most puzzled of all and the most active in the search for the missing key. It presently appeared that the Doctor's hat and his text- and record-book were all locked up in the office, and that the Seniors were due to recite to him in International Law the very next hour. By this time the man who had locked the door and hidden the key was somewhat alarmed at the situation. He took the man whose pocket held the key to one side and told him where the key was. The latter was indeed startled. After a hurried consultation the janitor was called in and told the facts, and the key was given to him. It was understood that at the end of the Senior recitation the janitor told the Doctor that the key had been found "where it was not lost," giving the Doctor the impression that *he* had mislaid it; and no further questions were asked.

It may be of interest to know that in spite of their periods of frivolity, the members of the little German band all passed creditable examinations in the early summer and were duly graduated towards the end of June. They are now gray-headed men, but, at their occasional meetings, it is not difficult to understand why they laugh when certain incidents of their undergraduate life are recalled.

The Change from the Free Academy

Robert Abbe, '70

THERE is a middle period in the life of an institution somewhere between the first struggles of infancy, when all the promise and evidence of greatness is conspicuous, and the later period of manhood and matured greatness, during which a sort of adolescence and forcing one's self before the world is the most noticeable part of existence.

The claims of the young débutant may be fitly represented in the second quarter-century of the growth of our College.

Ambition was justified by an already fine array of noble graduates, by a well ordered and sustained college curriculum, and an array of officers and teachers of which any college could be proud.

At this juncture, then, the claims to representation in the sisterhood of colleges called for a new name. Those who entered in 1866 with the writer had the delight of joining in the christening of the College of the

City of New York, and burying the old "Free Academy." The new name was painfully long—every one knew that—but it was explicit. That was enough.

The day of the fateful change was a holiday, and the fête was as elaborate as imagination and precedent could make it. For the students, the night was the most memorable part of the ceremonial.

Those were days of torchlight processions such as were never seen before. Several years of civil war had accustomed the city to processions whenever a great battle had been won, and though the war had ended, the habit remained.

On the miniature campus surrounding the fine old gothic structure there was enough grass to harbor as loyal and lusty-lunged a lot of lovers of alma mater as any college needed, to celebrate its great renaming. Let us recall the forming of classes in procession,—each man with his torch,—marching and counter-marching, shouting and echoing, crowding and jostling, within and without that old iron railing; thronging the streets, bullying policemen, anathematizing Columbians. We owned the town that night.

Speeches by the Seniors and chosen orators, which seemed to us undergraduates brimful of eloquence, were made at the angle where the flag-pole has so long stood. Never can we forget the impassioned eloquence of the poem by our renowned Edward M. Shepard, then chosen from the Freshman class as already a marked man. Raised a little above the crowd, backed up against the

The Philosophy Room.

old flag-pole, his face lighted only by the glare of a hundred torches, he seemed to the boys about as eloquent and brilliant as any orator who ever spoke. I have heard him a score of times since, in the momentous public gatherings of recent years, where he has been potent for good influence with his choice diction, stainless principles, and great moral force, and it seems to me he looked then, as since, the embodiment of calm severe dignity, the champion of justice and right.

The night was given up to shouts and revel. The "burial of the ancient," a delightfully carried out mock burial (in another corner of the grounds) of the now defunct "Free Academy," to which were added some dry-as-dust books we all voted odious, was followed by a noisy torchlight procession in hollow squares up and down Fifth Avenue. I think we extended our tramp to the gates of our supposed rival, Columbia, then at Forty-ninth Street and Madison Avenue.

But it may well be remarked that the boys of our College were never given to rowdy proceedings such as often marked the university sports of other colleges. There seems to the writer to have been always in the minds of the City College boys a sense of serious work and responsibility, and of careful conservation of other people's welfare, because we are essentially children of the people, and in a socialist sense a product of the public purse. In this view I feel a touch of pride, as if the fundamental facts of social order were deeply rooted in the breast of every well disciplined scholar graduated from that great institution, the public school.

To the graduates of the classes of that day, the distinguished and venerated figure of the president, Dr. Horace Webster, will stand out as long as memory lasts. A large, classic-featured gentleman, whose searching eye and mobile lips fixed one's attention, taught us all a better way to do everything which we already had thought we were doing well. His frequent unexpected advent in the class-room was always pleasant to the boys. Professor Huntsman, in his arid way, taught us philosophy, but we felt he was ably seconded by Dr. Webster when once in a while he would drop in and help elucidate matters. I recall a day when the discussion of "responsibility" was to the fore. "Pop" Webster, as we irreverently called him, said to the classman reciting, "If a bird flies over your head, you are not responsible, are you?" "No sir! " "But if a bird flies over your head and makes a nest in your hair, you are responsible are you not?" This was one of the self-evident and clarifying ways by which he often helped out.

How our views change with the years, and how interesting and valuable now seems the dry learning of philosophy and metaphysics and political economy!

Dear old Professor Barton, who taught us English by the homely but impressive method of making it pleasant, who can forget his admonition to a rough member by forcing down his throat the definition of Sir Philip Sidney of a "gentleman," "high thoughts

The English Room.
A Section reciting to Professor Mott.

seated in a heart of courtesy!" What student did not know that the dear old Professor saved some of the crumbs of his frugal luncheon to feed two little mice who always came out of their hole under his platform when the class had gone?

Professors now gone have all left a sweet memory behind. Professor Docharty lightened his dry mathematical course by immensely dryer humor. Professor Owen was most serious in his pride of the Greek he taught. "Poluphloisboios," he would say, "the loud resounding waves," and suiting the action to the word the reverberation in his deep mouth would almost sound like breakers on the shore.

Professor Koerner, who looked the old German artist that he was, was so full of the defence of simplicity and truthfulness in art that he would even go into fits of anger after a Junior exhibition, when the speakers had been showered with flowers packed in cord-bound bouquets, and tell the class that it was "zutch a pity to dhrow doze dr-r-readful bumshells."

Then we, too, had Professor Doremus, the incomparable Doremus, florid, graphic, entrancing. His words of fire stirred and impressed us; as the glow of electric sparks he delighted to send in showers, or the phosphorus and red lights he could display as no one else. Never should it be forgotten that he was the pioneer in making the dry subject of chemistry alluring by the brilliancy of his experiment and demonstration; or that he represented a power in the social and public eye in the city that was a large factor in popularizing our noble institution. No one was ever more loyal.

Frobisher (no one called him "Professor" Frobisher) left a strong impression on the boyish mind—and what more can be asked of a teacher? He was so serious, and so insistent on repetition of a sentence, until one could himself see that he spoke better with every utterance. And then, what a picture this tall serious being left on the mirror of one's brain, with his long wind-mill arms agoing; but so patient, as if all the future life of the student depended on his instruction in elocution. And then our dear Professor Tisdall, who seemed to know so much that was profound and beyond our ken of Latin and Greek. How we envied him!—but he made us love the subject-matter. That was enough.

Out of the very loins of our own College came one of the best teachers who ever won the esteem of his pupils, Adolph Werner. His life-long service to the intellectual growth of the horde of city youths who have entered our College and gone out into commercial life (the wealth-producing part of the community) cannot be estimated by the meagre total of salary paid to such valued teachers.

Of all the fascinating subjects, though, that were laid before us, none captivated as did Professor Compton's. He has seen the coming and going of more classes than any one ever in the faculty, and has had the affectionate regard of more thousands of students than any one, perhaps, in any college in this great city.

PROFESSOR HUNT'S ROOM.

Sacred to descriptive geometry and mechanical drawing.

His was a delightful subject, physics and astronomy, music and the stars. With him we ran the gamut, from surveying and drawing most perfect roads upon the hillside (which he called "ramps"), to an estimate of the orbit of a planet. In my class it was understood, and told with awe, that in the previous class there was a man named Burchard who had exactly calculated the return date of a comet; such were the accuracies of mathematics applied in our class-room.

In a room sacred to history and occupied by bare benches and a wonderful safe full of valuable coins of every age sat Professor Anthon, long since passed away. So brimful of historic facts, and yet so lenient for our failures! How much pain we must have given him! How sweet now those hours would be to us, and what would we not pay in coin to have them back!

The days of the studies, the songs, and quartettes of the classes now forty years old have been replaced by years of success in every field of human work; and we look on the growth of the enormous classes and throngs who come to drink at the worshipful font of knowledge to-day, with eyes accustomed to larger horizons but still dazed and delighted with the vision of our new college buildings, grown up like Aladdin's palace in a year.

In our day such things could not have been even dreamed of, and we but echo the philosophic remark of the Chinese sage—"We can imagine a limited number of things, but there is nothing that may not happen."

The Later Seventies

Lewis Sayre Burchard, '77

LINKING the later with the earlier '70's, like Bismarck's cigars, "chain-smoked," lit each upon the remainder fire of its predecessor, let this writer take the torch from the man ahead by saying that his very first hour as a student of the Introductory class was passed under the tutorship of the author of the preceding article. I remember that hour well. It passed in what was called the Introductory Chapel, then new, and presided over at matins by Professor Scott, as viceroy or proconsul. Afterwards christened "Natural History Hall," it came to be described by Noble, of '80, as containing "a menagerie of unearthly-looking skeletons, a whole cart full of peculiar stones, and some unpleasant models of people's insides, together with a festoon of intestines employed for decorative purposes." "By what possible means," asks Noble, "can it be assumed that this blood-curdling precinct was ever an Introductory Chapel?"

Yet there it was that Dr. — then a slender,

THE LARGE MATHEMATICS ROOM, NUMBER TWENTY-ONE.
Professor Sim sits where Professor Mason sat before him.

graceful Mr. — Abbe lifted the curtain on our five-act, five-year Chinese drama with an hour in drawing. His opening statement, that his personal, practical instruction in sharpening a lead pencil was at our service if necessary, mightily impressed me, to whom the preparation of a lead pencil was always a strenuous whittling solo without inches of pencil ever yielding a satisfactory point. Here at last, thought I, was a place where teachers appreciated what a fellow really wanted to acquire, and where "Learning" approached respectable practicality.

We were a very young and impressionable lot, and I had had whatever additional impulse to susceptibility to tradition a little boy might get from having two older brothers at the College ahead of him. I had heard that in "Pop" Webster's time some students, looming in an Ossianic mist of heroic legend, had conveyed a goat into chapel, and that others, moving on a lower plane of laudable endeavor, had put assafœtida in the stove of the Doctor's classroom. I had heard at our breakfast table some one read in the morning paper of the students taking the horses out of Christine Nilsson's carriage the night of her début, and drawing her around to Professor Doremus's villa on Union Place. That seemed like the right thing, and suggested caps and gowns, Burschenkorps, and the Latin Quarter. The stuccoed Flemish turrets of Lexington Avenue had also a certain attractive uniqueness, and the Avenue front looked like Eton; but in total all these hardly sufficed to make a satisfying atmosphere of tradition and background of picturesqueness.

When I came up, a mere number, to take my admission exams for the Introductory class, I caught with a keen anticipatory delight at a fine antique smell of dead animal as something richly promising scientific mysteries; but whatever glamor of tradition my willing imagination fondly attached to that was shortly stripped away when Harry Van Kleeck of the Seniors told me that it came from an alligator that Professor Draper was stuffing, and I realized that our own humble household had sent ahead of me the very cause of the biological mustiness that had entranced the olfactories of hope. Was there to be in the antique line "nothing new under the sun"? That six-foot alligator corpse had been examined by me to satiety in our own backyard. My elder brother's taxidermical enthusiasm, which had been equal to gulls and prairie-chickens, had quailed before the job of stuffing a part of a ton of alligator, and, to get it off his hands, he had solemnly "presented" it to the Department of Natural History. To the relief of our family and the misery of the College, Draper had accepted it with a collector's ardor and proceeded to prepare it for his cabinets. I believe it decorates "Natural History Hall" to this day; but it represents for me the first dispelled illusion of my college years.

If one may quote his old Fraternity song, which to

A Board in the Mathematics Room.
Where sixty generations have left their record.

this day serves some of us better for "Marching Through Georgia" than the tune's original words,

"When we went to College, we were all on study bent;
Hazing, smoking, *et id om.*, were far from our intent;
We'd not the faintest kind of thought *what* College really meant;"

and I'm afraid that, if all the truth must be told, our "college days" for five years were, in a cheerful, laborious sort of way, pretty monotonous. Four hours of recitation a day for five days a week allotted us no "study hours" in College, such as had afforded the boys of the '60's some sort of opportunity for getting acquainted with classmates, getting up "Joke Clubs," and concocting other schemes. One o'clock or half-past found a growing youngster in the condition of a large spheroidal appetite surrounded by a thin coating of boy, which outvoted what little temptation there was to linger, even if Bonney *pater* had allowed. So, except as we foregathered in the halls in the five minutes between recitations on our way from room to room, or in the streets on our way to and from our homes, or at occasional tumultuous class-meetings, or in the literary societies Friday nights, or in the chapter rooms of our fraternities, there was almost no opportunity for the students to "get together." I suppose that is why we to this day cheer and sing so wretchedly. There was little opportunity for the development of that "human interest" that makes one's four years at any residential college so formative and full of tradition, and so rich in reminiscence. I devoutly hope the boys of the years to come may find more of it on St. Nicholas Heights.

But, as the child's enjoyment of his toys is largely subjective and quite spontaneous and insuppressible, so that all he needs is a soap-box and the disc wheels of an earlier civilization to taste the joys of motoring, so our hungry imaginations roamed seeking what they might devour. We must have been a comical and inventive lot of gossips. The fact that Professor Anthon washed his hands after each recitation, added to an authentic report that at home he smoked an enormous meerschaum pipe, seems in reminiscent examination to be all the ground there could have been for my being told that he had adopted "some kind of an oriental religion." One professor they used to say was the son of a king and received a monthly subsidy as the result of some mysterious treaty renouncing all pretensions to the crown. At any rate he drove in good form a high-stepping pair of hackneys to a high cart, and had written a text-book on cavalry that in some way we connected with West Point; and some of us had seen an aquarelle of him in a dragoon's cuirass, moustachioed and whiskered *à la* Count d'Orsay. He told me of leading charges with 100% of casualties and of taking part in the siege of Antwerp (1830); and whether his disabled leg was crippled or "cork," and how it happened, were subjects of respectful but curious discussion. As a politely respected but inspiring and undownable mystery, that leg shared

THE SMALLER MATHEMATICS ROOM.
An hour with Professor Legras.

honors with the beloved enigma as to how the dashing Doremus had lost his arm. Another tradition was that a venerable professor of philosophy habitually lunched upon pea-soup brought to College in a small tin pail, and that a famous corpulent strawberry had been named in his honor "the Huntsman Seedling." Tutor Tisdall wore a certain aura of renown because our unwritten chronicles had it that he could play several games of chess at once blindfold, and that he had met defeat with honor in the lists of Caissa at the hands of the invincible Paul Morphy.

Thus, half in hunger for imagination's food, half in college patriotism, we cherished the veriest tags of interest that tended to prove a man anything other than a hearer of recitations, and welcomed a hint that Barton, who looked like a Hebrew prophet or a high Druid in a parson's coat, would tramp the countryside with a gun, or that he had a clandestine interest in a certain friendly mouse in his section-room wainscot and daily fed it scraps of lunch. Thus, John Jason Owen, whose books had been read at Oxford, was a personage, despite the fact that his wife fussed in upon him at recitation. They say she would irrupt for carfare—some financial accident I suppose—and wait while he patiently fished out the required six cents and called her "me dear," or "Medea," as George Baker's song had punned it to round out the couple's classical relationship. So, too, was Docharty a celebrity in our eyes, and Draper, Frobisher, all those who had "published."

The tradition of Compton's many-sided practical and scholarly ability inspired us with a sort of reflected pride; while above all was the glorious memory that President Webb, as the newly assigned commander of a raw brigade, had, without losing ground or formation, received the impact of the greatest charge of the Civil War,—Pickett's at Gettysburg.

Every differentiation from our public-school standards of scene or person served to stimulate this sense of and appetite for a peculiar or "student" atmosphere. Welcome, therefore, was the evolution from the three peripatetic or visiting teachers of our Grammar School—drawing-master Miller, with his neat sheets of patterns; delightful old George Moore with his zöological collections in his side pockets; and the burly, bearded Hyatt, calling with baskets of bottles and performing with a Bunsen burner, a retort, and an assortment of glassware, sundry more or less spectacular muddlements, some of which "went off" delightsomely—to casual glimpses of Koerner's room with its talented amateurs sketching Venuses and Caryatids, of Draper's skeletons, or of the amphitheatred wonder shop of Doremus.

What picturesque reminiscence attends that Herman Joseph Aloys Koerner, Professor of Drawing, Descriptive Geometry, and Æsthetics. A little figure, bent, in a foreign-looking cloak and an exotic

THE OLD GERMAN ROOM.
Professor Werner and a few of his friends.

hat, with long white hair and beard, the hair brushed straight back and cut off square at the seventh cervical vertebra, and the beard surmounted by a jolly red nose and adorned as to its centre with a well-marked Nicotian halo, he seemed like a Teutonized combination of Clement C. Moore's St. Nicholas and Joe Jefferson's Rip Van Winkle. Yet he, too, carried the glamor we sought, for had he not exchanged the *bursch's schläger* for the revolutionist's sword with Carl Schurz in the '48 and, like him, fled, an exile for freedom, to America; and had not a certain ponderous, unreadable, great book of his in German, on *Æsthetik*, received high praise from President Porter of Yale? Do you remember his disdain of English as "a jargon," and his strings of blackboard notes, elaborately subdivided and numbered with Roman and Arabic numerals and large and small letters, liberally parenthesized, and abbreviated on the principle of leaving out the vowels; how he emphasized the importance of shadows by a droll dramatic rendering of the old German story of Pieter Schlemihl selling his shadow to the devil; how he told of creeping by the Domestic building at 14th Street and Broadway with its cast-iron statues, praying that it would not fall on him, it was so "oogly"?

I recall once, when I was mulling along on a hideosity *à deux crayons* which was supposed to represent the familiar mask of Dante, very undecided in my mind as to what was shadow and what plain dirt on the nose of the original, how he took me by the nose, most comrade-like and genial, and said, "Here, you, Boorkart, mek dat nose black, *black*, blacker'n Hell! Yes! Hell, Dante, *Inferno, siehst du?*"

How I wish I had taken the right kind of notes of his Senior lectures in "Æstetics, or the Principles of *Biooty.*" Memory brings me these:

"Here, you, doan' spik! Now! Arabic noomeral seex—The biooty (very long "u") of moation (very long "o") in annim'ls. Underline! Now, in a verticcle line, a, b, c, small lett'rs. Then, typiccle, a, the flea; b, the frog; c, the hare. A, the flea goes, so-o (gesture), three times so much perpendickler as it goes furder. B, the frog, so-o (jumping), simultaaneous; and c, the hare (a sudden pose that made his hair stand out behind him while the arm shot ahead), horizont'l.

"Now, seven, und last,—Underline. Mittic (mythic) annim'ls. Verticcle a, b, c. Typiccle. A, the dragoon; b, the griffin, and c, the Tevvle." Then followed elaborate descriptions of the zoölogical combinations which made up "a" and "b," wound up by this: "C, der Tevvle. Has body and het like a man, with hoarns, so-o, on the het; one foot regguler and one foot cloaven; and a tail mit a dart on the end, parentesis, not essential, und, note, some peeple thinks it 's a god! *Yes!*"

But this runs me off the track. As the sight of Koerner's rooms showed us horizons past the revealings of Miller, so did even the College's modest natural history collections surpass the museums of old

THE MECHANICAL SOCIETY.

A meeting in the Astronomy Room. Professor Compton and Professor Fox are on the front bench.

Mr. Moore's side pockets, and so we were impressed by Dr. Stratford's fascinating manikin and by a chance sight of Professor Draper sitting before one of his cabinets seriously dusting with a bellows the skeleton of a bird. That seemed such a knowing way to dust.

But above all did it open the pores of our minds to seat ourselves under the tuition of Doremus, and hear ourselves called generally "young gentlemen" and one's particular self "Mister," and plunge into stories of great things really done and doing in the living world outside, and how the reduction of atmospheric pressure above the boiling sugar syrup saved the sugar refiners some tremendous sum a year—or an hour—in coal. And that distinguished gentleman, who never deigned to harry us with small-boy recitation questions, but left us, like university men, if you please, to prepare an ambitious series of illustrated notes, had been known to present prizes, out of his own pocket, for superior performances in that line—once even the unheard-of munificence of a four-oared shell. A classmate's brother, Harry Dwight, as an Introductory, had won such a prize and so the Dwights and I spoiled several Saturdays on the opening chapters of an ambitious series of notes, with water-color illustrations taken from every text-book and encyclopedia we could lay our hands on, with gold-paint for the brass-work, which if our endurance had persisted, might have won for the next year's Freshman class at least a yacht.

There were others who impressed themselves on

memory. Professor Barton was a courtly old gentleman, finely deserving Dr. Anderson's noble eulogy, but a delicious inconsistency of his is perhaps worth a moment's gossip. In his little book and in his classroom lecturelets, he loved to hold forth upon the fitness and beauty and preferableness of Saxon words, if possible, monosyllables. Yet his speech was Latinistic, polysyllabic, and flowed in a dignified, cadenced, metrical rhythm. As Dr. Anderson put it,

> "Who can forget the method of his speaking—
> The shapely words of a well-ordered mind?"

It "burbled" in dactyls and trochees. Hearing him, one recalled Coleridge's

> "From long to long in solemn sort
> Slow Spondee stalks; strong foot! yet ill able
> Ever to come up with Dactyl trisyllable"

or noted how

> " One syllable long, with one short on each side,
> Amphibrachys hastes with a stately stride."

One could imagine his voicing even the "high-bred racer" of "Amphimacer" but never the jigging frivolity of an anapest. A sesquipedalian man, like Sidney Smith, he could have taken comfort unto himself in saying "Mesopotamia." And so, when you tilted your chair, he begged to be permitted to observe, oh, so gently and impersonally, and in a sentence that you could have scanned on the blackboard, that your chair had been manufactured on the model of a quad-

Apparatus Room of the Physics Department.

ruped—cæsura—*not* that of a biped. Every one of his students must remember his illustration of the Chartist banner bearing the "good old Saxon inscription" of "A Fair Day's Wage for a Fair Day's Work," and how if they had "inscribed upon their standard its equivalent in the Latinistic vocabulary, 'An equitable diurnal remuneration for an equitable diurnal operation' —cæsura—not a man would have joined them."

Yet he who asked for short, special, Saxon "picture" words rather than Latin, long, general, and abstract words, edited my chum Clark's description of Greece (or France) in a Junior oration, as the "light-bearer to the nations of the west" and changed it to the "glorious benefactor" of the same, greatly to Clark's bewilderment and indignation.

If, under stress of previous circumstances, you "improvised" your differentiation of a pair of Graham's synonyms, you stood an equal chance of hearing, "I like to commend a praiseworthy variation from a too slavish adherence to the exact verbiage of the text. I will give you 10. You may take your seat"; or, just as blandly and kindly, "Mr. ——, one should bear in mind that the author has devoted considerable research to his presentation of the subject under discussion and, unless one can feel quite confident that one can improve upon the language of our author, I should not recommend one to depart from it. I will give you zero. You may take your seat. That is quite all." To quote Dr. Anderson again, you received

> "His velvety rebuke, than sharp sword keener,
> And thrust home with an aim that never swerved,"

much as did the victim of Rupert the Headsman who never knew his head was off till the executioner politely handed him a pinch of snuff, when off it rolled and

> " the victim spoke no more."

Awesome he looked, in that straight-cut clerical coat, with those gaunt limbs,—with a handkerchief spread over one knee,— those "quaint gnarled hands," that shaggy, tousled head, that bardic beard, that glittering heavily-browed eye, now stern, now most kindly, but "take him for all in all" he was a most lovable gentleman, and we loved him and mourned him.

But the limits of space and the reader's patience forbid the detail that memory loves to gambol in. In hastiest perspective recall Draper, with his hand behind his ear, bidding you, in a thin, high, plaintive voice, that belied his rotundity, to "classify" the most unheard of animals, or giving you a pinch of seidlitz powder in a watch crystal, which, under your dudheen blow-pipe, would cut up the most ridiculous and un-classifiable shines that never could be found in that funny little "Bædeker's Guide to Magnesia," or "the Shorter Catechism of the Known and Unknown Salts,"—"the Youthful Alchemist's Own Handbook," —in which we used to look for "symptoms."

One ingenious youth devised the scheme of beating

PROF. COMPTON IN HIS WORKSHOP.

the book by tasting his powder, and, not being sure, kept at it till all was gone. As with the English railway's porter's little dog that "had 'et 'is tag, and nobody knew where 'e was goin'," investigation was at a standstill, and, like Oliver Twist, he had to go back to Draper for "more—" to find out that it was arsenic!

Do you remember the suddenly exploded "Ouch!" and smothered cuss-words of your neighbor who, absorbed in the performances of his parti-colored "bead," had forgotten how long a glass tube can stay hot? You do? So do I. Let 's pass on.

Then there was Frobisher, author of *Voice and Action*, descendant of polar Sir Martin, trainer of the Demostheneses of the '60's, black-bearded and hollow-cheeked enough to pose for Captain Kidd. He 'd put you through five minutes of exercise with a rubber strap to get your blood up and then bid you "speak LARGE and WIDE!—speak to that window up there at the other end of the chapel." When you spoke your piece on the stage and heard your own voice somewhere in the remote distance sounding something like a tiny dog in distress under a barrel, he sat in grim solitude at the right of the stage, just where your wobbling knees showed worst—in profile, because they *would n't* stay back,—and put down marks ag'in' you.

> "Frobisher (and Faculty) to right of you,
> Faculty also to left of you,
> Faculty (and President) behind you,
> Volleyed and thundered"

with their horrible little books and pencils, and when you ambled in a blue funk down those steep stairs you indeed

> "rode back again
> *Not* the six hundred."

It was a blood-curdling experience.

And there was Godwin, bearded like one of the beloved bushrangers of youthful reading, who bade you "promenade" or "take two pieces of chalk" if you said "Draw the parallel lines AB and CD," instead of "the line AB and, parallel to it, the line CD." With him you really learned to talk. More than any man we knew, he taught us orderly, *inevitable* reasoning.

Then dear, polite old "Barney" Sheldon, forever "shooting" his cuffs as, like a great crane, he paced, oh, so quietly, in chapel, always on downward and outward pointing toes and with straight knees, as if he had passed the days and nights of an orderly youth in alternately teaching sarabands and minuets and playing the ghost of Hamlet's father.

And Dr. Eustace Fisher, warm and tender friend of so many of us, with his rearwardly-curving legs, his red lips and pink complexion, his far-legended smile:—how,

> "as a bird each fond endearment tries
> To tempt her new-fledged offspring to the skies,"

he strove to lead us to dote appreciatingly on all the tropes in the samples of poetry we had to memorize.

The South Chapel Stairs.

We doted, hypocrites avid of marks that we were, but, I fear me, perfunctorily.

Then there was Fiston, whom you could always get a rise out of by saying "*À bas les Prussiens!*"; and Fabregou, ever so courteous, with French like a crystal bell, so contrasting with the deep-chested *Pays-Bas* French of his chief of the black-ribboned monocle and the grimly-clipped white moustache—a French that always conveyed to me the conviction that indeed they *must* have sworn terribly in Flanders. It seemed to come

"Acrross the sound of rrolling drrums."

Old as he was,—and he had led his dragoons in 1830,—he had a magnificent grip, taught me a *jiu-jitsu* trick in '77, and once rolled out in that jolly old word-of-command voice of his, "Burrcharrd, you're a good fellow: but your French is *dammnnable!*" rolling drum accompaniment again with a bow and a laugh and a polite wave of the hand which made us all feel good and whose *bonhomie* warmed our hearts. He had the air of the old world, the high world. One missed the gold lace, the ribbon, and the order.

Another vivid memory Kodak is that of Doremus in his photometric room. A travelled American woman, who knows her galleries, said, when she saw the photograph of Boynton's painting of Doremus in his cap and gown, "He looks like a Doge." Against the soft, rich, dark of that photometric room, where everything was painted a sooty, velvety, lustreless black, the flame of his single "standard candle" threw the noble lines and contours of his face and head into simple masses of black and white, without reflected lights, —the darkness suppressing the modern clothing; it was a subject to invite the ghost of Rembrandt.

One other painting of our day was less successful. They tell me the chapel of to-day looks "dingy and classic" as ever; but '77 saw Alma Mater, perhaps suddenly becoming conscious of her age, and true to her sex, blossom out in gay attire. It was a most sudden, startling, and frivolous change. The *Microcosm* recorded, "Chapel transformed into a mixture of rainbow and tea-store, and defiled by the presence of Introducts." The *Echo* called it a "chameleonic outburst," and printed a parody on Dryden's *Alexander's Feast* about it in which the Glee Club at the Alumni Meeting was supposed to inflame President Ketchum of the Alumni and Chairman Crawford of the Executive Committee, as follows:

"Now strike the Steinway Grand again;
A louder yet and yet a louder strain.
Keep his lemonade off yonder.
Rouse him, *tenori*, like a peal of thunder!
Hark! Hark! that last great chord—
Like a slip signed 'McG.'
Or, worse, the dreaded 'P.'—
Has brought him to his feet and leans him on the board.

"'Revenge! (keep time!)' the leader cries—
See the painters rise!
See the scaffoldings they rear,

THE CHAPEL, LOOKING EAST.

Showing the Columbus banners along the walls, and the empty stage from which every alumnus has held forth in oratorical turn.

Dangling paint-pots in the air;
See the yellow paint—and drab—spare our eyes!
Behold a ghastly band,
Each a brush in one hand,
And a contract in the other to protect 'em.

"Now, *Alexander*, *Ketchum*,
And to their just doom fetch 'em!
Look on high!
Oh, my!

"Behold, how they rub their red brushes on the beams—
And now within your very view
They paint your chapel roof a sickly blue!
The Alumni rise despite the paint-fiends' screams:
Alexander seized a window-pole with zeal to destroy;
Holmes (sweet Holmes!) led the way,
To light him to his prey,
And, like another Helen, fired another 'Sealed
Proposal for Painting, Kalsomining, and Decorating
The Chapel of the College of the City of New York.'"

And so we blossomed from schoolboys into, at least, potential classmen such as we had heard of and read of, susceptible to every suggestion that promised to realize college "life."

So some of us (I remember Nelson Henry was my cicerone in this) carried torches from the Worth Monument up Fifth Avenue with the Columbia boys in a "Burial of the Ancient" and cheered or serenaded fondly-imagined Rutgers girls who were supposed to live in the picturesque round-towered Rutgers "Female" College buildings opposite the Reservoir, brought

President Barnard out on the porch of his house on Columbia's 49th Street campus, and attended a songful and hilarious *Kneipfest*. Again we journeyed to Rutgers,

"On the banks of the old Raritan,"

Princeton, and five or six other colleges, to learn how initiations and class-days were carried on.

A vacant block in Harlem—there were plenty of them then—on what is now called Lenox Avenue, overlooked by the Convent of the Sacred Heart, saw under the Class of '76 as Seniors the beginnings and, indeed, all of our football. We ranged up in "twenties" then, with red stockings, but innocent of the guards and pads and jackets of modern armor. The game was the old "open" American game. You might not carry the ball or tackle your man. There were no signals nor formations nor mass plays nor flying wedges nor any of the war science of Deland and Walter Camp. But we did a power of running, and the writer carries a broken nose gained from a spirited but unplanned collision with one of the '76ers of mighty name—Wood or Riblett or Ormsby. Judge Vernon Davis, '76, was a captain then, and Ed Weed, '77 (now a prosperous automobiling physician), Adjutant-General Nelson Henry, '77, and his brother Howard, '77, the three Kenyons, '76, '78, '81, Rushmore, '76 (auspicious name—lately candidate for the Supreme bench), Birkins, '77, Putnam, '78, Shethar, '80, recall

THE CLASS OF '05.
Grouped about the Chapel Stage, with the star flag, old clock, and electric class numerals in background.

themselves as "scouring the plain" or clustering in scarlet-legged scrimmages against the twenties of N. Y. University, Stevens, Rutgers, and Columbia. Going down in the train, after a game, from the 125th Street station to 42d Street, there would be much cheering, but our random, ill-trained "C. C. N. Y." never prevailed against the disciplined orthographic cheer of Columbia,—much to the writer's humiliation and sorrow. As my class went out of college the Rugby game began to come in, with, I think, a son of Professor Fabregou as a star player. In November, '77, our Freshmen held the Columbia Freshmen to a tie score of zero in a Rugby game which the *Herald* called "the most remarkable contest of the season." But we had too little opportunity for practice and were too light and lathy ever to amount to much on the then ungridironed field.

We had certain "functions," though. There used to be a "Junior Exhibition" every year in Steinway Hall, with eight or ten proud orators who took themselves very seriously and carried from the stage, with many bows, a series of bouquets and baskets of flowers, as unconscious of what now seems the funniness of it as so many "sweet girl graduates." I remember, as a boy of less than eleven, the Junior Ex. of the Class of '69, and how I doted upon the fiery oratory of Julien, and my rapture when Shepard, (to me then already a sort of historic hero,) throwing back that dark, romantic lock of his, quoted with immense emphasis and a rearward pointing gesture, Holmes's lines as "the words of our old college song,

> 'Gone like the tenants that quit without warning,
> Down the back entry of Time.' "

No one but the famous Shepard, this small boy thought, would have dared venture such a humorous—why, even frivolous—quotation on such a dignified occasion and in the very presence of the majestic Dr. Webster.

At these Exhibitions, the Sophomores — hardened and desperate wits, and to us eminently mirth-provoking — distributed "Mock Programmes" — the product of laborious committees solemnly elected in class meeting after much campaigning and much Cushing's Parliamentary Law. These seemed daring things, (undoubtedly the product of some sort of subterranean printing-office visited only at dead of night,) whose venturesome authors, after flinging before a shocked public such a *jeu d'esprit* as "Grabyourcap" for the eloquent Gratacap, '69, simply took their futures in their reckless hands and lived, even at home, furtive existences, ever shadowed by visions of visits from "the authorities."

Then the Clionian and Phrenocosmian Societies—fondly called "Clionia" and "Phrenocosmia" —used to have gorgeous "Anniversaries" in the Academy of Music with Eben's band and more floods of oratory and more flowers. At one of these George A. Baker of

THE COLLEGE ORCHESTRA.

On the Chapel Stage, under the direction of Instructor Schoen.

'69 read a brilliant poem in the Saxe manner, entitled "Fifth Avenue," in which he roasted Columbia and apostrophized the newly-named College. To these Anniversaries, the Board of Trustees used to vote a modest "subsidy" of $200, the last being received by the Clionian Society for its twenty-fifth Anniversary, at Chickering Hall, over which Loth, of '77, presided. When the Phrenocosmian came to its twenty-fifth Anniversary in the spring of '77, we, to our high indignation, were denied the subsidy. So in a fine burst of heroics we determined to have it anyway, and without any Chickering Hall tapering-off, but in full old-fashioned splendor at the Academy. And we were greatly fortunate in one thing,—that the "Graduate's Poem" on that occasion was the Rev. Dr. Joseph Anderson's tribute in the "In Memoriam" quatrain to Professor Barton, who had died shortly before, perhaps the high-water mark of our College's poetical output, certainly of its occasional poetry.

In those days, the chair always placed in the centre of the stage for the presiding officer at all meetings at the Academy of Music had been provided by some diabolically ingenious practical joker with a gilded head of Mephistopheles in the centre of the top of its frame, carefully located so as to pierce with a very sharp nose the exact centre of the back of Mr. President's head every time he sat down flushed and absent-minded with the fervor of his eloquence or the intermittent fever and ague of his stage-fright. Mr.

President would then have to put his head on one side, checking as dignifiedly as possible the agonized swiftness of his movement, and let the gilded mask grin over his shoulder at the audience, and so involuntarily realize the mischievous artist's grim and curious fancy. I am sure every one who ever sat in that chair, from General Webb down to the most sadly rattled of society presidents, (which was I,) will remember the torment of that nose and the vicious prod it gave to his brief hour of presidential dignity, and his occipital bone. I used to notice them and enjoy their surprise when they sat down and their feeble pretence of choosing that pensively inclined pose not too suddenly but as if they happened to prefer it.

Then they used to have "Kelly Prize Debates" at the Academy with more music and flowers, and more proud Freshman marshals fluttering in a beribboned ecstasy of publicity and carrying neatly-turned mahogany batons adorned with long lavender streamers.

In '77, the Kelly Prize Debate had been omitted for some years, and a committee of us—a joint committee from the Clionian and Phrenocosmian Societies—went before the Board of Trustees to have it revived. President William Wood, a doughty Scotch veteran, with a fine great snowy beard and a bright frosty eye, told us we might have the debate if we would argue the question (as he put it,) "Whetherr Frree Trrade or Prrotection werre prreferrable forr Amerrica." How he "burred" those *r*'s at us! Each society expressed

A Corner Room in the Chapel.

The crowding of later years compelled the partitioning of the Chapel for class rooms. This is a German section under Instructor Richter.

itself as ardently willing *if* it might have the Free Trade end of the argument, but there came the deadlock, and so the debate again fell through.

It was also in '77 and at my own suggestion that, instead of two prizes for debate, half of the Kelly Fund was devoted to a prize for literary criticism. I remember coining the phrase "Kelly Critique"—it sounded so alliterative. The proposition was brought up in Phrenocosmia, suggested to Clionia, and the two societies successfully petitioned the trustees of the Kelly Fund to establish two prizes,—one for debate and one for criticism. Yancey Cohen, '78, won the first "Critique" Prize on "The Bard" of Gray.

The Junior Ex. was usually signalized by the Sophomores appearing in high hats for the first time and by a grand Sophomore-Freshman rush in the streets, but a more intimate "function," perhaps because it was more at home among ourselves, and came around oftener, was the old Joint Debate in the Chapel.

Like the May Regatta, there seemed to be something spontaneous and indigenous about this. It was less pretentious than the performances in Steinway Hall and the Academy. There was no music, except such as happened to come from the weird, recurrently sporadic "college orchestras," (Oscar Weber, of '80, had one of thirty pieces,) or an occasional moribund and anæmic glee club that would solemnly file up on the high stage, swallow, get ready for the plunge, and attempt to rollick correctly and with careful part-singing through "The Mermaid," or "Rolling down to the Bowling Green," or "The Flowing Bowl," in order to give fond female relatives and visitors an idea as to what devils we were, or again would essay the classical and bumble through "The Artillerist's Oath" or "The Knight's Farewell," and then as solemnly file down again. There were no beribboned ushers and no family flowers, and the speakers were not so apt to be scared to death.

After Hanford Crawford had proved to the satisfaction of the judges in spite of desperate opposition that Thackeray was a better or bigger or greater satirist or novelist than Dickens, and after Paul Krotel had nearly stood your hair on end with his thrilling declamation of Poe's "Telltale Heart," or made you raise the dust on the Gothic rafters over his solos, and the judges had unburdened themselves of their decision, and we had cheered our way down-stairs, then would form the usual serenading army. With 'Gene Oudin, the bright particular star of all our singers, to lead and to take the mellowest of fancy top-notes in

"Then come, love, come, and do not fear;
My bark lies on the other shore;
And all I ask is Sally" [top-note] "dear,
And then I'm off" [with a turn by the top-note man]
"to Baltimore,"

and with Huber's eccentric tenor, remarkable for being sung with his mouth nearly shut, because he "felt so,"

Howard Henry's well-trained baritone, and Krotel's ringing, beautiful,

> "boisterous, midnight, festive clarion,"

we felt quite proud of the noise we could make. Starting with General Webb, next door to the College, we 'd "roll along" Lexington Avenue and down a side street to Professor Docharty's, but always wound up for a climax on Doremus's lawn. For were there not ever the memories of the horseless carriage, and stories that amazed students had been taken in by the genial Doctor to see real "wine" opened, to join in toasts to his "Queen of Women," perhaps even to see Booth, or Ole Bull, or the radiant Christine Nilsson? Had not the Philharmonic assembled on this very lawn to serenade its President on his return from Europe? Here were grass and trees and a fountain and the open air, and we were wearing the mantle of the mightier men of the '60's, who had brought out the great *Collegian*, packed applauding Academies, serenaded a prima donna, borne torches to the burial of the Free Academy, and shot up into the night air their songs and cheers in welcome of the new College. From our hearts came our cheers when that gallantly upflung hand waved us its greeting. Then tradition hung heavy in the air above us, and the quest of a student atmosphere found its own.

The Eighties

Lewis Freeman Mott, '83

THE recollections of a student of the early '80's begin with the numbered green card and the three days' examination for admission, more terrible to the schoolboy than the three days' fight with the dragon sustained by Spenser's Red Cross Knight. A week or two later came the portentous list published by the *Herald*, where, in most cases for the first time in his life, his name appeared actually printed in a daily newspaper for all New York to read. After a summer's mitigation of this triumph, he returned to the field of action, submissively joined the section to which he had been assigned, learned his programme and his way around the buildings, and entered upon his five years' climb toward the bachelor's degree.

But recitations and lectures are not the whole of college life. More memorable, if not more important, is the social element, the contact of young minds, the joyous ebullition of youthful spirits. One of the first student associations formed in my own class was the Diokonian Society, an organization of high seriousness, if one may judge from the preamble to its constitution. This passage is, indeed, worth transcribing: "We, the undersigned, do declare ourselves an association for mutual improvement and enlarging our fund of general intelligence, in the pursuit of which objects, we desire to maintain perfect harmony in all our intercourse, to seek for truth in all our exercises, and have adopted for our government the following Constitution and By-laws." But seeking truth was not our only recreation. We also had a football club, which played enough successful games to puff us up with pride. The physical, alas! seems to have been more enduring than the spiritual, for at the end of the term the Diokonian Society peacefully died, while the football club continued a vigorous and tumultuous existence throughout a span of three years. We used at first to play in a vacant lot at 130th Street and Sixth Avenue, but later received permission to hold our games on one of the greens in Central Park.

The minutes of this football club contain some items of interest, particularly on the financial side, for Mammon does not seem to have smiled upon us. On account of the cost, there could be no cut in the *Microcosm*, and it was even necessary to levy an assessment in order to raise the three dollars required to pay for the indispensable insertion of the names of the officers. One treasurer's report showed the club to be thirty-five cents in debt. A little later a committee on procuring for the team purple caps with gold bands and tassels reported that these gorgeous adornments were too expensive. On another occasion there was a prolonged discussion of a resolution authorizing the treasurer to levy twenty-five cents on each member for the purpose of purchasing a new football, the outcome of it all being that a committee of three was appointed to have the old football repaired.

Obviously our happiness was not based on riches. One of the duties of the recording secretary appears to have been to write in the minute book at the close of each session a glowing panegyric of the club with a lofty record of its glorious victories, a task which often called for the exercise of considerable imagination. We stood on our dignity, too, for as Sophomores we thought it beneath us to challenge the Freshmen, and decided to wait for them to challenge us. That our meetings were not always models of parliamentary procedure is proved by such an entry as the following: "At this point Mr. P. (who, by the way, was presiding) had an umbrella fight with Mr. M., in which Mr. M. was badly wounded and fell heavily against a bench almost breaking it to pieces by the shock."

I fear that our class meetings were often quite as disorderly: certainly they were almost always uproarious. Even in the literary societies there were evenings which would make the most excitable European parliaments seem tranquil; the dignified president imposing right and left upon the obstreperous fines of ten and even of twenty-five cents, all of which were,

One of the Small Rooms off the Chapel.

Where older generations studied, others violated the laws, and more recent classes hung their hats—now left to the dignified idleness of age.

as a matter of course, at the close of the evening excused by unanimous vote. Perhaps, on the whole, our most violent breach of the peace consisted of rushes between Sophomores and Freshmen, both in the lower hall of the College at recess and in the streets after every public exercise, these latter encounters being accompanied by vociferous class cheers and followed by parades of hoarsely singing hordes up Fifth Avenue and Broadway. After an exceptionally scandalous performance of this sort, the perpetrators would be lined up in the chapel, while General Webb brandished the sword of Gettysburg over their heads.

The chapel was more of a centre in the '80's than, owing to practical obstacles, it has lately been. The whole College assembled there every morning to listen to the reading of the Bible. Among the mischievous it was a favorite pastime of an afternoon to put back the book-mark, so that "Prexie" three or four times in succession would with fine unconsciousness exclaim in his sonorous voice; "Moab is my washpot; over Edom will I cast out my shoe": till the charm would be broken by Professor Roemer who, on mounting the rostrum, would read something—we imagined from Proverbs—in his inimitably unintelligible way, concluding with that majestic slam of the good book and removal of the reading-desk, which marked the transition to the equally unintelligible announcement of the student orator and his subject. For Grattan, Pitt, Webster, and Spartacus still thundered from the stage, while Seniors and Juniors expounded every human topic outside of "religion, politics, and the government of the College." What nobility of utterance, coldly marked by an unappreciative Faculty! "Awed by the immensity of the infinite"; "It is more than patriotism, it is philanthropic cosmopolitanism"; such phrases memory is loath to relinquish.

We were also rather fond of public speech-making in those days. In addition to the Joint Debates in the chapel, the Prize Speaking either in Chickering Hall or Booth's Theatre, and the Commencement at the Academy of Music, there was the Junior Exhibition at Steinway Hall with its ten orations varied by interspersed selections from the College Orchestra and enlivened with the Sophomoric Mock Programme, "Manhattan Gas Works, Grand Annual Let Off." The last of these exhibitions was held in '79, the ensuing disorders in the street having landed several of the offenders in the lock-up. But the oratorical impulse was too strong for suppression. The next year Phrenocosmia had a surplus on hand and, in order to spend it, the society celebrated its twenty-eighth anniversary at Chickering Hall with speeches, one by a graduate and nine by students: "The Scholar's True Position," "The Greatness of Macaulay," "True Charity," etc. In this same year, 1880, Clionia defeated the Euclean Society of the New York University in a debate held in the college chapel on the subject, "Resolved that the English system of government is more favorable to the production of great statesmen than that of the United States."

In all these activities of student life we were our own masters, wholly free from Faculty supervision and neither asking nor receiving outside assistance of any sort. Our elections, too, not only of class and society officers, but even of contestants at Prize Speaking and for the French translation prize, were altogether in our own hands. Objectionable features, it must be confessed, were not absent. Our bargains and deals would hardly have discredited the most expert practical politician, and doubtless many a political leader gained his earliest training in these contests. Only once, in my recollection, did President Webb interfere in a student vote. As the attendance at the weekly meetings of Phrenocosmia had become lamentably small, a group of enterprising members sought to arouse fresh interest in the proceedings by introducing an amendment to the constitution abolishing the reading of the Bible. For three weeks debate on this live question continued, earnest, vigorous, even violent, before a crowded house; until finally the Office got wind of what was going on, the wicked were obliged to cease from troubling, and humdrum resumed its sway.

There was, however, one field in which the authorities appeared to us egregious tyrants, the field of journalism. In the fall of '78 the "Echo" gave its last feeble flutter and died. A little over a year later the "Mercury" was started by a group of Freshmen. In its first issue there was an editorial on the decay of oratory in the College. "Fault of the Faculty" from mere Freshmen was more than those grave and reverend signiors could bear. The managing editor was suspended and the others dosed with a stern official Philippic. Meanwhile the newspapers had taken up our cause and "Emperor Alexander" was castigated by the press, while our leader was held up as a hero and a martyr to liberty. When things simmered down, as they soon did, the "Mercury" quietly submitted to the rules, and in later years was even taken into high favor, receiving officially inspired articles and publishing a lengthy philological disquisition by the distinguished Vice-President. Equally tractable were the "Mercury's" four or five short-lived competitors. The one rebel was the "Free Press," published anonymously and sold outside the gates by messenger-boys, a periodical the chief aim of which was to print, much to our naughty delight, disrespectful squibs about the President and Faculty.

The annual "Microcosm," issued by the secret fraternities, was then much less pretentious in form than its present representative. It consisted chiefly of lists of societies, together with their members and officers. It was, I suppose, an open secret that perhaps a third of these organizations never existed except in these pages, but such spurious clubs gave opportunities for students to see their names in print with official titles attached. At one time, for example, there was a Spanish Society with five members and six officers, so that one member

THE CLIONIAN LIBRARY.

Its dusty pride is established in one of the hat rooms off the Chapel. Here the treasured volumes are preserved under lock and key.

had always to serve in two capacities. On the other hand there was a society, The Owl and Scroll, which never disclosed even the real names of its membership. Its motto, *Perfectum Silentium*, was strictly enforced, and mystification, the very breath of its being, was a feature of all its proceedings. The brethren were designated by Greek names—Æschylus, Sophocles, Pericles, Thucydides—with an exponent added to denote the class. All the notices on its bulletin board were in cypher, which only the initiated could comprehend. At this distance of time, when Æschylus has forgotten who Sophocles was, and probably whether he himself was Æschylus or Sophocles, it will perhaps be no indiscretion to admit that, judging from the zest of the performance and the absence of any other noteworthy achievements, the sole object of this mysterious fraternity appears to have been the initiation of new members, a function which invariably gave more pleasure to the initiators than to the initiates.

The ritual of these dark and momentous ceremonies leads memory to another feature of student life in those older days, which is now, I believe, entirely extinct. I recall a little white marble tombstone which stood for years in one of the chapel hat-rooms, removed thither from a corner of the campus, it was said, on command of a certain unfeeling Trustee. It had been purchased by some class—I think '81—to mark the resting place of the ashes of a detested text-book. My own class performed a similar rite one evening at the close of the Sophomore year, the "Cremation of 'Analytics'" in what we called the *Campulum*. The yard between the buildings was adorned with strings of Chinese lanterns. A procession of black-gowned students, carrying torches borrowed for the occasion from a generous political club, marched around the buildings chanting a mournful dirge, and halted under the lanterns to listen to the funeral orations. The climax of the ceremony was the burning of a copy of the obnoxious mathematical work by the high-priest, whose head was surmounted by a gigantic fool's cap. The ashes were deposited in an urn which stood for half a generation among the bushes at the corner of Lexington Avenue and 23d Street. At the close of the ceremonial, solemnity vanished and, bursting out into a jubilant pæan, the noisy procession proceeded up Broadway to an obscure oyster-house for refreshment.

Such burials were at that time a feature common to almost all colleges; so, in the realm of athletics, were contests in football and baseball, and track-games out of doors, such as we used to hold every spring and fall on the grounds of the Manhattan Athletic Club at 56th Street and Eighth Avenue; but our College had one function which, so far as I know, was peculiar to ourselves. The May Week Vacation, established when all New York moved on the 1st of May, was marked by the Regatta. At a mass meeting of the entire College, held in the chapel a fortnight or so before, were elected a Commodore, always a professor or tutor, and a Vice-

Commodore, always a Senior. These two fixed the day and the destination, usually Baretta's Point. At the appointed time, swarms of students and many instructors, with lunch baskets and athletic paraphernalia, congregated on the shores of the Harlem River, hired boats for the day, and then rowed valiantly to the spot assigned for the picnic. Sports and good-fellowship filled the day: but woe to the venturesome tutor who entered a football game with the boys, for in such a case victory was not though of; the game consisted in getting the ball into that tutor's hands and then in the union of both sides to down him. At length the Sound steamers passed, and evening saw the tired oarsmen creeping slowly back to the Harlem boathouses. It was a good old custom, and we who enjoyed such outings cannot but regret its disappearance.

But the garrulity of reminiscence meanders like the ceaseless brook, and yet can never reflect even an approximately complete picture of the past. One word must be said, however, about the Faculty. To one looking back twenty-five years, it seems as though the average professor of that time had a greater number of strongly marked individual peculiarities than the professor of the present. Every one who attended College in the early '80's will, for example, remember the stentorian invitation to the sinner to write and, in another room, the frequently reiterated command to "cease all folly," together with the constantly recurring entry in the section-book of "Continued childish frivolity," while disturbers of the peace were obliged to occupy the bench which backed against the heating apparatus. Moreover, who can forget those easily successful efforts to "get the old man on a string"? The topic was Chinese literature, perhaps; any subject was of absorbing interest, provided that it could be made to last long enough. Then, too, one calls to mind the desperate and almost invariably futile efforts to keep the discourse going, so as to shut off those last fifteen minutes of remorseless questioning. Trivial as the incident is, I remember one of our oldest professors of that time, on a morning when the rain was pouring in torrents—such a day as our newspapers now generally announce as partly cloudy with variable winds—coming up to me as I stood by the window and saying, "This is a fine day." Then, after walking the whole length of the hall and back, he added with a chuckle, "For the ducks."

Some of these peculiarities encouraged disrespectful and occasionally riotous behavior on the part of the students. In one room, it may be recorded, there was a conspiracy among four Seniors to get each in turn sent out for disorder, a conspiracy that was eminently successful in its outcome. In another, tradition maintains that, of a class of only three, two were sent to the office for impertinence, while the third and only remaining one was demerited for "interrupting the recitation." How the Sub-freshmen looked with respect almost amounting to awe upon the Sophomore

The Work Shop, Looking South.
Showing Speed Lathe Room, with twenty-six lathes.

class that piled all the benches against the door so that the professor, who was in the hall, could not enter! How they hoped some day to emulate the great achievement! The boys were suspended, it is true, but that was a cheap penalty to pay for so heroic a reputation.

Of course, such occurrences were exceptional. Discipline was generally well maintained and, although one member of the Faculty was reputed to be "mean enough to die in vacation," we usually liked our teachers and felt for them a high regard. The frugal lunches at Chelborg's Bakery, where we often sat with Compton, Werner, and Sim, were to us feasts of the gods.

Among the most interesting characters of those days was certainly the Registrar and Deputy Librarian, Cana, with his immortal vocabulary of almost prophetic imprecation. One of the amusements of a dull afternoon was to enter the library and innocently address the old man as "Professor." The result was instantaneous and delightfully violent. The holder of a professorship was obviously no object of reverence to Cana, and he had no hesitation in volleying out his views in the most expressive terms at his command. But even this was not the topic which showed him at his best. No one could appreciate the full weight, volume, and velocity of his vocabulary who had not listened to his remarks upon Dutchmen, *à propos* of the receipt from the German publishers of a bewildering assortment of what he called "Bands, Abtheelungs, and Liferungs." On the whole, however, Cana was a fine old fellow, frank, hearty, and kindly, winning from almost all with whom he came in contact affection and esteem. When he disappeared, those who had been accustomed to frequent his office were haunted by a feeling of emptiness. The change there seemed almost like a type of the passing of the old and the coming of the new.

The Early Nineties

Arthur Guiterman, '91

DO you, or did you ever, keep a Memory Box? There is one at present lying under my desk, for I pulled it down from a dusty shelf and opened it a few days ago; and as I lifted the cover, out poured a whole flock of recollections of five lively years spent in the old red-towered building on Twenty-third Street. The box is a treasury of trifles that I haven't yet the heart to throw away;—old letters, of course; faded pictures of sober-faced boys who evidently took themselves very seriously; photographs of some of the same boys costumed and posed in thrilling scenes in college plays; a large group of the Intercollegiate Team of 1891, all wearing the white trunks and black running-shirt with the diagonal lavender band that was then *de rigueur*, and looking positively tragic in their earnestness, posed against the ivied background of the college buildings; copies of the college "Mercury" and the college "Journal" containing solemn editorials beginning, "Another term has passed away," or "Yule-tide has come again bringing with it—," to say nothing of inspired tales, and verse, excruciatingly funny jokes and witty personal paragraphs that have somehow lost their point; manuscripts of orations delivered on the chapel stage to grinning Seniors on the front benches who were far more interested in the *tremoloso* movement of the speaker's knees than in his perfervid periods; wine-stained menus of rollicking banquets; a crumpled marshal's badge; programmes of dramatic entertainments, and many other odds and ends that represent college life as it was in my day, which is, I suppose and rather hope, college life as it is to-day and as it long will be.

Perhaps distance lends enchantment, and, equally perhaps, it affords a clearer, truer perspective; but it seems as though fifteen years and more ago an essential harmony and unity pervaded our collegiate republic. To be sure we had our cliques and our keen personal rivalries; class politics often ran high; the "Mercury" and the "Journal" sometimes exchanged pleasantries in a style that would have delighted the heart of the editor of the Arizona "Kicker"; we had our share of good-natured class battles; for instance, one night after a prize debate, incited thereto by the fiery exhortations of "Kiss," '88 (now known to fame as the Honorable Gonzalo de Quesada, Cuban Minister at Washington), a small but compact phalanx of the Class of '91 rushed a large but undisciplined mob of the Class of '92, sweeping them across the car-tracks and out of Twenty-third Street. But aside from incidental clashes there was a noteworthy spirit of concord both among the students

THE WORKSHOP.
Looking north—speed lathes at work.

as individuals and between the classes. We stood together for the College.

I wonder whether Time has wrought many changes in the routine of college life? We used to tramp downtown in the morning carrying a greater weight of books than most of us would undertake to transport two miles or more in these degenerate days. With the iron gate ominously clanging behind us we entered the stone-flagged lower hall where, to quote a facetious contributor to the "Mercury," "in obedience to a sign that confronted us we took off our shoes and carefully wiped our feet." If we had time it was customary to linger a while below, reading the notices of the various societies on the bulletin boards and discussing the weighty affairs of our little world. Then we climbed up to the chapel, found our places, surreptitiously copied a kind seatmate's Greek prose exercise with a forbidden fountain-pen, listened, I hope with due reverence, to President Webb's sonorous rendering of a chapter from the Bible, listened with entirely justified irreverence to two hackneyed Sophomore declamations and a reminiscent Junior or Senior oration, and then descended to our proper lecture-rooms, changing these hourly according to schedule with the brief but welcome intermission of lunch-time, until the final bell set us free.

Was there ever a class that in its first passage across the "Bridge of Sighs" connecting the two divisions of the old buildings neglected to mark time until the resounding passage trembled perilously,—thereby incurring the Presidential displeasure as expressed in a severe lecture from the chapel pulpit on the following morning?

Was there ever a class that did n't amuse itself with mysterious reagents from the chemical laboratory—sulphuretted hydrogen by preference? On at least one occasion that odoriferous fluid was smuggled into the chapel and carefully sprinkled over the floor with wholly natural and satisfactory results, except that the zealous experimenter escaped detection and expulsion.

There was one rather thick-headed chap—in the late eighties, I think—who had a perfect mania for borrowing from the laboratory stores supplies of chemicals for original, if purely empirical, investigations. One morning two wily desk-mates so wrought upon him by their descriptions of wonderful reactions to be obtained with sulphuretted hydrogen that he carefully filled two large test-tubes with the baleful stuff and placed them in his waistcoat pockets to carry home for private investigation. As he hurried through the swinging doors of the lecture-room, his two abandoned classmates simultaneously "bodychecked" him from either side; the test-tubes, of course, were shattered and the poor victim fled home for a bath and a change of clothing, hating himself all the way.

Truly, as Professor Sim used to drawl, "The Freshman is a ver-ry wicked man. His wickedness culminates in the Sophomore year. There may be a slight improvement in the Junior and Senior terms, and about ten years after graduation he begins to become a fairly respectable citizen." In the light of experience I am sometimes inclined to believe that Professor Sim placed the time of reformation altogether too early.

Do undergraduates still sing,

> "Mike Bonney lies over the ocean,
> Mike Bonney lies over the sea,"

on gala occasions when the spirit of psalmody moves them? At all events I am sure that Michael Angelo Bonney, as we always styled the dominating janitor, is a no less important personage now than he was in our day, when his own unconscious phrase, "Me an' the President," pretty well expressed his position in the cosmogony.

Do Jim Reed's preponderant moustaches luxuriate in the atmosphere of the engine-room as they did in former years?

Is there—? No, I am sure there can't be any such flow of Elizabethan profanity in the library as there was in the time of little old Mr. Cana of cherished memory. His demise left forever vacant the chair of Objurgation and Denunciation. His bursts of torrid eloquence nearly frightened unsophisticated Sub-freshmen out of their little wits, but Juniors and Seniors, who by the study of literature had learned to appreciate expressive diction, were wont to gather round the little man and listen to his burning words in admiration and despair.

On one occasion a few of us belonging to a choice coterie known to the police as "Murderers' Row" paid a social call on Mr. Cana in his library where it was our fortune to find the old gentleman in a peaceful and reminiscent mood. He dived in among his treasures and brought out to us a large portrait. "Know who that is?" he demanded.

The picture represented a handsome young captain of cuirassiers, curly-headed, dark-eyed, wearing the enormous black moustaches typical of *le beau sabreur*, —but we did n't recognize him as an acquaintance and cheerfully admitted as much.

"Professor Roemer," briefly explained the little librarian.

Now Professor Roemer as we knew him in his kindly old age was like anything but that dashing young soldier; yet, to those with whom he became on really intimate terms, he would sometimes recount a few choice adventures of the martial past. With great animation he would tell how, brandishing his saber, he once led a desperate cavalry charge in the face of a murderous fire. "All at once," he would say at the most thrilling point of the narration, "I turned my head to shout to my troopairs.—Not a man was following me!"

"Why, where were they, Professor?" was the invariable question.

WORKSHOP, CARPENTERING ROOM.

Looking north,—showing class receiving lecture on cutting-edge tools from Instructor De Groodt.

"All dead," came the nonchalant answer.

"But what did you do then, Professor?"

"Oh," he would say, with a shrug, "I got anothair troop. Such things do not bothair a young man."

Dear old Professor Roemer! Sometimes there were little clashes that would wake the old fiery spirit, and then how the sparks would fly! Yet he was ever the embodiment of the fine courtesy of the French officer and gentleman of the highest order.

Just before graduation it was customary to acquire photographs, signs, and other college souvenirs, and I asked Professor Roemer for his likeness. Now as I had not elected to take French in my Senior year I very much doubt if the Professor even knew my face—much less my name, but he replied with a most charming smile, "Cer-tain-lee,—eef you will give me a photograph of yourself." And that, I think, was as delicate a bit of practical courtesy as I have ever encountered.

The Dramatic Association was a highly important institution in the days that were. We really had one of the best amateur organizations in the city; our plays were laboriously rehearsed for months, carefully costumed and well staged, and we not only financed the Athletic Association with the proceeds of successful performances in town, but we also proved our independence of friendly audiences by carrying the bright torch of histrionic glory into the outlying darkness of Yonkers and likewise elevated the stage in the benighted precincts of South Norwalk, Connecticut.

Our star was unquestionably Jimmy Hackett, who, though already a successful actor-manager, has not yet attained the pre-eminence on the stage that we, who knew him best, are confident that his great powers and earnestness will eventually win. Hackett was easily the most popular man in the College in our time, and his popularity was due, not so much to his talents, his handsome person, or his achievements on the lacrosse and football field and the cinder-path, as to his uniform good-fellowship and amiability. When he declaimed "Wolsey's Farewell" from the chapel stage the silence was simply awe-inspiring, and his victory at Prize Speaking was a foregone conclusion.

Our stage's second prop was the redoubtable Billy Wood of rotund figure and irresistibly infectious chuckle, a born comedian if there ever was one; and those who never saw him play "Little Lord Fauntleroy" at a weight of two hundred pounds and upwards cannot realize the true inwardness of that famous rôle. Billy's bulk was deceptive; it was more beef than fat; he was an agile dancer, an expert wrestler, a shifty, hard-hitting boxer, and a highly efficient tug-of-war man. He was, moreover, a most adroit politician. In the last year of his long and joyous course, at the head of a small but well organized ring, he successfully dominated the Class of '90 in the face of the opposition of a large and vociferous majority. How he managed this he still refuses to explain. Billy has now taken the

Island of Cuba under his august care and patronage and promises to make something out of the fair but tumultuous republic. If he really sets his mind to the task you may expect that the Empire of Cuba under William I. will soon annex the United States.

Our dramatis personæ likewise included Stevie Lutz, metamorphosed from the centre-rush of the football team into the most sprightly of elderly ladies; there was also Phil Stern, later Captain Philip H. Stern, veteran of two wars, whom we call "Filipino Phil, the Boy Terror of Luzon," though he is now quietly practising law down in Alabama; and there were others "too numerous to mention."

On the lacrosse field Mr. Mitchell was our tutor and Jack Curry was the captain who led us to victories that did not become monotonous by too great frequency. Yet the silver lacrosse stick, still preserved among the College trophies, remains as evidence that our boys, though generally far younger and lighter than their opponents, learned how to play the game. Curry after his graduation was long captain of the famous team of the Crescent Athletic Club, and J. H. Greenbaum was his worthy successor on the college team.

Field sports are usually considered a pretty good basis for military training. At all events Edgar Bell, who in practice once shot a goal past me clear from the other end of the field, afterward went to West Point and is, presumably, still in the service. Jack Oakes, who once stopped a goal with his eye (he came to college next day with the finest black eye imaginable), also went to the Point, graduated second in his class, and is now a Captain of Engineers at Washington. Incidentally, there were at least four men from my class alone who served as officers in Cuba and the Philippines, so it is probable that the College was well represented in the War of 1898 and its subsequent developments.

Scholarship? Oh, well, we took our A.B.'s or B.S.'s, but somehow I like best to remember that my class won the college games in its Sub-freshman year, and that it was the mainstay of the Dramatic Association, the lacrosse team, and the bicycle club. The courses not in the curriculum, after all, have as much to do with developing character, personality, and ability as have Latin, Greek, French, and the mathematics.

Yet we learned much and knew how to apply our profound learning. This may be gathered in a glance at the menu of the banquet that celebrated the end of our college days in which various viands are listed as: "Lamellibranchiata: Myolene Swallowi, in lime. Soups: Aqua-Regia with the Faculty in it. Pisces: Ganoids, Selachians, Placoderms, à la Devonian. Viand: Iguanodon steak, caught by Professor W. S. Punch: Ethyl Methyl Alcohol, Glacé. Aves: Archæopterix on carbonized cereal."—So you see we were wise as well as witty.

And to think that so many of these boys are now doing their share of the world's work, and doing it well!

Workshop Forge Room.

Looking east—Instructor De Groodt lecturing on steel.

Under the Changing Rule

Howard C. Green, '02

WHILE some may view with pride and fond recollection, as Alma Mater, those white-capped towers, rearing their stately beauty upon St. Nicholas Terrace, yet to many others will come, then, the memory of the quaint red towers of a smaller and vine-clad building, where amid storm and stress was laid the foundation of their careers. The impressions of those undergraduate days, and all their vicissitudes, are recalled to memory with mingled joy and regret. He of the "nineties" rejoices that the speculations of a new home for the College are now a grand reality, and he regrets that so many dear faces and many scenes must be now only the treasures of memory.

To the graduate of 1912 there will be no "old days," no fifty years of precedent to weigh upon him, to add veneration to the love which he also will feel for his Alma Mater. The man of 1902 is almost the last to remember "old days" in the old building as they always had been.

He well remembers the day he passed in line through the chapel and received his number for those dreaded entrance examinations; and how vividly appears the picture of that room of mystery, where, among strangers, and under the watchful eye of a "professor," he poured forth his knowledge upon large yellow sheets bearing only the identification number. How he wondered if he were a lucky number. Those long, anxious days again appear, during which he daily consulted the newspapers for that list which should foretell his fate. At length he was able to say to his friends that "he would enter college in the fall." During vacation he learned more of his future; that he was to be dubbed of the species, "Subby," a fact more deeply impressed upon him by the following October.

Eight weeks' probation passed all too soon, and some Special Invitations came to the section and, alas! the "invited guests" were seen no more. Despite the almost over-generous lessons and the fact that the battle had only begun, the survivor was happy to be still in the ranks. He had learned many things. He was convinced that the longest way over the bridge to the Drawing Room was the safest. A stentorian voice had called him back once, while others escaped, and at least one "historical record" had been added to his fame. What a history that section-book became. and what a study in rhetoric! "Subby" also learned the respective values of all the numbers from one to ten but almost believed that beyond nine no one of *his* class could go. There were intermediate fractions, too, between those fateful figures. He lost all faith in signs. The pen point might be tracing a zero when he was sure it was a six.

The prospects of attending chapel, and all the glamor thereof, were still denied him at this period, and he still felt himself on very precarious ground. This he realized very keenly when the fusillade of the first day of "Review Exam." was over. On the second Friday he breathed a sigh of relief and presently was again thankful that the Secretary had not invited him to an extra session in the lecture-room, where the voice is not that of the grand old Professor expounding the wonders of physics, but a briefer, bitterer announcement. That afternoon those of the chosen few who had heard the tragic summons of fate learned from sympathizing upper-classmen of the "petition" and the medical certificate, and each was comfortingly assured that "he 'd get back." But do you remember how many succeeded? How many only began to understand the advantages of the City College, and "left!"

Do you recall those exhibits of "professorial penmanship" behind glass in the lower hall, which all fortnightly consulted, and often to our dismay? Those sheets called forth many an impassioned speech that would have been held inappropriate in recitation.

By degrees our "Subby" learns the names of more of the stern individuals whom he meets in the halls "between the hours" strolling or chatting, and even joking, an attitude seemingly quite inconsistent with his recent experiences within the "Professor's" room. Every instructor to the "Subby" was a "Professor."

May we dwell a little longer on these earliest recollections? Remember those hours spent in the "family circle" where we were told to "write, you sinners, write, as you would to her," and "draw this, gentlemen—draw this," and the interjections of "George!" and "Mr. Mandel, take that young man's name," and those jokes—good old days! Yes, and did we, in that year, appreciate that genial face, that eloquent voice, and the "marvellous experiments"? Can we not hear some of those wonderful phrases ring in our ears? How many have the book and the beautiful drawings made by each of us with so much care—or begun and completed in a last wild scramble on the final night before the books were "called in for examination"?

We remember that O. B. P. might mean *out buying pretzels;* and that the cost for registering among the immortals was often ten demerits when the gate to the stairs had just closed in front of us. The bulletin boards, as we lingered impotent in the basement, suggested to Sub-freshmen eyes merely the possible distinctions one might acquire either as an artist or as a member of several societies—or of all.

We met the faithful old guardian of the repository, that unique character who was never too busy to plod from the "Office" to the dust-laden shelves to exchange a book or sell a two-cent note-book, which contained

Workshop, the Engine.

Showing end of cylinder, students at work studying engine.

"those" prose exercises that spoiled many a good recitation mark. We also made awed acquaintance with the "Boss" of the Institution, not meaning the President.

At the threshold of the General's room we all remember having waited for the kindly smile and searching look of "Prex," accompanied by the welcome "Come in"—and we have returned after a brief interview with our card either stamped "Excused," or "Examination for average." Then we must "present the card" for the hieroglyphic endorsements.

Now comes June, and again, indeed for the third time, the poor "Subby" wonders whether his recitation of yesterday was his last within the sanctuary. After more trials and anxious waiting he sees the great and the small fall while the victorious ones are allowed the pleasure of looking forward to passing the ordeals of the Freshman year—reported to be "the hardest year in college," or he still may be only a *quasi*-Freshman with weeks of cram for "re-exam." in hot September staring him in the face.

In a file of the 1896 "College Mercury" one may find not only a series of club notices, with their respective illustrated headpieces and hieroglyphs, but also the record of various other societies of those "old days." There was the roisterous banjo player, the soloist of the Glee Club, with seemingly distorted face, the hard peddling "scorcher," and the chairman of the Literary Society—trying to test the strength of his gavel—so each society notice was headed with its suggestive cut. More mysterious than all were the symbols of the "Greeks." There were, also, the Mandolin Club, Camera Club, Golf Club, Skating Club, Tennis Club, Chess Club, Cricket Club, Phreno, and Clio, and the Bible Class of the Y. M. C. A. Neither the "Mercury" nor the students could keep track of all the meetings of these "various and divers" activities.

We also learn from these ancient papers that in 1896 the first glimmer of hope for new and larger quarters was realized when the bill authorizing the new buildings was passed at Albany.

The following year the College lost by death Professor Hardy of the English Department, a man beloved and respected by all whose privilege it was to have known him. He had been with us only three years.

After the Easter vacation of '97 some students in the Department of Natural History met the perplexing situation of calling their instructor by a new name. They were corrected "frequently"; and often, when the instructor, forgetting the change himself, would correct the new form and demand the original, the dilemma was greater and the prospect of "maximum" dimmer. But this man was a father to all who came under his instruction, and his sudden death was a personal loss to all who knew him.

In the early part of '97 we remember how overenergetic the Freshmen and Sophs became in the neighborhood of Madison Square. Directly the press was full of articles describing how college students had forgotten their dignity even to the extent of a "riot." After this chastizing, students of C. C. N. Y. gained little newspaper popularity, until the subway gave opportunity for further picturesque journalistic exaggerations.

Subs and Juniors—forgive the comparison—may remember the "monster Holtz machine," which visited us on its way to Washington, D. C.,—and how shocking it was!

In '98 the Senior class obtained the temporary abolishment of the section-book, but the resulting order or disorder caused it to be restored to the Seniors of the following year. The men of '98 even rose to the dignity of the Cap and Gown. This not only awed the underclassmen but also incurred much silent ridicule from other quarters. Again and again some learned Seniors ventured such scholastic insignia only to abandon them until that night when, sweltering in them, they received "all the rights, privileges, and honors," etc.

The stirring war time of '98 is fresh in all our minds, but how few of us students realized how nobly the College answered the call to arms.

Two undergraduates put aside their college careers for the camp and field—Messrs. Brockway and Inevado. The latter never returned, but succumbed to the fever camps. Not to do injustice to many valiant alumni, we cannot help but mention among those who saw active service, the fearless and noble Major Frank Keck of '72 who waved his red bandanna as he led the way up San Juan.

By Christmas, '98, the appropriation for the new buildings was approved and more commodious quarters seemed nearer than the horizon of distant hope. The first decided evidence of growth emphasizing the need for more adequate class room took the form of a year's lease of a floor in the Metropolitan Life Insurance Building, where five Sub-freshmen and four Freshmen sections reported about April, 1899—a pleasant change from the dark and unquiet curtained chapel rooms where both students and instructors labored under great difficulties.

Mention of the chapel will remind the men of '99 of the elaborate ceremonies then instituted, when the numerals of '99 were illuminated upon the stage, the occasion being celebrated by speech and poem. Few there are who have not some recollection of their own part in some morning entertainment in the chapel or in the Natural History Hall—either the declamation eloquent, or the learned oration. You remember how the result of your efforts was told by a flourish of red ink upon a little white card, posted up in the lower hall, and how seldom you agreed with the value there recorded. The memories of the chapel are perhaps more numerous than those associated with any other one part of the building. It was the scene of "oratory" and remarks, class elections, class plays, the Alumni reception, and a host of minor events too numerous to specify.

WORKSHOP, THE MOLDING SHOP.

Showing bin for molding with sand, and models ranged on walls for lead castings.

In April, 1899, some reckless chap attracted unwarranted attention by a fire scare in the newspapers, and there followed much talk about the dangers of the building, the increasing number of the students, the lack of sufficient exits, and so on. This discussion, however, soon subsided. The guardians of the halls and stairways by various "gentle reminders" had well accustomed us to habits which made all dismissals as orderly as a fire drill.

The century year was one of both joy and of sorrow; the Junior class was given more electives and we remember how many profited by experience and tried to avoid what seemed likely to be "dangerous." On May fourth Governor Roosevelt signed the bill which provided a Board of Trustees to control the College. These were to be appointed by the Mayor. As the Alumni had well served their Alma Mater in the Board of Education, now they availed themselves of this new opportunity and the rapid strides and growth of old C. C. N. Y. into a new C. C. N. Y. attest well their earnest efforts and the wisdom of their plans carefully executed and aided by our President, Dr. John Huston Finley.

When we returned in the fall of 1900 how sadly surprised we were to find our campus narrowed and fire escapes added to nature's adornment of the old pile.

Real sadness and deep regret fell like a cloud upon the whole institution when we learned that Conrad H. Nordby had passed away October 28th. The tribute of the "Mercury" but faintly expressed our sorrow:

Conrad H. Nordby.—A kind and respected instructor, a loving husband and father, a sincere and affectionate friend—Conrad H. Nordby was in turn loved and respected by everybody. A man who was truly loved by all who knew him.

It is often remarked that there was not much college life in the social sense, but one must remember that he may have failed to take advantage of the opportunities offered. There were the two Literary Societies, with open arms to suitable men, there were a variety of Clubs, as we have seen, each for some special trend of mind; there was the Athletic Association, so generously encouraged by some of our professors. It held the annual games. Think of the results of those contests under the handicaps of lack of practice. We did have a baseball nine. There were the great and stirring debates and the filling(?) class dinners, each with its own aftermath. There was also the mutual contest among the Fraternities for new and valuable members, a struggle wherein those precious fifteen minutes at noon were so enjoyably passed as to lead one almost to forget the lunch counters in the yard. Many will long remember the happy groups of good fellows who obstructed the various passages to the stairs, and other traditionally established "corners."

The class of 1902 was first to experience the new curriculum intended to extend over the seven years' course, but upon the men of '02 the full advance was not rigidly enforced. This was also the last class whose diplomas were signed by General Webb. In the fall of

1902, on behalf of the students, a beautiful loving cup was presented to the retiring president in appreciation of his long, faithful, and valuable services in the interest of the young men of our city.

The Present System

James Ambrose Farrell, '07

THE College has come into so many things within the last few years that it requires considerable restraint to avoid the superlative in talking or writing of it. Twenty-five thousand dollar organs, thirty thousand dollar murals, and seven thousand pound bells do not encourage modesty. The "new era" has been dinned so blatantly into our ears that some of us forget that the four years that compass our direct association with the College are not the beginning, the middle, and the end of our Alma Mater's history. Yet, on the other hand, we did not spring full-armed from the Jovian brow of Harris. We had to grow and to forge our armor. For a half-century and over our forbears busied themselves with the making of the panoply. Without the skill that they put forth in the fashioning, or the courage and strength they displayed when they used it before it was completely wrought, we have taken from them the goodly armor to gird upon ourselves. The greater part of our work has been done for us. The mail is

ENTRANCE FROM THE YARD.

Looking north, to the right stood the "pie shop" in older days. The covered walk is a recent innovation.

ours, ours to use, if strength is given us, with foreknowledge that from the armet to the sollerets, with equal care for the little rose and the heavy cuirass, every part is perfectly tempered.

Fortunately, something was left to the present collegiate generation, for no work is so good but that other workmen can improve it. We of the past four years, everybody from our beneficent genius, the City, through our Trustees and Faculty down to the younger tutors and the youngest student; from the master workmen to the humblest apprentice, all have burnished the well-made armor that lay darkling in the sight of men, until it has taken on a polish that makes the poorest of sight to see that the armor is there and that it is good. It is of this "polish" that I may be able to tell something of interest to him who would know the College, from the standpoint of the student, who, as a spectator, has seen at work some of the forces that have brought about the polish.

The new buildings leap at once to the mind, but they are the result of twenty years and not of the last four. The graduate of the College and every other friend of the College knows of their history, their size, their equipment, and their beauty, but he knows nothing of the effect they have had on the men in College whom they have inspired with a desire to be worthy of the new home and all that goes with it. The news of every delay in the progress of the work has been received with impatience. The completion of any part of the work that ought to be a finishing touch has been hailed with joy. Washington Heights have formed the background in every plan made by the students; every society in the College has mapped out its work with reference to the wider field of opportunity offered by the new buildings.

Hundreds of new plans have been made in every direction of student activity; and the right spirit, the indefinable atmosphere that at its best we call "college spirit," has become tenfold more potent. The strengthening of this force has come about partly as a reflection of the possibilities foreseen in the promised land, and partly as an inevitable consequence of the equivalent of the spirit or another variety of it in the man who came to us as our president in September, 1903. President Finley at once put himself in touch, at every point, with his students and has kept in touch with them ever since. This personal contact has meant much to the men in College and with the co-operation of the personal force and enthusiasm of a young working president many things have been accomplished that without this co-operation might have been left undone.

The administration of the College is an immense burden. The president wants a dean to relieve him of a great part of the work connected with the supervision of the four college classes. The need, too, for such an officer is apparent, but we hope that it will be years before the Trustees can see their way to his appointment. The fear of offending the modesty for which the president is known forbids even an enumeration of the things that are to be attributed entirely or in part to him. About a year after Dr. Finley's inauguration, a lower-classman had the privilege of writing, for a paper read by men in all the eastern colleges, of the president of City College and what he had done for it in a year. In an appreciative letter Dr. Finley said: "Thank you for the article about City College. You say too much in praise of its president—" The young man to whom the letter was addressed had at that time a firm conviction, and believes still more firmly now, that to say too much in praise of the president was a task that surpassed his powers, if it was not, indeed, impossible.

With that same treasured letter, which is valued as the president himself prizes an encouraging letter from Edward Everett Hale, to "a young college president in the West," as he speaks of himself in an article, there came just a slight feeling of resentment—though the word is perhaps a little too strong,—a sense that thanks were superfluous. It seemed like a father thanking his son for aiding his own brother. In the College, surely, the students were all members of one family with the Trustees and Faculty, a family working together for the good of the College. That feeling, for which Dr. Finley must hold himself responsible, that all are laboring shoulder to shoulder for the good of the College, all striving for the good of what is dear to them simply because it is dear, has reached its best expression under our new president. He has the feeling deep-rooted and exemplifies it every moment of his busy day. The most diffident, the least enthusiastic Freshman cannot fail to absorb some of it in spite of himself. With the spirit the president combines enormous energy. He is one of those few men to whom the awed praise given to Sir Walter Raleigh by an admirer who said he could "toil terribly" may be applied without sacrificing the vigor of the expression in the application.

About three years ago each section in the College was invited to elect a delegate with a view to forming a body representing the four classes. The plan was cordially received and a Student Council was organized. The function of the Council is the same as that of student boards of representatives at other colleges and universities—it is a medium through which the students and Faculty are brought closer together. Our Council has justly earned the reputation of not being a "meddlesome body." It has thus far been merely the mouthpiece of the students in matters in which undergraduates are interested, and it has aided the president of the College in arranging for the observance of anniversaries and in ascertaining student sentiment on different questions. Its creation was one more instance of the liberal policy of the new administration, and its attitude has proved the wisdom of giving students a fair measure of participation in affairs in which they are immediately concerned.

The Yard and the Bridge of Sighs.
View looking east with main College on left, Twenty-second Street annex on right, and laboratory building in background.

The spirit of self-reliance has been helped further by the establishment of the elective system. The students who pass out as the first products of the *à la carte* service are thoroughly satisfied. Contrary, perhaps, to general expectations, their intellectual appetite and thirst for the waters of wisdom have shown no appreciable diminution. If the theory that a man who has reached the sophomore year at college is capable of exercising his own judgment holds good at other colleges, it is at least equally sound at City College.

The formation of a department of physical training was so obvious a concomitant of the new order of things that the coming of a new associate professor out of the West created no sensation. The good work done by the new director and his assistants shouts out, in refutation, its answer to the good old souls who contend that physical training should have little or no place in the course at City College. The new gymnasium has brought highly improved facilities for training that have already resulted in winning teams. If there is anything that nourishes in her sons a healthy pride in the College more vigorously than do teams whose victories are followed by a keen, proprietary sense of interest, we shall all be willing to deck ourselves in cap and gown and take our exercise in scanning Archilochus.

With the interest in physical work there has come, inevitably, an increase along intellectual lines. Whether the quality of our debates has improved or not, there has been an undoubted increase in quantity; more men can speak well and debate well and the average ability is far higher than it was a few years ago. Our range has been increased from the moss-covered joint debates of the past sixty years to inter-collegiate debating. Before our teams the best men in a college known for its work along forensic lines, Hamilton, have twice gone down to defeat.

Of other roads along which we have taken long steps in the right direction, passing the good marks reached by our predecessors, much might be said. That we are new, however, should not be too strongly insisted upon; it is only because we have had a period of sound youth and a healthy and true maturity that we can put our manhood strength to its best use now. No one can realize more surely than we who stand at the meeting of the old and the new, just how much we are indebted to the old.

We who are still in the College have new ideas, else were we falling short of our early promise, but we have old ideas too. We have with us now new men—men of full strength—but, worthy Senior, vain of things your betters caused to be, with us, also, as Eliphaz the Temanite said to Job, "are both the gray-headed and very aged men, much elder than thy father." To the old men our debt is great. May we go forth with the obligation to pay some part of it worthily, and the will and strength to do. So we who form the pointer, the small finger between the weight of the old, on one side, and the new metal that is undergoing test, on the other,—an uncertain index, unimportant in itself but significant—we feel the old and the new. We shall stand ready to favcr either, with great love for the old and trusting confidence in the new.

The College in the Civil War

The College in the Civil War*

Henry Edward Tremain, '60
and
Charles F. Horne, '89

ABOUT the old "Free Academy," as the College of the City of New York was officially styled, until the legislative change of its name in 1866, there was a something in the atmosphere inducing, if not inspiring, individual public spirit and personal activity in an enlarged and intelligent citizenship. How this atmosphere was created, or sustained, it matters not. Certain it is that it was historically reflected in the careers of large numbers of graduates and non-graduates among the first dozen of the Free Academy classes. Perhaps the special atmosphere sprung from the fact, then freshly in mind both of students and instructors, that the institution itself came into being as the product of a popular vote.

* Despite the labor given to the compilation of this record it is far from complete. Any one who can furnish additional, and especially personal, information as to the Civil War record of any graduate or non-graduate student, will confer a favor on the Associate Alumni by communicating with Mr. Horne at the College.

Undoubtedly there was much to encourage this patriotic spirit in the course of instruction pursued, particularly as it progressed to the higher classes, and entered the historic realm of statehood and nationality, with explanatory and legal expositions, extending into the elementary law of nations.

Indeed the history and purport, even to a memorizing, of the Constitution of the United States were not omitted in the instruction given to some of those earlier classes. That this factor was not without its reflection upon individual careers is illustrated by the incident of one zealous graduate who on his first enlistment carried in his knapsack a copy of the U. S. Constitution, which he still preserves as a personal relic of the war period. Moreover, the honored president of the Institution, himself a graduate of West Point, was foremost in promoting this line of college sentiment and work. Indeed by his own instruction and pronounced convictions of its educational value he secured for himself and his topics peculiar attention from his students. He believed in the building up of "*character*."

Through his personal alliances, too, there came occasionally into the class-rooms for higher mathematics eminent military officers from West Point, who were also instructors and authors, and whose text-books were used at the United States Military Academy. It goes without saying that when the professor's chair at the Free Academy about examination time was

The Yard Looking West.
Twenty-second Street annex, and President Webb's house on the left.

relinquished by its rightful possessor and occupied by a gentleman in army uniform, the picture was not without its impression more or less permanent upon the youthful student.

However all these features of academic life may have asserted themselves, certain it is that public life, and the great questions of that day that engaged it, furnished by no means a silent factor in the educational work of the old New York Free Academy. It is no wonder then that the continental agitation growing out of the repeal of the Missouri Compromise in 1854, and the Kansas-Nebraska Bill, and the Lincoln-Douglas debates of 1858, and the proceedings in Congress—then more closely and fully represented in the daily press than unfortunately is the custom of to-day—should find some reflex in the ranks of youths approaching manhood; and approaching it too with a sense of public duty, more or less happily grounded on some reciprocity for the privileges afforded by the city and State.

At all events there was no discouragement to this line of sentiment; and it found more or less expression in various individual developments among those who were tutored within the walls of the honored Free Academy, under Horace Webster, its esteemed first president.

Thus possibly, if not probably, it first came about that the Alumni have ever been ready and eager to acknowledge their special obligation of public duty and patriotic service. The city of New York had honored them above other citizens, had selected them by severe tests to become the recipients and beneficiaries of high educational training.

If this be a debt, these men have sought ever to recognize it, and have done somewhat to repay it in every walk of life; some of them perhaps in every action of their lives. The broad opportunity came when the great national discussions culminated in "grim-visaged war." The outburst of the terrific struggle of the War of the Rebellion found the men of the classes, from the class of 1853 upwards, youths all of them, in the full vigor of youthful manhood, ready and zealous for any public duty that claimed their intelligent effort. It is only fair to say that they were in general young men without special so-called rank, or wealth, or family, or political influence to speed their careers. But they entered the lists, and won their way to an honorable death, or to an honorable survival; some with distinction of rank as generals and field officers, and some in the less eminent but equally honorable rank of line officers or enlisted men.

It has been found impossible at this late day to collate a complete and comprehensive list of all the college names in the military service. In doing as best we can, we may glance at the men of this type from the various classes, beginning with the earliest.

From the first class graduated, that of 1853, there went to the front James R. Steers. He had already

SENIOR MECHANICAL CLASS.
Taken in the yard on steps leading to the Chemical Laboratory, Professors Compton and Fox in front.

established himself as a lawyer, but when in 1863 General Lee's advance into Pennsylvania threatened the Northern States, as indeed the very existence of the Union, Mr. Steers joined the Seventh Regiment, N. G. S. N. Y., and did duty with it as a private in the vicinity of Baltimore. He was summoned back with his regiment to quell the draft riots in New York, and saw active service in that work.

Among the non-graduate members of this class of '53 who saw service were General STEPHEN WEED and General GILBERT H. MCKIBBIN. Weed was only at the College a little over two years. Then he went to West Point and became an officer of the regular army. Hence as a professional soldier he should rather be credited to West Point. He was killed at Gettysburg, where his conduct was notable and famous. General McKibbin remained at the College until within a few months of graduation. His military record is well known. At the first outbreak of hostilities he joined the Seventh Regiment (Company C) as a private. In October, 1861, he was made a Second Lieutenant in the U. S. service and attached to the 51st Regiment, N. Y. Vols. He rose to be Colonel of this regiment, receiving the rank Dec. 9, 1864, but was not mustered, as he had already (Dec. 2, 1864) been commissioned Brevet Brigadier-General, and was assigned to the command of a brigade. He was afterward appointed to command the sub-district of the Blackwater, Department of Virginia (May 25, 1865), and was mustered out of service Sept. 19, 1865. General McKibbin was engaged in much of the fiercest fighting of the war, being present at the battles of Roanoke Island, Newbern, Second Bull Run, Chantilly, South Mountain, Antietam, Fredericksburg, Vicksburg, Jackson, Knoxville, the Wilderness, Spottsylvania, Tolapotamoy, Cold Harbor, and Petersburg. At Petersburg he was severely wounded by a rifle shot through the head. He was invalided home, but immediately on recovery returned to the front, and resumed his gallant and notable service to our country.

Of the twenty-two graduates of 1854, seven laid aside their prosperous civilian careers to aid the nation in its peril. One of these, Edward King Wightman, perished in the strife. He had already won repute as a journalist on a New York paper; but at the first call to arms he cast advancement to the winds and entered the military ranks as a private in Hawkins' Zouaves (Ninth N. Y. Vols.). All through the war he fought, participating with his regiment in no less than fifteen engagements, rising step by step to be Sergeant Major; and then in January, 1865, in the final successful assault on Fort Fisher, he won his way among the foremost into the heart of the fortress and there fell dead, sword in hand. For his bravery he was brevetted Lieutenant-Colonel.

Also of this class of '54 was Rodney G. Kimball, Ph.D., Professor Kimball of the N. Y. State Normal School. He laid aside his professorship, and in '62 formed a company, the "Normal School Company," of which he was made Captain. This company was attached to the 44th N. Y. Vols., "Ellsworth's Avengers," and Captain Kimball commanded it at Fredericksburg. In February, '63, he was sent home on sick leave and in April was honorably discharged for disability incurred in service.

A classmate and fellow-teacher of Kimball enlisted as a member of his company. This was EUGENE DOUGLASS, A.M., M.D. Douglass afterward rose to be Second Lieutenant in the 47th N. Y. Vols. and fought at Gettysburg, where a comrade describes him as seated on an exposed rock shooting away "as if at turkeys in a Thanksgiving match." Being urged to seek a more sheltered place, he responded unconcernedly, "Oh, I guess I won't get hit."

NICHOLS H. BABCOCK * of this class served as a private in the 22d N. G. S. N. Y., during both its terms of service at the front in '62 and '63. In less violent but not less useful service were CHARLES B. WHITE, ROBERT F. WEIR, and GEORGE E. POST. Dr. White was commissioned as an Assistant Surgeon in May, '61, and served through the McClellan campaign, and at Chantilly and Antietam. He was afterward U. S. Surgeon at Pittsburg, and for his services was brevetted Major in the U. S. Army in March, '65. Dr. Weir had a similar though more exciting experience. He entered as Assistant Surgeon in the 12th N. Y. S.

* See Mr. Steers's reminiscences.

militia in April, 1861, and was transferred to the U. S. Army service in August. From January, 1862, till March, 1865, he was in charge of the U. S. hospital at Frederick, Md., a building which proved a centre of military operations. It was the base hospital for the Shenandoah campaign, and for Antietam and Gettysburg; and Dr. Weir was twice made prisoner by the Confederates.

Dr. Post, whose career as a missionary to Syria has since made him widely known, served as Chaplain to the 15th N. Y. Vols. in '61. He acted also as a doctor and thus saw double duty through the campaign of McClellan and at Fredericksburg. In February, '63, he resigned to take up his missionary career.

The class of '55 sent to the front WALTER BRINKERHOFF, HAMLIN BABCOCK, ELIHU D. CHURCH, THORNDIKE SAUNDERS, and WILLIAM M. COLE. Mr. Cole enlisted at the first call and fought as a private at Bull Run in the 71st N. Y. militia. He served for two years and rose to be First Lieutenant in the 158th N. Y. Vols. Hamlin Babcock, a brother of Babcock, '54, was First Lieutenant of Company I of the 22d N. G. S. N. Y. during its first term of service at the front, and rose afterwards to be Captain, taking an active part in the suppression of the draft riots in '63. Mr. Saunders was commissioned as Paymaster (Eleventh N. Y. S. militia) in April, '61. Later in the year he enlisted in the volunteers, and in August was commissioned Captain. He was honorably discharged

The Twenty-second Street Annex.

Originally the introductory department under Professor Scott. View from Twenty-second Street. The lower building, with ivy-covered windows, on the left, is the last addition built on the old College grounds.

in February, '62. Mr. Church enlisted in April, '61, in the Seventh Regiment (Company I) and served until honorably discharged in July, '63. Mr. Brinkerhoff enlisted in the Ninth N. Y. S. M. in July, '61, and served as a private through the entire war, receiving his honorable discharge in June, '65.

From '56 came Dr. JOHN HOWE, who promptly entered as Surgeon in the First N. Y. Vols. in April, '61. He served through the entire war until July, '65, and rose to be Brigade Surgeon and Medical Director. From this class came also General JAMES LYMAN VAN BUREN whose career is here recounted by his old-time friend and classmate Mr. RUSSELL STURGIS.

In 1852, at the summer examination for admission, James Lyman Van Buren was admitted to the Free Academy. He applied immediately for advancement by one class; and he and two other newly-admitted students, having been examined in mathematics and English, were so advanced. Immediately afterward, the classes were rearranged and renamed, and in this way Van Buren found himself a Freshman, and a member of the class of 1856. After graduation, July, 1856, he began the study of law in the office of Charles Tracy, in New York. In 1860 he travelled in Western Europe, and lived for some months in Germany.

When the Civil War began he was eager to enter the volunteer army, and in the autumn of 1861 he received a commission as Second Lieutenant in a Zouave regiment, which was sent immediately with the expedition to the coast of North Carolina. General Burnside commanded the land forces; and General Foster the brigade in which Van Buren's regiment was included. The forts at the inlet had been occupied by the U. S. troops in August; and the army landed almost immediately on the Southern end of Roanoke Island. Van Buren's private letters, describing the fight and the capture of the forts, were printed in a journal of the day, and were found a most spirited and intelligent account of the fight. About this time the system of signalling by means of flags was introduced; the most intelligent officers were told off to study the method, and Van Buren became signal officer on General Foster's and then on General Burnside's staff. From that time on, he was continually with General Burnside, and was promoted to the rank of Major, and finally made Brigadier-General by brevet.

In November, 1862, Burnside was made commander of the Army of the Potomac, but, during the two months of this command, Van Buren was ill, and on sick leave, in New York with his father's family. He joined the staff again before Burnside took command in East Tennessee, when, in August, 1863, Knoxville was taken by the United States forces, and in November was defended against Longstreet's army in a memorable siege which ended in the relief of the place by Sherman after the battle of Lookout Mountain. Letters from Van Buren during the siege are full of the interest of warfare seen, close at hand, by a capable and scholarly observer. But Burnside, in command of the "Old Ninth Corps," came East with his staff to help in the final movements in Virginia, and at first, with his headquarters at Annapolis, was busied with reorganization, and the filling up of his decimated ranks. It was May 1864, when Van Buren reached the front in Virginia, after the Battle of the Wilderness. The operations of the Ninth Army Corps were, from this time, merged in those of the Army of the Potomac, and Van Buren was able to join personally in the assaults upon Petersburg which closely preceded the final evacuation by Lee's Confederate army of all their advanced posts.

The war was over: Van Buren, already suffering with an increasing languor, evidently the result of the malaria of North Carolina, many months earlier, broke down altogether in health when the life under canvas was given up. He was confined to his chamber from midsummer, 1865, to the beginning of the following year, and died in New York in the early spring of 1866.

In the class of '57 was CLEVELAND ABBE, A.M., Ph.D., LL.D., the esteemed head if not the actual founder of the U. S. Weather Bureau in Washington. He served in the U. S. Coast Survey from October, 1860, to June, 1867.

'58 contributed to the service, J. WESLEY PULLMAN, Doctor WILLIAM K. HALLOCK, and Brevet Colonel

Alexander P. Ketchum, LL.B. Mr. Pullman, whose long mercantile career has been associated with Philadelphia, served briefly in the Fifth Pennsylvania Reserves, which were called to the field during the Antietam campaign. Dr. Hallock offered himself as a volunteer surgeon at Bull Run and died of the illness brought on by exposure and over-exertion in care of the wounded.

The record of Colonel Ketchum extends to greater length. Few men have rendered fuller service to their country. Even before the war his vigorous anti-slavery convictions had brought him into notice, his "Senior Address" at the College being so earnest an exhortation upon this theme that he was in danger of being refused his graduation diploma, "because of his radicalism." At the outbreak of the war Mr. Ketchum was studying law at Albany; after receiving admission to the bar he secured an appointment in 1864 as First Lieutenant in the 56th N. Y. Vols. In May, '65, he was appointed Captain in the 128th U. S. colored troops, and as aide to Generals Saxton and O. O. Howard he did important work in controlling the negroes and their relations to old landowners and in re-establishing order in Georgia, South Carolina, and Florida. He stood in the very midst of the "reconstruction" storm and by resolute discharge of duty advanced to the brevet rank of Colonel, remaining in the service until September, 1867.

The class of '59 had among its members Mr. Reid

Entrance to the Bridge of Sighs.
Passage from the main building to the annex, Drawing Room stairs to the left.

SANDERS, who served upon the Confederate side and became a prisoner of war, remaining as such for a long time in a Northern harbor. To the Union camps this class sent five men. Dr. BENJAMIN E. MARTIN served as Assistant Surgeon in the Fifth N. Y. Vols. from April, '61, until February, '62, when he resigned and entered the U. S. Consular Service in Germany. Dr. LOCKWOOD DE FOREST WOODRUFF rose to be Surgeon to the First Brigade, N. Y. S. N. G. Dr. ABRAHAM W. LOZIER served as an Assistant Surgeon during Grant's peninsula campaign of '64. OSCAR B. IRELAND was appointed in March, '63, to be Second Lieutenant in the Signal Corps, U. S. Vols., and was employed in important service until his honorable discharge in August, '65. ASA B. GARDINER, LL.D., L.H.D., entered the U. S. Vol. service in May, '61, was appointed First Lieutenant, 31st N. Y. Vols., and was honorably discharged as Brevet Major in '66. He has since served in the regular army, including a detail as Professor of Military Law at the West Point Military Academy, and is now on the retired list with the rank of Lieutenant-Colonel.

Among the non-graduate students of about this period who enlisted were W. G. HOWEY, WALTER ABBE, and EDWARD N. KIRK TALCOTT. Mr. Abbe served as a private in the N. Y. City Home Guards in 1861, and in the 37th N. Y. S. militia in 1862. Mr. Howey enlisted in '61 as First Sergeant in the Sixth N. Y. Cavalry. He was made prisoner and kept in Libby

Prison for over a year, contracting malaria from which he finally died. Mr. Talcott, a member of the Seventh regiment, went to the front with his regiment. He was soon appointed a captain in the volunteer Engineer Corps, and served throughout the war, acting on the staffs of Gen. Gilmore and Gen. Meade.

The class of 1860, young and eager, gave fourteen of its graduates to the war, beside several non-graduate students. The alumni who served as privates were SAMUEL G. ADAMS, BYRON E. CHOLLAR, HENRY L. HARDT, STEPHEN B. HYATT, HERBERT G. TORREY, and EDGAR KETCHUM; the latter, although not a swimmer, was one of a few fortunate survivors who made their way through the breakers from a wreck off Hatteras. OSCAR G. VOUTÉ and WILLIAM ELLSWORTH (13th N. Y. Vols., '62–'63), non-graduates, also served as privates in the Union army. FRANCIS MARKOE was from a Maryland family, and he fought against the Union side, rising from a private in the First Maryland Regiment (May, '61), to be a Captain and staff-officer in the Confederate service. He was wounded in '62 and lost the use of one arm; he was included in the surrender at Appomattox. Dr. WILLIAM THURMAN was acting Assistant Surgeon at Fortress Monroe in May, '62, and was commissioned Assistant Surgeon Fifth N. Y. S. N. G. in July, '64. FREDERICK HOBART enlisted in the Second N. J. S. militia, in April, '61, and afterward in the Ninth N. J. Vols. He rose from the ranks to be Sergeant, Lieutenant, and then Captain in his regiment. Four times he was wounded in battle, at Roanoke Island and again at Goldsboro in '62, at Conuto Swamp, N. C., in '63, and at Walthall Junction, Va., in '64. In a still later skirmish Hobart had a bullet plough a furrow through his hair, leaving him practically untouched. Disability resulting from his wounds finally compelled his resignation in October, '64.

Less fortunate than Captain Hobart in his narrow escapes were four members of the class who perished in the war. The earliest of these to die was WILLIAM CULLEN BRYANT GRAY, a relative of the poet after whom he was named. Gray was studying for the ministry, and had also, even in his undergraduate days, won repute in literature. At the call of his country, however, he laid aside his own career and entered the army as First Lieutenant in the Fourth N. Y. Heavy Artillery. His brief service at the front resulted in pneumonia, and he died at Washington January 1, 1863. On his grave is carven a sentence from one of his own letters home: "I do not fear the battlefield, for I look beyond it to the delights of heaven."

CHARLES CLARENCE TRACY KEITH came of a South Carolina family; but so passionately had he become devoted to the anti-slavery cause that he abandoned the profession of law sooner than as a lawyer swear allegiance to the United States Constitution, which permitted slavery. At the celebrated New York "war meeting" held in Union Square in April, '61, Keith sprang suddenly into fame as the "boy orator" who swept the vast crowd away with him in his impassioned plea for action, and freedom for the slaves. The orator confirmed his own devotion by enlisting in the ranks. He was soon transferred to the Signal Service, and rose to be First Lieutenant in the Signal Corps (March, '63). While on duty at Plymouth, N. C., he was thrown from his horse. His head struck upon a stone, and his brain was so injured that, after lingering for nearly a year in hopeless misery, he died in April, 1864.

More fortunate, as men count fortune, was FRANKLIN BUTLER CROSBY, for he died suddenly in battle. In August, 1861, he was commissioned Second Lieutenant in the Fourth U. S. Artillery. He rose to be First Lieutenant, and in the great fight of Chancellorsville he was in command of his battery. A fellow-alumnus tells of seeing Crosby on the second morning of the battle and calling to the youthful commander in protest at the danger to which he exposed himself. Crosby was on horseback beside his guns directing their fire. A splendid giant in physique, he offered too fair a mark and a bullet pierced his breast. His own men carried him a few rods to the rear. "Tell mother I die happy," said he, and his life was over. His parting words became the burden of a war-song among his comrades; and a relative, the poet William Allen Butler, wrote of him the following lines:

Lower Hall of Twenty-Second Street Building.

Looking north, entrance from the yard in background. The passage to the left leads to the newest addition. The stairs lead up to the Bridge of Sighs. Professor Horne's room opens from the last door on the right.

He was our noblest, he was our bravest and best!
Tell me the post that the bravest ever have filled.
The front of the fight! It was his. For the rest—
Read the list of the killed.

On the crown of the ridge, where the sulphurous crest
Of the battle wave broke, in its thunder and flame,
While his country's badge throbbed with each beat of his breast,
He faced death when it came.

His battery planted in front, the Brigadier cried,
"Who commands it?" as fiercely the foe charged that way,
Then how proudly our gallant Lieutenant replied,
"I command it to-day!"

There he stood by his guns; stout heart, noble form;
Home and its cherished ones never, never so dear,
Round him the whirlwind of battle, through the wild storm,
Duty never so clear.

Duty, the life of his life, his sole guiding star,
The best joy of his being, the smile that she gave,
Her call the music by which he marched to the war,
Marched to a soldier's grave.

Too well aimed, with its murderous, demonlike hiss,
To his heart, the swift shot on its errand has flown—
Call it rather the burning, impetuous kiss
With which Fame weds her own!

There he fell on the field, the flag waving above,
Faith blending with joy in his last parting breath,
To his Saviour his soul, to his country the love
That was stronger than death.

Ah, how sadly, without him, we go on our way,
  Speaking softer the name that has dropped from our prayers,
But as we tell the tale to our children to-day,
  They shall tell it to theirs.

He is our hero, ever immortal and young,
  With her martyrs his land clasps him now to her breast,
And with theirs his loved name shall be honored and sung,
  Still our bravest and best!

Also of the class of '60 was EDWARD FRANCIS YOUNG. He had been, in College, the leader, the valedictorian, of his class. His brilliancy seemed to all who knew him to assure him a wonderful career. Moreover when graduated he was already married. Although a young father, the call to arms induced him to enlist. He was made Captain in the Fourth N. Y. Heavy Artillery (June, '62) and rose rapidly to the rank of Major. The fort where he was stationed in the fall of '63 was near Washington. Here, while he was making a night tour of inspection, his horse tripped and fell upon him. The young Major was so cruelly crushed that death came to him as a relief (Dec. 22, '63). His funeral and burial in Greenwood Cemetery, Brooklyn, were attended with the full military honors due to his rank.

Such were the deaths by which the class of 1860 paid the debt of the education which its members owed to their country. High army rank was also attained by a non-graduate, CHARLES MCLEAN KNOX, who in November, '61, was commissioned Major in the Ninth

N. Y. Cavalry. He was honorably discharged in January, '64.

Of all the members of this heroic class the one whose military career carried him highest in official rank was HENRY EDWIN TREMAIN. Entering the army as a private in the Seventh Regiment N. Y. militia, in '61, he was commissioned First Lieutenant in the 73d N. Y. in August. In November '62, he was made Captain, and in April, '63, Major and Aide-de-Camp. In March, '65, he was brevetted Lieutenant-Colonel, in June, Colonel, and finally in November, '65, he received his brevet as Brigadier-General. General Tremain by his own efforts recruited a company for the Second Fire Zouaves (or 73d, N. Y. Vols.); and won his way from private to brevet Brigadier-General by arduous service through four years of war.

He served a year in the line, and afterwards on the staff; being promoted from the "Excelsior Brigade" staff successively to Division, to Corps, and to Army of the Potomac Headquarters. By the consolidation (1864) of the Third Army Corps he was temporarily rendered a supernumerary; but his volunteered services for field duty elsewhere were promptly accepted. He participated in many campaigns, battles, and skirmishes, including the great engagements at Williamsburg, Fair Oaks, and Malvern Hill in the Peninsula campaign under McClellan, at Bristoe and Manassas under Pope, at Fredericksburg under Burnside, at Chancellorsville under Hooker, and at Gettysburg under Meade, where he was senior aid-de-camp to General Sickles, commanding Third Corps. After an inspecting tour to all the Union forces in the West and South, including a brief service in Sherman's Atlanta campaign, General (then Major) Tremain while in front of Petersburg joined the Headquarters of the Cavalry Corps, and there continued to serve under Generals McGregor, Gregg, George Crook, and Sheridan, during the campaign and battles terminating with the surrender at Appomattox. After the disbandment of the Cavalry Corps he was ordered on Reconstruction duty in the Carolinas; until finally at his own request he was mustered out of the army April 20th, 1866, five years after enlisting as a private soldier April 19th, 1861. He was frequently commended in the official reports of his Generals, fell a prisoner in a countercharge at the second Bull Run battle, experienced the hospitalities(?) of Libby Prison, and for "distinguished gallantry" in battle at Resaca, Georgia, was awarded the Congressional "Medal of Honor."

Turn now to the class of '61. These young men had not yet finished their schooling when Sumter was fired on. Hence few of them were, like the men of '60, among the first to enlist, nor did they attain to such advanced military rank. Yet ultimately twenty of them found place in the roll of our country's defenders. Of these, eight were content to serve as privates. Their names, inscribed upon our roll of honor, are

The Latest Addition.

Row of three classrooms added to ground floor of Twenty-second Street building, viewed from Professor Ilgen's room, looking north.

Theodore G. Ascough, Charles P. Kirkland, who enlisted in April, '61, in the 71st N. Y. S. M., William C. Kimball and Edwin F. Hyde, now vice-president of the Central Trust Co., N. Y., both of whom served from May to September, '62, in the 22d N. Y. Infantry, James H. Pullman and Frederick J. Slade, both also in the 22d N. Y. S. M. in '62, Roland G. Mitchell, a member of the Seventh N. Y. militia in Company K., and David J. Starkey, who served in the Thirteenth N. Y. Cavalry from '62 to '65. Among the non-graduates of this class was another private, Francis Hull Cowdrey, recently deceased at the Soldiers' Home in Hampton, Va.

George Roberts rose to be Orderly Sergeant of the Ninth N. Y. Infantry; and Edwin M. Cox to be Color Sergeant in the 37th N. G. S. N. Y., in which rank he served with the militia column co-operating with the Army of the Potomac during the Gettysburg campaign. Lawrence Kiernan was appointed secretary to General Thomas Francis Meagher, and was commissioned a Second Lieutenant, but did not serve. William West held a Lieutenant's rank in the 176th N. Y. Infantry. David D. Terry was commissioned Captain of Company E, 176th N. Y. S. Vols. in September, '62. He served in Louisiana until November, '63, and was honorably discharged. Frederick H. Man rose to be Captain and afterward Brevet Major. Alfred H. Taylor became clerk of a depot of volunteers in N. Y. City in 1861, and in 1862 secretary to General Hillhouse at Albany. He rose to be Acting Assistant Adjutant-General of N. Y. with the rank of Major; and in later years was Assistant Adjutant-General with rank of Colonel. His services as an organizer of the vast army of N. Y. volunteers were of sterling value, though his only active military service during the war was in connection with the draft riots in New York.

Among the commissioned officers of '61 in more strictly warlike service, was Lieutenant HENRY C. SELVAGE. Immediately on graduating from the College he aided in raising a N. Y. State regiment, the McClellan Infantry, and was appointed one of its First Lieutenants. This regiment was incorporated with another; and Mr. Selvage, beginning his recruiting work again, helped form another company and in February, '62, was commissioned Second Lieutenant in the 87th N. Y. Vols. He served with his regiment in McClellan's campaign, fought at Williamsburg and Fair Oaks, and in the latter battle was wounded in the hip. Invalided home, he recommenced his recruiting work, and in 1864 was appointed First Lieutenant of U. S. colored troops, but the war was practically at an end before he had an opportunity to serve in his new rank so he resigned. He was afterward brevetted First Lieutenant of N. Y. S. Vols.

WILLIAM H. SANGER immediately after graduating enlisted as a private in the First N. Y. Mounted Rifles. He was commissioned Second Lieutenant of his company in November, '61, First Lieutenant in December, and Captain in August, '62. For three years he saw active service in Virginia, commanded the advance guard at the capture of Norfolk when the "Merrimac" was blown up, and was the first Union soldier to enter the city. In '64 he went through the Shenandoah campaign as Captain in the Second N. Y. Cavalry under General Custer. He was twice wounded by bullets and once with sabre, and was once captured by the enemy, but escaped on the same day. He resigned from the service in May, 1865.

Hon. William H. Wiley, Representative from New Jersey in the 59th Congress, enlisted as a private in the Seventh Regiment, militia, and was afterward commissioned First Lieutenant in the N. Y. S. Vols. (Company I, Independent Battalion) and set to the work of recruiting. In June, '62. he was ordered to active service in Virginia. He was transferred to the artillery and took part in the expedition against Charleston in 1863, was commissioned Captain (March, '63), and put in command of two companies of artillery during the bombardment of Fort Wagner. The extremely youthful Captain was not yet twenty-one, and when the consolidation of regiments that followed on the capture of Fort Wagner threw him temporarily out of service, he returned to his professional studies. He was graduated as a civil engineer in '66, and in the interim was brevetted Major for his services at Charleston.

Even more striking was the career of GILBERT ELLIOTT, the ablest student of the class, whose untimely end is here narrated by his brother RICHMOND ELLIOTT.

Colonel Gilbert Molleson Elliott, class of 1861, son of Jason and Ruth B. Elliott, was born in Thompson, Conn., October 7, 1840.

His career in the City College was marked by more triumphs than have fallen to the lot of any other of her students.

Entering the Introductory class in February, 1857, from Dr. Thomas Hunter's famous "No. 35," he at once took the front rank, and maintained it during his entire course. During this his first term, he came within two marks of the maximum, and even this extraordinary record he excelled in his first Senior term, when he achieved the unparalleled distinction of obtaining maximum for term and examination!

At four successive commencements he was awarded the Pell gold medal, the highest prize in the gift of the faculty. At his own commencement he was awarded not only the Pell medal, but also the Burr gold medal for excellence in mathematics, the Cromwell gold medal for excellence in history and belles-lettres, and six Ward bronze medals for marked excellence in as many subjects.

Devoted as he was to his studies, he was none the less patriotic. Immediately following the attack on Fort Sumter, April, 1861, he borrowed a flag from

Captain Ward, commandant of the Brooklyn Navy Yard, to be raised on the College.

In an enthusiastic and earnest speech at the ceremonies of unfurling the flag (the first to be raised on any institution in this city) he said, "I am willing to offer up my life in defence of my country."

After his graduation, abandoning his intention of studying law, he at once gave himself to the work of recruiting, and in October, 1861, he was mustered into the United States service, as First Lieutenant in the 102d Regiment, N. Y. Volunteers. In March, 1862, with his regiment he went to the seat of war. The young officer brought to the discharge of his military duties the same ardor and mental energy that had so signally distinguished him in his college career. He was specially commended for conspicuous gallantry and bravery at the battle of Antietam and was advanced to a captaincy. His rare intellectual and executive ability attracted the attention of Brigadier-General John W. Geary, commanding the 2d Division of the 12th Army Corps, who requested his assignment to the position of ordnance officer on his Staff. In this position of increased responsibility he won the commendation of his superior officers. In the memorable battles of Fredericksburg, Chancellorsville, and Gettysburg, he had provided necessary ordnance supplies not only for his own division, but he was able to fill requisitions for other division commanders.

After the battle of Gettysburg, upon the recommendation of Generals Geary and Hooker, for meritorious services, he was made Major in his regiment. Before retiring from his position as ordnance officer to take command of his battalion in the 102d N. Y. Vols., the Adjutant-General of his division, on behalf of General Geary, wrote him as follows:

> The General commanding, desires me to convey to you, on leaving his staff for a more extended sphere of duty, his warm appreciation of the ability and untiring energy with which you performed the arduous duties of your late position, and to thank you therefor. He tenders you his best wishes for your success in your new field of action in the great cause, and trusts that your present advancement is but the beginning of an elevation such as you deserve and will undoubtedly secure. On behalf of the General Staff, I have to express our regret at parting with you, and to hope that the fraternal relations so long existing between us, may not be disturbed by your separating from us.

In September, 1863, the 11th and 12th Army Corps under General Hooker were transferred to Tennessee to reinforce the Army of the Cumberland. On Nov. 24, at the desperate battle of Lookout Mountain, Geary's division of Hooker's Corps was in the first line of battle. Major Elliott with the advanced line of skirmishers while climbing the steep ascent of the mountain fell mortally wounded by a rebel sharp-shooter. In a few moments as gallant and intrepid an officer as ever drew the sword had poured out his young life's blood for his country. Fully cognizant of his approaching end, he said to the surgeon, "Tell my family I died

Microscopic Examination in Room G, under Dr. Bryan.

a brave man." His commanding general says of him, "He fell nobly leading the skirmishers. He has died the death of a brave soldier, gallantly fighting for his country."

His patriotism was not of that kind assumed for honor or distinction merely, as is evident from an extract from one of his letters to his family just after the Gettysburg campaign. "It is little I can do towards helping my country in her hour of peril, but what I can, I will do cheerfully, even though it cost me my life. If I live to see the end of the war, I should be ashamed of my name, had not some member of my family helped put down the rebellion."

In recognition of his distinguished services and heroic death, the posthumous ranks of Lieutenant-Colonel and Colonel were conferred upon him by President Johnson.

His remains are interred in the family plot at Woodlawn.

To this sketch might be added that Colonel Elliott was descended from a patriotic family. His great-great-grandfather was a Captain in Putnam's regiment, and lost his life at the Battle of Bunker Hill. It might not be amiss to add that Colonel Elliott's nephew and namesake, a graduate of the class of 1886, and the first son of an alumnus to be graduated, served in the late Spanish war in the capacity of surgeon in the First Maine Infantry.

With the class of '62 we approach still younger men. Yet twelve of these mere lads saw service. As privates there were AUGUSTUS RENIER ADAMS, WILSON BERRYMAN, KNOX MCAFEE, NATHAN ROBERTS, JAMES DAVIDSON (non-graduate), and WILLIAM E. SLOCUM. It was Mr. Slocum who came home on furlough and graduated in the uniform of his regiment (71st N. Y. S. militia). On the college commencement programme of '62 appeared a notice: "Messrs. Brower, McAfee, and Slocum are absent at the seat of war serving their country. They would if present be entitled to speak on this occasion." Mr. Slocum, unexpectedly fulfilling the obviously necessary condition, appeared upon the platform when another's name was called and despite President Webster's rather doubtful approval delivered an address amid great applause.

JOHN L. BROWER rose to be Captain and Lieutenant-Colonel of volunteers. DAVID E. BREKES was an Acting Assistant Surgeon on the field and at Fortress Monroe and helped succor the released prisoners from Andersonville. JAMES MATTHEWS TRIPPE rose to be Lieutenant-Colonel of the 24th U. S. colored troops in March, '65. CHARLES ROBERTS was commissioned Second Lieutenant in the Signal Corps in 1863 and served in Virginia, South Carolina, and Georgia until mustered out of service in August, '65. OTHO MICHAELIS, the valedictorian of his class, enlisted as a private in the 23d N. G. S. N. Y. In September, '63, he was appointed Second Lieutenant in the Signal

Corps and in November was transferred to the Ordnance Corps. He saw field service in the Gettysburg campaign, and in Tennessee as Chief of Ordnance on General Thomas' staff, being not yet twenty-one. In September, '64, he was promoted to be a First Lieutenant in the regular army, and in March, '65, was brevetted Captain. Remaining in the service after the war, he rose to the rank of Major before his death.

RICHARD POLK STRONG of this same class enlisted as a private in Company H of the 71st N. Y. S. M. in April, '61. He returned to the College for his final year and then in September, '62, was commissioned Second Lieutenant, 139th N. Y. Infantry. Through the winter of '62 he was in active service in Virginia and then (June, '63) received his appointment as First Lieutenant in the Signal Corps. He was made a member and then president of the examining board for commissions in this newly organized corps. In '64, he served at the siege of Petersburg and in the memorable cavalry raid through Florida and Alabama. In March, '65, he was made brevet Captain and Major of volunteers. Remaining in the regular service after the war, he was later assigned to the artillery, and rose to be Lieutenant-Colonel.

The class of '63 sent to the war only three of its graduates, HENRY SMITH STEELE, who as a private in the Seventh Militia Regiment took part in the suppression of the draft riots, ABRAHAM KIPP VAN VLECK, who was commissioned Captain in the 102d N. Y. Vols., and H. RAYMOND HOWLAND, who served as Commissary Clerk with General Butler's command in Virginia. Being, like his predecessors of '62, absent at the seat of war Howland was deprived of the pleasure of delivering his "Honorary Oration" at commencement.

Of youths of this period who did not wait to complete the college course, but left studies unfinished and courses incomplete, to serve the nation, there were several. WILLIAM C. ABBE enlisted three separate times. From June to September, '62, he was in the 37th N. G. S. N. Y. In 1863 he enlisted for a month, and was wounded in the neck in a skirmish at Carlisle, Pa. Later in the year he secured a commission as Lieutenant of U. S. colored troops and served at Ship Island and in the capture of Mobile, receiving his honorable discharge in '65. CHARLES HENRY O'CONNOR, enlisting as a private in the 22d N. Y. Infantry in '62, rose to be Second Lieutenant in the 2d R. I. Infantry (March, '63) and served on the staff of General Wheaton. He resigned in July, '63. APPLETON STURGIS served as First Lieutenant and Aide-de-Camp. HENRY WALTON GRINNELL entered the navy. He was appointed Acting Ensign in November, '62, rose to be Acting Master in January, '64, and Acting Lieutenant in May, '65. RICHARD B. GREENWOOD, who was studying with the class of '64, enlisted in the 22d N. Y. militia as early as '61. John T. Nagle of the same class served as Acting Assistant Surgeon from

THE "COLLEGE MERCURY" EDITORIAL ROOM.
A gloomy den on the ground floor of the Twenty-second Street building.

May, 1864, to June, 1865. He was commended for conspicuous bravery in action in the battle of Kernstown, Va., and was commissioned Assistant Surgeon in 1865.

Of graduate members the class of '64 sent only two men to the front. A. QUACKENBUSH, Jr., served as a clerk in the Ordnance Department at Chattanooga from September, '64, to January, '65. JOHN ABBOTT CLARKSON enlisted in the ranks immediately on graduation. He was soon made a clerk in the Ordnance service, but had already contracted a camp fever at Chattanooga, and he died in hospital.

Younger still, the last victim of a tragic record was EDWARD STURGIS. A student in the class of '65, he left college in February, '64, having secured his commission as First Lieutenant in the 20th Mass. Infantry. He was killed in action, May 10, 1864.

The Literary Societies of the College

The Literary Societies of the College

Edward M. Colie, '73

A LARGE part of the traditions and reminiscences associated with the old college building are intimately connected with the history of the two literary societies, which practically began with the life of the College, and many phases of their development throw interesting light on the conditions at the institution during the early days. Nearly all of the older Alumni have been members either of Clionia or Phrenocosmia, and a large number of the students who have not taken a degree, for some term of their college life enjoyed their benefits, and all cherish the memory of the days of their membership as among the most interesting and helpful of their student life. On their rolls are the distinguished Alumni who have brought honor to Alma Mater. A special interest is to be found in the fact that these societies were no part of the institution as planned by its founders. They were not ordained by the faculty, but were the spontaneous expression of a felt need by the students of something to supplement the prescribed course of study, and to deepen the sense of comradeship and create a college spirit. Their persistence, prosperity, and usefulness for these many years indicate that they represent and express ideas and ideals that are lasting.

The Free Academy opened its doors January 15, 1849. Students were admitted from the schools every six months, the first class entering February, 1849, and in the autumn of 1851 six classes had been received, each called after the letters of the alphabet, the oldest designated "A," in accordance with the plan at West Point, from which the Academy adopted many ideas besides its mathematical course. With a free field, without traditions, without precedent or experience to guide them, with no bond of union between the different classes, the students conceived the idea that the classes could be best united and a college sentiment developed by the foundation of a literary society constituted of the members of all classes. Clionia, the older of the two societies, originated in this idea and was established to realize it. Seemingly one of the causes which led to the founding of the society as a broad collegiate one was the fact that there already existed a class literary society known as the Amphilogian. This, the earliest literary association, was formed by the members of Classes A and B, afterwards constituting the Class of '53. Its membership was limited strictly to that class and it ceased to exist, so far as the College was con-

Natural History Hall.
The Assembly Room at the top of the Twenty-Second Street building.

cerned, upon its graduation, although the organization was continued by members of that class for some years thereafter.

The genuine college life began with the founding of Clionia by students of the Classes E and F, September 25, 1851. The founders were Joseph Allen, Simeon Baldwin, Jr., Cleveland J. Campbell, Irving S. Campbell, James W. Mason, Russell Raymond, and Charles C. White. The name adopted was the Free Academy Union. Its first debate, at which ten members were present, was held October 17, 1851, upon the question "Whether the assistance afforded to the Cubans by the Americans in the late disturbance was justifiable," then a burning question, growing out of the aid given by some altruistic Americans in a recent attempt at revolution in Cuba. The question was decided in the negative. The debate was held in a room hired especially for the occasion. The other exercises consisted of a declamation by Simeon Baldwin, Jr., entitled "A Parody on Lord Ullin's Daughter" and an essay by James W. Mason on "The Orators and Statesmen of Greece." This was evidently a great occasion, but the luxury of a hired room could not be ordinarily indulged in, and for some time thereafter the meetings were held at the houses of the members. The class feeling, however, was so strong that the members of the higher classes would not join a society originated by members of the lower classes, although every effort was made to induce them so to do, and the organization of the

Society was announced to be a temporary one, subject to change at the will of the incoming members from higher classes. The Society became one of all classes only by the process of the advancement of its members towards graduation. No student graduating before '55 was a member of it. In some way shortly after its organization, permission was obtained to hold meetings in School No. 20, afterwards No. 35, the famous Thirteenth Street School, of which Dr. Hunter was for so long the Principal. Old-fashioned candles furnished the artificial light at these meetings, which were held in the evening—the days of kerosene having not yet come. The permission to use the schoolroom was before long revoked upon the charge that the wear and tear on the room was unduly great, and thereafter, for a while, the Society met at the houses of the members, until permission was later given to meet in the Academy building, by which time the Society had grown in numbers and influence and value. About this time the name was changed to "Alpha Delta" (*A Δ*) and "Certamus Amicitia" was adopted as the motto. These Greek letters stood for *αδὲλφοι διαλεκτικοί*—"Brothers skilled in debate,"—but this meaning was a deep secret carefully guarded by the members.

The success of Clionia evidently led to the founding of Phrenocosmia in the late fall of 1852. Its name was then spelled Phrenacosmia and its Greek letters were "Phi Kappa" (*Φ K*). It, too. was founded by a small number of lower class men, among whom was

Natural History Hall, Platform.

Showing cases of "rocks" and a glimpse into the private workrooms of the department.

Dr. Joseph Anderson, '54, who was also one of its early presidents. The records of Phrenocosmia, which are extremely fragmentary, begin in 1854. About this time the friction began between the Board of Education and the two societies, growing out of the attempt to regulate and control them, and the adoption and the promulgation of the rules that they must meet in the daytime, must choose members by a majority vote, could initiate no member of the Introductory class, and could have no library. Both of the societies then left the college building and found quarters in Clinton Hall. Clionia occupied rooms in Clinton Hall from '53 to '57. During this period the name was changed to Clionia, and the Latin motto was dropped and a Greek one adopted αδελφικῶς διαλοῦμεν—"We fight as brothers"— which is said to have been the suggestion of Prof. Barton. After some years both societies came back for awhile to the college building, and later Clionia met in rooms constituting the Armory of Battery A of the National Guards on West 33d Street. These quarters were expensive, but the members had no difficulty in raising the needed funds. In more recent years both societies have held their meetings in the college building.

Clionia early began the collection of a library, which came to number several thousand volumes, consisting mostly of fiction, installed in one of the small rooms surrounding the chapel. In 1871 it was catalogued, and the extravagance of printing this catalogue was indulged in by the Society. The library still remains but its usefulness seems to have disappeared.

Phrenocosmia in 1854 had about ten members, eight of whom held official positions, and of the two not blessed with office, one immediately resigned, leaving a sole non-official member. There are signs in the fragmentary record of other dissensions. One member who resigned carried off a book which he had been authorized to buy for the purpose of recording the minutes. This may explain in part the breaks in the record. Graduates continued their membership, but after '55 they were not permitted to hold office, and thereafter gradually ceased to attend. The first recorded oration had for its subject Pollock's "Course of Time." The first recorded debate was upon the proposition "Political themes are fit subjects of discourse for the Pulpit."

In the records under date of February, '55, it appears that the Society requested the Board of Education to alter the offensive rules, already referred to. The resolution among other things, recites that the Society should be "reinstated into all their former privilages [*sic*] in the Academy, without infringing on the independance [*sic*] or honor of either party." This dignified proposition produced seemingly no effect on the Board of Education, but apparently did increase the enthusiasm of the members, for they continued, according to the record, to hold meetings up to July 16th of that year. On December 17, 1855, they held a private "Anniversary Meeting" at "Gramercy Lodge Room" and the "Hon. Horace Webster" made a few remarks. A public anniversary was arranged for the following spring. At this public meeting it appears that the "Marshal" disgraced the membership by appearing in an intoxicated condition. This was the occasion of much debate and many resolutions, and resulted in a demand for formal apology which was delivered in writing, and finally accepted on motion, to which an amendment was offered, but lost, that the Marshal be further instructed to "refrain from boasting" of his offence. It was in connection with this same celebration that it was resolved by the Society to "request the several speakers not to expatiate longer than ten minutes."

The second public anniversary was held in 1856, after which it was voted to discontinue the custom because of the expense, and the subsequent recognitions of the date were private affairs. In 1857, the "obnoxious by-laws" which kept the societies out of the college building were repealed. In October '57 members of the Introductory Class were barred from membership thereafter. The records of this year contain an account of a stranger who entered the meeting, apparently as a visitor, and interrupted the proceedings until he was invited to make a speech. He then started "a flow of derogatory remarks," which led to the conclusion that he was not sober, and he was conducted with "due solemnity outside." During this year there was waged also a mighty war of words, because a member felt that he was insulted by some remarks addressed to him by the President. This charge resulted in many resolutions and much argument, and a private meeting was held at a member's house for the discussion and decision of the matter, which resulted in the exoneration of the President. After 1858, the minutes entirely disappear until 1871; thus the entire record during the war is lost.

As early as November, '55, members of the two Societies were invited to attend each other's meetings, and such friendly relations continued until '57, when Clionia proposed the holding of joint debates. Phrenocosmia agreed to this, but first demanded an apology for some supposed insult to her by some overzealous Clionian, when on the floor of his Society he discussed the proposed project of joint debates. As Clionia professed ignorance of any insult, while Phrenocosmia insisted on an apology, and the apology was not made, Phrenocosmia withdrew from all intercourse with her rival for a considerable length of time. Subsequently, all friction between the two societies apparently vanished. Indeed, we learn from General Tremain, a leading Phrenocosmian of that day, that matters were entirely harmonious after 1859, and in that year he took part in what he believes to be the first joint debate between the two societies. It was held in Dr. Doremus' Chemical Lecture Room, and the question was: "If the South should secede, would it be able

Natural History Hall.

Looking north, showing cases of specimens mainly the gifts of Professor Stratford and Professor Dean.

to maintain itself as an independent Confederacy?" Phrenocosmia held the negative of the question, and the vote taken after the close of the debate was overwhelmingly on that side. The records after '71 show that meetings were held sometimes in Masonic Hall and sometimes in the College. The joint debates were again re-established. At a debate held January 12, 1872, in the Chemical Lecture Room, there were about seventy present. Professor Compton acted as Judge. John Bach McMaster of '72 won for Phrenocosmia, and the prize was a copy of Bryant's Iliad. The honors have been very nearly even since the re-establishment of the joint debates between the two societies.

In 1868, James Kelly, Esq., by gift of $1000, established a prize to be awarded to the best debater among six elected annually by both literary societies, and these annual debates became a great source of emulation between the two societies, and, as in their joint debates, the honors to the two societies have been practically even. In the writer's time, this debate was held in Steinway Hall on Fourteenth Street. It was a great public function and tested the capacity of the large hall to its utmost. The College paid all the expenses, including the furnishing of a large orchestra. Owing to this great expense, however, these debates were held subsequently either at the college building or in the Hall of the Board of Education.

In 1887, Hon. Elliott F. Shepard, then acting as a referee at a joint debate, offered a sum of $500 to be contested for in prizes of $50 each. Clionia won the first prize, and thereafter the honors again were practically even.

During the years covered by the writer's term in College, both societies were in a flourishing condition and on most friendly relations. The writer was a Phrenocosmian.

A great event for both societies at that time was their Annual Exhibition, as it was called, which had been held for a number of years at the Academy of Music. Eight members were elected to deliver original orations, and a large orchestra was furnished to discourse music between the speeches. The old Academy could hardly contain the crowds that enjoyed these occasions. Expenses were paid by subscriptions by the students who could afford to pay and by money raised on the sale of the boxes. The expenses were between $500 and $600 on each occasion, but there was never any difficulty in raising the amount needed. In 1872, these functions were discontinued because there were so many members of limited means that it was felt to be indelicate to have an entertainment to which so many were entirely unable to contribute.

About this time also took place the first joint debate between one of the literary societies of the College and one of the literary societies of the Normal College. It was between Clionia of the College and Alpha of the Normal, and it was voted a very successful affair. The Clionian records of the contest have unfortunately been lost but those who participated in the excitement recall it with vivid satisfaction.

In 1873, for the first time in the history of the Kelly Prize Debates, Clionia took both prizes, the winners being Lewinson and Kohn of '73.

In 1877, Phrenocosmia held its Twenty-fifth Anniversary in the Academy of Music, an entirely worthy affair. Lewis S. Burchard, '77, presided; General Tremain, '60, delivered the Graduates' address; and, Dr. Joseph Anderson, '54, read a poem on Professor Barton.

In gathering the data for this sketch, the following letter has been received, which is of so much interest that it has been decided to print it in full:

73 AVENUE KLEBER, PARIS,
Feb. 16th, 1907.

PROF. CHARLES F. HORNE,

Dear Sir:

My mail from America brings me, this morning, your letter of January 29th.

Right glad am I to hear of your proposed Memorial Volume concerning the College of the City of New York—my Alma Mater.

But I am sorry to reward your Phi Kappa inquiries with only a meagre and nebulous response.

It is true that in 1852 (or perhaps a year later) I co-operated with some of my fellow-collegians of Class C in founding the Phrenocosmian Literary Society, and in editing (with their help) its organ or gazette:—which was a wee bit of a newspaper—not printed, but handed about in manuscript,—issued not regularly but at odd times, the total edition always consisting of *one* copy only,—and which, in passing from borrower to borrower, was sometimes lost, or more usually worn out and finally reduced to its primitive rags!

In fact, the Phrenocosmian "early records" (as you call them) did not include any formal and permanent Book of Minutes, or journal of proceedings, but were simply a few haphazard contributions such as might chance to be flung together to make up the tardy next number of a semi-occasional fly-sheet.

I think I am right in saying that nothing like a "file" of this spasmodic publication existed either under my régime, or during my college-term.

Nevertheless, any student who wanted to wreak himself on expression, and to commit a burst of eloquence, was allowed a generous latitude.

It was a free press!

My small corps of the more regular and sedate contributors, such as never on any occasion had fireworks to let off, were Joseph R. Anderson, Edmund Belfour, Franklin S. Rising, and E. Tanjore Corwin:—so that strictly speaking the whole editorial staff, except only the editor-in-chief, consisted of clergymen in embryo!

But I never found that these sober-minded gentlemen objected to innocent fun. So our little sheet bristled with a crispy secularity—a breezy worldliness especially adapted to "well ordered minds" and hence its contents were specifically and etymologically "Phrenocosmian." It irradiated Murray Hill and Lexington Avenue with Baconian Wisdom in the form of college-jokes and with vivacious comments on passing events, all set forth with an adolescent freshness of style far more sparkling than much of the weary waggery which I now read daily in the *Figaro* in its "*Nouvelles à la Main.*"

Let me tell you an anecdote of those golden days of Phi Kappa.

One of the non-clerical luminaries of Class C (a splendid comrade whom we never saluted by his name but always by his

A CORNER OF THE NATURAL HISTORY HALL.
A class in mineralogy under Professor Stratford.

initials) said to me one day, "Our college newspaper would be much better if it were not so good," and his remedial suggestion was "Less comedy and more science!"

Whereupon I challenged him to contribute to our very next number a brief résumé of his most solemn views on the Descent of Man.

His lucubration (as nearly as I can recall its phraseology) was as follows:

The Problem of the Origin of Species.

Question: Why was Eve created?
Answer: For Adam's Express Company.

This *bon mot*, on its first appearance in our Phrenocosmian sheet, was signed G. F. S.

It was at once stolen by the whole American press—no credit being given either to the author, or to Phi Kappa.

So I take the liberty of mentioning that the G. F. S. of half a century ago is to-day the celebrated physician and surgeon Dr. George F. Shrady of New York.

I close my letter, my dear Mr. Horne, by adding that my long-ago editorship of the Phrenocosmian journal was terminated by the graduation of my college class in 1855.

Good luck to your Memorial Volume!

Cordially yours,

THEODORE TILTON.

The societies have not been without their troubles during succeeding years. The Kelly Debates were not held for a number of years, the fund for some reason not having been productive, but they have now been resumed; the most recent joint debate, held in December, 1906, was won by Clionia, and singularly this victory made the record of joint debates between the two societies once more exactly alike.

A number of literary societies have, from time to time, originated in some one or other of the sub-Freshman classes in recent years; most of them have had a short life, but one, the Adelphian, has not only maintained itself for three years in those classes, but now has members who are of the Collegiate classes.

The establishment of the "Department of Oratory" under Professor Palmer has brought debating practically into the curriculum of the College and the interest in that subject has greatly increased, especially since the success of the College in its two debates with Hamilton. Nevertheless, the two leading societies have maintained their traditional independence. Standing thus as peculiarly and emphatically student organizations, they have grown in strength and in numbers and are in a condition satisfactory both to the College and to the members.

College Journalism

College Journalism

Julius M. Mayer, '84

And The Editors

THE idea of "college journalism," that is of magazines chronicling student life and published by the students themselves, is essentially American. Only very recently has it taken root in Europe at all, while in America it dates back to the beginning of the last century. The *Literary Cabinet* was started by Yale students in 1806. It was stupendously heavy of thought and slow of movement; and it did not last. Yet it was a beginning; and the idea soon spread to other colleges. It is to be noted, however, that Yale was founded in 1701, hence it took her over a century to evolve a college paper. Our own Free Academy reached a similar stage of development in nine years. To be sure we began existence in a faster moving age. Moreover our environment and associations with our great metropolis led us naturally into journalistic lines. So that perhaps we should rather seek excuse that our magazines did not spring even earlier into existence—as early as our literary societies. Such excuse is to be found in the expenses involved in printer's ink. The desire, the ambition for print, existed in our very earliest classes. We have record of the *Phrenocosmian*, a journal laboriousy written out by hand, far back in '52, and circulated from student to student until it perished, as more pretentious volumes seldom perish, from actual use.

In 1858 appeared our first printed paper, the *Microcosm*. It could scarce be called a journal, for it was intended only to be what it still continues to-day, an annual record. Toward literary effort, it made no pretence whatever; nor was it in a financial sense a "venture." It was prepared by the fraternity chapters of Chi Psi and Alpha Delta Phi; and the projectors first went about the College and secured subscriptions in advance, sufficient to defray expenses. They then proceeded to "cut their coat according to their cloth" and issued only a four-page sheet, 12 x 16 inches, giving the names of the faculty, members of the classes, societies and similar rather deadening details.

The *Microcosm* had in 1860 a rival similar to itself, the *Cosmopolitan*, which sprang into existence under spur of the healthy rivalry roused among students who felt themselves too little noticed in the other publication. The *Cosmopolitan* lasted through three years.

Encouraged by the success of both these annuals a real journal was attempted, the *Free Academy Monthly*. In this enterprise the students were encouraged and

A Corner of the Natural History Hall.

A class engaged in the work of dissection, diagramming results.

advised by Professor Anthon and several others of the teaching force; and the first and alas! only number of the *Monthly* ever published was a really admirable production. It appeared in the winter of 1860–61; then came the tumult of the Civil War, and the *Monthly* was forgotten.

During the war the *Microcosm* continued as the sole printed representative of the students. Then in 1866 came the change of name of our institution to the City College, and with the change, as though inspired by it, appeared that ambitious magazine, the *Collegian*. The first number of this was issued November 21, 1866; it was published by the class of '68 under the editorship of Richard R. Bowker, then a member of the class. The paper was planned as a bi-weekly; it published news of student doings in brief; but was devoted mainly to literary purposes and included in its pages some poems which have since won considerable repute. Really admirable as the paper was, it failed of financial success. Of advertisements it had practically none, and while the students liked the articles and approved their general tone, yet the price per copy, twelve and then fifteen cents, was higher than most student purses could afford. So the *Collegian* died after issuing eight numbers.

Warned by this serious and decided failure our embryo journalists kept out of print for several years, if we except a single number of a paper published in 1870, and called the *Introductory* because issued by members of the Introductory class. Then in 1874 there came a sudden startling outburst of the journalistic fever. Papers sprang up throughout the College like mushrooms and some of them to the genuine astonishment of their perpetrators proved financially successful. First to appear (February, 1874) was the *Clionian Magazine*, issued as a monthly under the editorship of Mr. Samuels, '74. It was severely literary, deeply impregnated with student wisdom, and was not among the pecuniary victories. It was discontinued after three issues.

In that same spring appeared the *College Budget*, which enjoys the distinction of being the first C. C. N. Y. magazine that *paid*. Let us with all humility confess that nobody ever accused the *Budget* of the journalistic crime of being "literary." Its first issue was published as a joke by H. C. Kahrs, '75. Indeed if we may believe the *Budget's* own assurance Mr. Kahrs, or H. C. Shark, as he placarded his name in thin disguise, not only edited and published but also printed the sheet himself. It was certainly printed execrably, full of errors, on a 3 x 5 sheet of cheapest paper. But it was crowded with fun and impudence and the rather vapid personalities which please the lad who thus for the first time sees his own name in public type. So it "took." Kahrs was joined by some of his classmates, Henry Jenkins, now principal of the largest public school in our city, and others; and among them they kept the *Budget* alive until the spring of '75. They increased its size too and improved on its respectability, without losing its ingenuity of wit and sarcasm. Jenkins, "our paid poet" as the editorial page denominated him, had a ready power of rhyme which has not deserted him, and his squibs would have made good reading in far more pretentious columns.

The *Budget's* success soon brought it rivals of similar type. This class of '75 was certainly a remarkable one in its thirst for print. Its first effort had been the *Introductory*, then came the *Budget.* Then another faction of the class published an opposition piece of impudence called the *Firefly*, and edited by Wilbur Larremore, since editor of more ambitious works. The Freshman class, '77, started the *Mosquito*. Next year the incoming Freshmen of '78 issued the *Flea;* and '79, still an Introductory class, produced the *Meteor*. The names of these sheets form sufficient indication of their spirit and style.

Perhaps the editors themselves were a little ashamed that in the rapidly developing world of college journalism our College was no better represented for we find that all of these buzzing little insects lent generous aid to an attempt to re-establish the defunct *Collegian.* This effort and the use of the old, revered name were sanctioned by Mr. Bowker, editor of the former *Collegian*. The new paper, founded on the lines of the old, appeared in January, 1875, under the managing editorship of G. N. Messiter of '75. Both Larremore and Jenkins were on the editorial staff; so was J. V. V.

Olcott of '76, now Congressman Olcott, Hanford Crawford, '75, Nelson S. Spencer, '75, in short all the literary talent of the College.

Even these men, however, could not make a purely literary paper pay by its sale among undergraduates. Four numbers of the *Collegian* were published in the spring of 1875. But when the class of '75 was graduated, '76 made no effort to continue the profitless undertaking.

Yet the determination to have some sort of paper, to serve as a more dignified representative of the College than the slangy little insect buzzers, was steadily gaining strength. As '76 did not take up the work, two men of the following classes attempted it. They were L. S. Burchard of '77, and F. S. Williams of '78. Between them they planned the *Echo*, a journal which should by being part literary, part newsy, combine the glory of one style with the profit of the other. They secured the approval and support of the former editors of the *Collegian* and so were able to advertise their paper as the legitimate successor of that dignified failure. Then they formed an "Echo Association" in which several members of the Senior class, '77, and also of the Juniors and Sophomores joined to aid them. In December, 1876, the *Echo* began its career.

In seeking to gather the forgotten data for this sketch I obtained from one of the *Echo's* early editors an account so characteristic that I make no effort to

Dissecting Work.
In corner of Natural History Hall under Dr. Sumner.

change, but quote it entire. No reader of our college literature will fail to recognize the genial pen of Burchard, '77, the first president of the Echo Association.

When '77 entered its Senior year, steps were taken to launch a new college paper. An association of members of the three upper classes was formed and the *College Echo* was launched. I was in the literary subdivision of the board of editors, Sigismund Pollitzer, '79, hounded us for copy, and Frank S. Williams, '78, was business or managing editor. The *Echo* was criticised by one of its contemporaries for "spreading its new-fledged wings too ambitiously," but attained a small sort of distinction. Perrin, '79, composed the dedicatory verses beginning

> "'Tis related that Echo, a lovely young Oread,
> Sat beside Juno and chatted so long,
> That old Jove slipped away and clandestinely sported
> With all the fair nymphs in that heavenly throng;"

and Emil Andrew Huber, '77, began a series of poetical contributions which for sheer, simple, inexplicable genius—a Poe-like melody and unearthly weirdness or eerieness, a Keatsian splendor of landscape—had never been equalled in the history of the College.

During the first two or three months of the *Echo's* career, there occurred the funniest little journalistic scrap the College ever saw.

Just before the first number of the *Echo* came out, and while we "editors" were all somewhat aghast at the amount of writing it took to fill the maw of the unpresentable monster that "took so long a-borning," the class of '80, then in the Freshman year, brought out a comical little mishap of a paper called the *Star of '80*. Its first number was written almost entirely by a lovable, blundering, energetic, harumscarum Freshman named Oscar B. Weber, who afterward became rich and famous as a builder of really beautiful chimneys of so-called "radial" brick for gas works and factories, and who died only recently. The paper was printed in some German printing office over in a small Jersey town and was full of amusing typographical errors. For instance, the opening "poem"—we all had to start life with "poems" in those days—began by comparing itself to "a bird" that "first assays its maiden flight" and, after cavorting around, sometimes without bothering to rhyme its quatrains and sometimes without waiting for a fourth line, soared to its noblest height by chanting:

"O'er the far-extended earth,
Clouds will hide, thy light appearing,
Truth will wear [*sic*] its noble head,
Drown the voices of the snearing."

The *Budget* had been Bohemian—having a bit of literary flavor in its fooling, the *Mosquito*, neat and tiny, the *Festive Flea*, flippant and ribald, the *Meteor* solemn and priggishly literary, but this *Star* had nothing but a heavy German-American clumsiness. Here was grist for the despairing *Echo* millers. And so I wrote a review and pounded the poor little *Star*.

Then came my punishment. To fill up that awful first *Echo* I had taken a Sophomore composition on "The Dream of Eugene Aram" (subject assigned) and a "Junior Oration" on Thomas Hood and tacked the two together into an "article" on Thomas Hood. It was turgid, wordy, Sophomoric (pardon, '09!), and deserved all that "came to it." But imagine the astonishment of the Seniors in general and poor me in particular when, within a few weeks of the publication of the *Echo*, out pops a "No. 2" of the *Star of '80*, correctly edited and printed, and containing two of the wittiest and most scathing roasts of the *Echo* in general and Thomas Hood in particular that could be imagined. Slashing, dashing criticisms of the first order, worthy of Charles A. Dana in his raciest moods, they left neither hide nor hair of poor Hood's eulogist. Evidently, they were the work of mature minds, of writers who had read far more than any undergraduate we had ever seen. It seemed to me like an aggravated case of calling in a big brother. They estimated my flights as of the style of "a pale, interesting young clergyman, the recipient of many slippers," and compared them to "the emotional effusions of Theodore Tilton in the days when Tilton wrote with purity of feeling" (this was just after the Beecher-Tilton trial).

They were reminded "of a virgin with yearnings," quoted Artemus Ward—"Let her gush! I roared, as loud as I could holler," and accused me of "silly half-plagiarism" because I called the air "multitudinous."

Aldrich's Tom Bailey used the text-book description of the earthquake of Lisbon to express his sensations during his first "blight." I felt reminded of the lines in *Horatius*—

"All shrank,—like boys who, unaware,
Ranging a wood to start a hare,
Come to the mouth of the dark lair
Where, growling low, a fierce old bear
Lies amidst bones and blood."

In the second number they roasted a second Sophomore composition of mine refurbished into another *Echo* "article," and turned the kreese in my wound by displaying the masterly critical taste to recognize and praise most heartily, and with really scholarly and poetic appreciation, Huber's first remarkable verses in the measure of *Tears, idle Tears*, beginning—

Sea, open sea; it heaves and sinks amain
In long, low swell of heavy-lifted waves,
Hollows and hills, and caves of moving sea,
Near plash and distant boom; and, on the verge,
Still, stealthy lines that creep against the sky—
And all is glossy in the cold, white moon;
The corpse is silent with its ghost, the moon.

The *Star* reviewer, recalling the many phrases descriptive of the sea, "from the much collegian-

Professor Stratford in his Office.

A secluded nook cut off from Natural History Hall to be the headquarters of the department.

mimicked 'multitudinous seas' of the greatest immortal to the 'sea of unshovelled graves' of Walt Whitman," found the poem a "surprise," the first five lines "astounding," "true, unmistakable poetry," and "a student of our upper classes (which before we did not know to be great in the brilliancy of their members) saying something . . . fresh and free and as good and life-like as it is new"; and, whether rapping one of us over the knuckles or patting the other of us on the head, conveyed the tremendous impression of a veteran *littérateur*, say, like our own Anthon, in some incomprehensible manner amusing himself contributing to an aforetime absurd Freshman paper, making Riggs's Essay men and Seniors stand around like schoolboys and treating eloquence carefully modelled on Shaw's *Literature* as "gaspirations."

To help "fill up" that ravenous maw of the *Echo*, when we came to print the second number I could n't resist the temptation of inserting what I thought the gem of all the Riggs Essays as preserved in a book in President Webb's office—one written by Edward Morse Shepard, '69, when a Junior, on the assigned subject of "The Gentleman." On this, in the third number of the now redoubtable *Star*, the unknown critics fell. Probably crediting this to the unfortunate *Hood* man, —and greatly flattering him thereby—they proceeded to "skin him again." "This time," they found it "not ludicrous but only dreary and impossible to review because no one would think of reading it," because the *Hood* man had the "air still pulsing with rich vibrations"; they managed to "dip into the vague ocean," of Shepard's essay "at points, and of course pick up, first thing, a stock *Echo*-essay pearl,—'aerial pulsations.'" They called his gentleman "the real old Sunday-school-book bore" and recommended him to the reading of "a wicked man called Thackeray," all of which, we heard, was highly amusing to Shepard, now chairman of the Board of Trustees of the College, and nuts and ale to me. If the great and brilliant Shepard of '69, already an heroic figure in our tradition, was to catch it, I could grin in my pillory.

Who were these astounding Freshmen?—if they *were* Freshmen, which seemed incredible, impossible.

We soon came to know them and found them to be Henry G. S. Noble, now one of the Governing Committee of the New York Stock Exchange and one of the committee that built the new Exchange, and Francis Dane Bailey, himself a poet, philosopher, and critic. With R. Floyd Clarke, later first prize man at Columbia Law School and author of the *Science of Law and Lawmaking*, and Harry W. Mack, they carried on the *Star* intermittently till graduation, when the *Star* published a Class-Day Book in pamphlet form in which Noble produced a *History of the Class of '80* with illustrations by the author, which, with the January and February, '77, numbers of the *Star*, remains to this day the wittiest and funniest piece of undergraduate writing that the College has ever seen. To this Class-Day Book Bailey contributed a series of sketches in the style of Edward Lear's immortal *Nonsense Book*, the *Pictorial History of the Class of '80*, illustrating '80's intellectual development.

Thus the *Star* swam out of our ken, while the *Echo* kept on a-coming out. Bailey wrote for it a screaming review of Shaw's *English Literature* and Freeman's *History;* Professor Werner gave us a wise and fastidiously worded essay, "On Scintillation"; Huber, Bailey, Theodore Ives, Perrin, and Merington, all of '79, wrote verses; Professor Roemer gave us a menu in Latin; Larremore, '75, two charming essays, "A Brief Homily," and "The Dilettante"; Spencer, '75, "A Dogma in Criticism"; Marcus Stine, '76, two letters from Leipzig, one describing a student duel; and other graduates contributed and we kept up quite a gait. We of the *Echo* were, if I am not mistaken, the first to recognize the decorative possibilities of the College seal and make it part of the "make-up" of our title, as the *Mercury* does to this day.

For this, one of the exchanges said we sported the "spiciest motto" of all the College papers.

L. S. B.

The *Echo* maintained itself vigorously through 1877 and 1878, a credit to the College, as highly honored in other institutions as in our own. But in 1879 it faded and disappeared, the Echo Association having failed to recruit sufficient new members from the lower classes. The little *Star* of '80 revived for a moment to dance in triumph over the remains of its defunct antagonist. The College was thus again left with no representative print except the *Microcosm*, which in 1878 was enlarged from its merely perfunctory list of names to a pamphlet somewhat resembling its more recent issues. It contained class histories and a chronology of college events. Moreover its editors were able to "point with pride" to its having a cut for a frontispiece. Stiff covers, giving the annual a right to be called a "book," came later, with '87 I think for the first time. And then finally in '89 came the heavy board covers and the two hundred pages or more of contents which gave the *Microcosm* a place in the first rank of elaborate college publications.

Meanwhile in March, 1880, there appeared two claimants for the post left vacant by the *Echo*. These were *Eboraciana*, issued by the Sophomores of '82 under the editorship of Everit Brown, and the *College Mercury*, issued by the Freshmen of '83. *Eboraciana* lasted only half a year. The *Mercury* is still in existence after twenty-seven years. Let Mr. Mosenthal, one of its founders, tell its story, as he told it twenty years ago in his farewell number of the paper.

When the *Echo*, in December, 1878, finally passed out of existence, matters looked very gloomy for our college journalism. No upper-class man was willing, with the failure of such brilliant prospects as the *Echo*

THE DEPARTMENT OF PHYSICS.

had, staring him in the face, to risk the establishment of a new paper. In consequence, from this time till March, 1880, our College had no representative. It was left to lower-class men, who knew little of the *Echo*, except that their subscriptions had never been returned them, to prepare a new venture.

The idea of founding the *College Mercury* originated with E. J. Newell, '83, and was talked over by him with several of his classmates during their Introductory year. It was not, however, till the middle of the Freshman year that the plan was carried out. In December, 1879, Mr. Newell and Mr. E. G. Barratt, then also of '83, finally agreed on a mode of procedure. By subscribing the necessary funds themselves they became the sole owners of the embryo paper. Before anything further was done, P. J. Mosenthal, '83, was taken into confidence, and, purchasing a few of the so-called shares, became one of the future editors. L. F. Mott, '83, was the next one chosen, and he, with Messrs. Channing and Bayles, who, however, never had more than nominal connection with the paper, completed the editorial board. The semi-annual examination coming on at this time delayed the appearance of the first number. However, toward the close of February, 1880, a notice appeared on the bulletin, surmounted by a figure of Hermes, cut from an old newspaper, and announcing that a new paper would shortly appear under the management of E. G. Barratt, '83.

Its coming was awaited with considerable curiosity, not unmixed, on the part of the Seniors, with disdain at Freshman audacity. For a time prospects were not very promising. The examinations had proved disastrous to one of the board. Advertisements were not easily procured and such "copy" as came in was of no great degree of excellence. But matters took a more favorable turn. Two or three Seniors, who had been connected with the *Echo*, good-naturedly became interested in the enterprise. One of them wrote the opening editorial, which arduous task the new editors did not dare to undertake. The modesty and good sense of this bit of writing did not a little toward creating a favorable impression for the paper, at home and abroad, when it finally appeared. But the *Echo* men did the *Mercury* another service, by giving it permission to call itself the successor of their paper, and thus freeing it at once from the imputation of being the representative only of the class from which its editors were drawn.

Finally, in March, 1880, No. 1 of the *College Mercury* appeared. It was of about the same size as at present, contained sixteen pages, and was printed in long primer type on good tinted paper. E. G. Barratt's name was the only one placed at the head of the editorial page. He was called the managing editor, but, though he supplied part of the funds for starting the paper, he never did any active work on it. E. J. Newell was the real manager and editor at this time. The others had

The Department of German.

absolutely no experience in writing even for a limited circle, and, as far as we can now remember, only one of them supplied any of the matter, beyond a few news items. With what fears and tremblings did not the editors await the appearance of the first number. We well remember driving down town one afternoon to take a look at the wonderful sheet, which was almost ready for publication. And when we saw it, how weak and puerile did the efforts we had spent time and trouble on sound to us, as we imagined ourselves in the position of a disinterested or even inimical critic. Well, it finally appeared, and as an immediate consequence we, the editors, almost disappeared from the scene of our journalistic achievements. There was in that first number a certain editorial which in no way agreed with some faculty rules passed at the time of the *Echo's* difficulty, for the delectation of college journalists. For a time the paper's existence was precarious. The second number appeared in April, and by trying to explain matters only made them worse. The unfortunate editors were suspended, and soon afterward the whole affair got into the papers and created a most ludicrous sensation. The New York papers embroidered a beautiful legend on the facts of the case and their rural contemporaries caught it up, and received from their city correspondents heart-rending tales of the attempts to infringe the liberty of the press. The truth of the matter is that none of the editors were suspended longer than a few days; that all were taken back into grace long before the issue of the third number; and that finally the *Mercury*, so far from being suppressed, has ever since enjoyed the complete favor and sympathy of the college authorities.

The second volume of the *Mercury* began in October, 1880, with E. J. Newell as managing editor, and P. J. Mosenthal and L. F. Mott as assistants. The rest of the board had by this time left college. The small number of editors necessitated the frequent printing of contributed matter, thus giving an agreeable variety. Vol. II, No. 2, saw the success of the paper assured. Hitherto it had been a monthly, but now, conforming to the general custom, it became a fortnightly, which it has since remained. With every succeeding number it rose in favor among the readers it catered to, and completed the second year of its existence with a large commencement number, containing prize lists and sketches of the members of the graduating class.

The third volume was begun under a different management and proprietorship. Mr. Newell having left college, an association consisting of Messrs. H. E. Brown and W. H. Rachau, '82, purchased from him the property and good-will of the paper. Mr. Newell had founded it and had by judicious management made it a complete success, and he parted from his former associates with the best of feelings. P. J. Mosenthal became managing editor and L. F. Mott first assistant. In order to assure C. C. N. Y. of a permanent paper, the new Mercury Association resolved, on the graduation of its then members, to make a free gift of the paper to the succeeding editorial board, who were to pass it on in a similar way to the next. Under a still later organization this plan was retained, but alumni members were given a voice in the paper's affairs. Thus, while always in the hands of the students of the College, the *Mercury* has in its alumni, anxious for its welfare, a means of support in case of need.

The third volume was thoroughly prosperous. The college authorities showed it their approval in a number of ways, among others by giving it a permanent office, and by frequent contributions. In Vol. IV. Messrs. E. F. Todd and J. M. Mayer, '84, took the places of the '82 members who had graduated. The success of the paper was in every way kept up.

This plan of passing the *Mercury* from class to class has indeed preserved it. It has even become a sort of "school of journalism" within the College, not unworthy of the institution which it represents, and sending out year after year men trained in the practical business of journal-making. Many a former editor, rising at the quinquennial dinners held by the *Mercury* graduates, has declared his *Mercury* labors the most valuable of all his college work.

Secure in its strength *Mercury* has watched generation after generation of papers rise and pass. Some of them it is even possible (an old *Mercury* man can not be expected to admit more than that) have temporarily equalled *Mercury* in wit and scholarship. But they have each and all been the work of individuals, perishing with the single brain.

Most formidable of these rivals was the *College Journal*, which began in December, '82, before *Mercury* was firmly established. It was published by men of the class of '85 and by them passed on to men of '88. For about five years its lively though at times indecorous and distinctly "yellow" pages kept the *Mercury* editors busy to "keep ahead." In 1892 Clionia revived its former magazine, but continued it for only two volumes. In 1893 Phrenocosmia also started a literary journal equally profound. Bernard Naumburg, '94, was the editor of this. It was a quarterly and persisted through four volumes before Phrenocosmian patience, funds, and literary genius ran short. Then there were the *College Epigram* and the *College Review*, severely literary, and *Quips and Cranks*, really bright and newsy, and *Cap and Bells*. With the separation of the introductory classes uptown came an era of introductory papers, chief of which has been the *Academic Herald*, which began in November, 1905, and still survives.

Of older papers kept alive by alumni help we have recently had two. In January, 1904, M. Gaston Laffargue, instructor in the French department, started a French paper, *La XXième Siecle.* While relying

THE LATIN DEPARTMENT.

partly on student support and material, this drew mainly upon the graduates, and after two volumes M. Laffargue abandoned it.

On December 30, 1904, was issued the first number of the *City College Quarterly*, a magazine devoted to the maturer interests of the College and its alumni. It was edited by James W. Sheridan, an instructor in the English department of the College. Mr. Sheridan died suddenly and tragically, and the *Quarterly* was continued by an association formed for that purpose. It is now under the editorship of Professor Mott, head of the English department and, as this article has recounted, one of the founders of the *Mercury*, the only other college paper which has persisted, as the *Quarterly* seems likely to persist.

The Fraternities

The Fraternities

Frank Keck, '72

AN interesting feature of a student's life in an American college is his membership in one of the Greek letter secret fraternities, and the existence of these fraternities at colleges and universities located in large cities helps much towards the enjoyment of such advantages as come to the student attending a similar institution located in a small town even where such fraternities do not exist.

The student attending a college or university in a large city lives at home, perhaps at some distance from the college buildings, and sees very little of the social side of his fellow-student unless he be a member of one of these societies. Perhaps he is inclined to fall behind in his studies; whereas a fraternity man always finds a brother ready with words of advice and encouragement to help him on to better work.

A very short period had elapsed after the founding of the Free Academy when its students felt the need of some such organization, and a local society known as Sigma Xi was established, renting a house on Fourth

Avenue near 18th Street. Among its members were Professor Alfred G. Compton, Hon. John M. Hardy, Brevet Brig.-Gen. Gilbert H. McKibbin, and James H. Steers. It was not a secret society, but purely a social club, and it maintained an active existence only a short time after the establishment of the first regular college fraternity in the Academy. Its members have met, however, once a year at dinner, and at the dinner given this year at the Hotel Astor no less than twenty were present.

In the year 1855 several of the students were approached by William W. Goodrich, an Amherst graduate, since deceased but in his lifetime a judge of the Supreme Court of the State of New York, on the subject of the establishment of a chapter of his fraternity, the Alpha Delta Phi, at the Free Academy. He succeeded in enlisting the interests of the following students of the class of 1855: William H. Abel, Simeon Baldwin, Lewis C. Bayles, Francis A. Mason, James W. Mason, Henry A. Post, Luis Fernandez, and Dayton W. Searle, and of the class of 1856 Franklin S. Rising, Russell Sturgis, and James L. Van Buren, who petitioned for a charter and became the founders of the Manhattan chapter of the Alpha Delta Phi fraternity at the Free Academy. They made their existence known at Commencement in July, 1855, by wearing the badge of the society for the first time. They selected their members from the students who were noted for their scholarly attainments, and scarcely ever had at any one time more than six members from any one class.

This exclusiveness on the part of the Alpha Delta Phi left some excellent material without the advantages of membership in a secret fraternity, and in the spring of 1856 the Nu chapter of the Delta Kappa Epsilon Fraternity was organized. Henry Davis, Frederick A. Leeds, Adrian H. Muller, Jr., John Howe, Jr., John E. Ward, of the class of 1856, Jared S. Babcock of the class of 1857, and Theodore A. Blake William Kirkland, and Henry Bausher of the class of 1857 were its founders. They continued their existence in secret until the Commencement in July, 1856, when they "swung" not only the founders but four additional members. This chapter did not restrict its membership solely to those who excelled in their studies, but looked more to the qualities that go to make a generally popular classmate.

The establishment of these two fraternities at the Academy did not absorb all the elements that go towards the making of college fraternities, and the year 1857 saw the organization of a chapter of the Chi Psi fraternity, which made some pretensions to regard simply the social position of the families of the students whom they invited to become members; and to emphasize this a noticeable smartness in the apparel of the student was observed by his fellows almost immediately after he became a member of Chi Psi.

Fraternity conditions as thus observed remained

the same for a period of nearly nine years. During this time these three fraternities had the field all to themselves, and did about at they pleased. Their control was considerably felt in college politics. With the opening of the Free Academy there had been at once organized two literary societies known as the Clionian and the Phrenocosmian, the officers of which were elected by the members. Public debates and public literary exercises were annually given at some public hall; and the debaters and orators for these exercises were also elected by the members. Naturally the fraternities would frequently control the election to these positions, rarely giving the students who were not members of the fraternities any representation. This condition could not go on forever, and so at the election for the orators to take part in the literary exercises to be given in the spring of 1866 at Irving Hall, much to the astonishment of the fraternities apparently no fraternity man was elected; but on the night of that function a chapter of another fraternity appeared and many of the orators, marshals, and committee men wore its badge. Thus was proclaimed the establishment of the Upsilon chapter of the fraternity of Phi Gamma Delta, the founders of which were Charles H. Smith of the class of 1865, William R. Allen and James C. Hallock of the class of 1866, William H. Clark and Fred L. Underhill of the class of 1869. It "swung out" with a membership of fifteen after having kept its existence a secret for more than six months.

THE DEPARTMENT OF GREEK.

The Phi Gamma Delta up to this time had been a distinctively Western and Southern fraternity, its chapters being located in the South and Southwest, while the other three fraternities were distinctively Eastern institutions. It can therefore readily be understood that the new fraternity on account of the manner in which it had made its debut, met with much opposition from the older fraternities, and every effort was put forth by them to refuse it recognition. Its members were at once dubbed "Fee Gees," their right to send representatives to the editorial board of the society annual the *Microcosm* was disputed, and for a time things waxed warm; but as is almost always the case this so-called persecution only helped to establish the "Fee Gees" more firmly, and it was finally deemed best by the other three that Phi Gamma Delta should be considered in the fold.

Heretofore the question of membership was one which had been easily determined: it was generally understood that certain men would go to Alpha Delta Phi, others to D. K. E., and still others to Chi Psi. But on the advent of the "Fee Gees" the situation was entirely changed and the "rushing" for members became a serious and difficult piece of work; it was done secretly, so secretly that very often the other fraternities were not aware of the so-called rushing of a student until he appeared in college with his badge of membership. Very often the proposed candidate was pledged while still attending some preparatory school, and the issuing of the college register was watched for eagerly so that the field of contest might be transferred from the college halls to the home of the intended member. Not alone was this secrecy observed in the rushing of members: the time and place of meeting of the four fraternities were kept a profound secret and everything was done to mystify those without the pale. In 1874 a chapter of the so-called anti-secret fraternity Delta Upsilon was organized, but it had only a short-lived existence, surrendering its charter in 1879. In the meantime the chapter of the Chi Psi had given up its charter when its representation in the class of 1872 graduated. Almost sixteen years after the establishment of the Upsilon Chapter of Phi Gamma Delta, the Theta Delta Chi established one of its charges, and it still continues to maintain with the other three fraternities its existence at the College. In 1884 a chapter of the Phi Delta Theta was organized, but it also had but a short existence at the College. There have been many local secret fraternities established from time to time, but their existence rarely continued for a longer period than four years.

Many of the students who were selected by these fraternities have attained some distinction in the professions that they followed, and reflect much credit upon the fraternity in whose chapter hall they may have received their first inspiration to follow a calling which has led to their success in life.

Songs of C. C. N. Y.

Songs of C. C. N. Y.

Henry E. Jenkins, '75

WHENE'ER and where'er the College Boy foregathers, he shows his pure delight in living by bursting into melody. Even his cheer that thrills the benches at the great games is rhythmical and he sings, as the bird sings, for such his nature is.

The college song of to-day is an evolution from the old English drinking choruses, the eighteenth century glees, and last, but not least, the songs of the German universities and their corps. *Carmina Collegensia* may be divided in two great classes—general and local. The general are the common property of all colleges, and, though attempts are made here and there to localize with new lyrics, yet so strongly wedded are melody and words that such attempts are mainly vain and fleeting. Shining examples of such are "Lauriger Horatius," "Integer Vitæ," and "Gaudeamus Igitur."

There are, however, many old melodies which are themselves general and classic, but to which the words are not so strongly attached. These form the bulk of the earlier local college songs; but the tendency is growing to use the popular song of the day as to air, while the words express the local atmosphere of the college. The burden of the college song has always been Wine, Woman, and Song, while to-day has been added the glorification of the various athletic teams.

President Hadley of Yale says that the great American college song remains yet to be written, though he claims that "Old Nassau" of Princeton approaches nearer perfection than any other.

Where, however, in all this stands C. C. N. Y.? What has she done and wherein has she done it? The lack of dormitory life and the immediate contact of college and home would seem to militate against any great result. The community of interest arising from the total dispersion of home ties and the welding of boyish friendship without a single outside disturbing element are great factors in the production of the local college songs; and if C. C. N. Y. had failed to produce any result the failure could easily be excused. But she has not so failed. Despite most unfavorable circumstances she has given to the college world songs that could well be compared with those of other institutions.

It has been difficult to compile a true history of the efforts in this direction. Data have been hard to find and oral tradition has been the greatest dependence.

The first book of songs of which we have any record was published in 1859 under the title of *Sans Souci Songs*.

The Department of History.

It would seem that Sans Souci was a society of the students of that day, and on the copy at hand appears the name of Adolph Werner, June 20, 1859. It was evident that the classics and the French and German languages appealed to the editors, for the authors have written delightful and clever songs in almost every tongue save English. A Latin song opens the ball. It is clever, and signed Chas. L. Balch, '60. Then comes one signed "Free Academy," to the air of "Sheepskin." Is there any one living who could give that air? Then come three original French songs signed "Free Academy." Oh, that modesty had not forbade us to know the real name of that jolly Frenchman! Then comes a truly poetical lyric called the "Song of the Birds," by "Incognitus Quidam, A.M." This we know now to be our dear friend of long ago Professor Charles E. Anthon. This we must give, and hope that it may be sung. Some academic composer should fit this to appropriate music, for it would be still a great song for alumni gatherings.

SONG OF THE BIRDS.

While on the board our glasses ring,
And eyes look bright and hearts grow tender,
Old Academia we 'll sing,
And all who honor and defend her;
"Fröhlich und Frei," in this our day,
We 'll think on those who 've gone before us,
And chant their praise in merry lay,
And join in loud and hearty chorus.

To the Birds who 've left their mother's wing,
Though their old nest they rarely come nigh,
To them we drink, and gayly sing:
"Here 's to the health of old Alumni!"

Like us they delved in antique lore,
Shook the rich boughs of the tree of knowledge,
Then set the table in a roar
With all the fun of friends at college;
Like us they pored o'er problems deep,
Sweated at tough examinations,
With Bartlett's puzzles banished sleep,
Made laughing love in long vacations.
Then here 's to the Birds who 've taken flight
From banks of Tiber and Clitumnus,
A health and rousing cheer to-night,
As we drink "Success to each Alumnus."

But now they 're scattered far and wide,
Some dwell in castles, some in attics;
Some preach against sin, lust, and, pride,
Some teach Belles-Lettres, some Mathematics;
And some in wealth already roll,
Amaze Broadway with haughty carriage;
And some have gained their wished-for goal
In chaste delights of holy marriage.
Happy, thrice happy may they prove,
Like old Pomona and Vertumnus,
And little birdlings crown the love
Of every virtuous Alumnus.

As they are now so we shall be;
We think of them with hearts o'erflowing;
The road they 've travelled travel we,
Whither they 've gone we now are going:

To mighty Platform's sacred height,
Whence graduate learning's strong aroma
Sheds influence through the festive night,
And perfume on the great diploma.
Of the Birds who leave their mother's wing,
Seldom their former nest to come nigh,
To them we drink and gayly sing,
"Long life to new and old Alumni!"

Next we find a Graduation Song to "Litoria," written by Asa Bird Gardiner, '59—no less—and a Song of '59 by E. A. Howland, '59. Then again the modest youth who dubbed himself "Free Academy." His song about the "pony" is just as *apropos* to-day to the wretched youth toiling and moiling at his Greek as it was then. It's well worth preserving. Here it is:

THE "LIFE PRESERVER."

There was a class went up and down
To seek a "pony" through the town.

What wretches they who "notes" forsake
Of "ponies" to advantage take.

At last they halt before a stand
Where books are sold as second-hand.

'T is advertised a "right cheap place,"
They enter in with brassy face,

The dusty books they toss around.
But nary "pony" could be found.

Behold them now in blank dismay—
"Must we get 'zero' every day?"

Some noble youth his mind devotes
To translate Greek with only notes.

The morrow sees an eager crowd,
Whilst one among them reads aloud.

Their warmest thanks the class outpour,
And praise him for his classic lore.

Then out speaks one: "Here 's joy to all!
I met a tutor in the hall;

"He says a manuscript they pass,
A legacy from class to class."

Thus we obtain the precious prize
Which neither love nor money buys.

No weary brain with labor racks,
But yet there comes the constant "max."

DEDUCTUM.

Then long live ponies great and small,
Who rides them well will never fall.

If ponies fail, and notes won't do,
Get manuscripts or "fizzle through."

The remainder of the book is made up of the songs of Yale, Harvard, etc., with a few old popular favorites such as "Cheer, Boys, Cheer!" Does n't that last bring back boyhood days to the old timers? How we lustily shrieked those inspiring words in every grammar school in old New York in the '60's and '70's. Never again for us!

This little book *Sans Souci* was a credit to the men of C. C. N. Y. of that early date. It showed the

THE DEPARTMENT OF NATURAL HISTORY.

beginning of a healthy, manly college spirit and the commencement of our college singing.

The next song-book on record is dated 1866. It is very handsomely bound and a well-set-up volume, being the most elaborate ever presented by C. C. N. Y. It is styled *Songs of the College of the City of New York, published by the Class of '68*. It has for its motto "Music hath charms to soothe the student breast." An aphorism as true to-day as 't was then. We cannot but note how properly, in the preface, the editors recognized that "song is the most pleasant, most refreshing, and least injurious of college amusements."

As usual with the Classic spirit of the day the book opens with the old Latin favorites, and in deference to the "moderns" an original French *chanson*, unfortunately unsigned, shows a knowledge of the *Café Chantant* that is rather apocryphal. Then there is a song signed J. R. S., '68, on the "New Life" and another glorifying '68. There then seem to be several original songs, but as they are not signed, and are more poetry than song, we can no more than allude to them.

Again appears Professor Anthon's "Song of the Birds," but this time it is marked as "Air by Jas. A. Jackson." We have not been able to find out that air. Next, to the air of the great war song "Tramp, Tramp, Tramp," comes the first song of one who in the early '70's was the college poet best known—George A. Baker of '68. Then J. R. S., '68, to the air of

"Duncan Gray" wrote a clever song called "Fortune's Ball," but it was overshadowed by the next—unfortunately not signed. This latter, to the West Point air of "Benny Havens," we ought to sing:

ALMA MATER O!

We're gathered now, my classmates, to join our parting song,
To pluck from memory's wreath the buds which there so sweetly
throng,
To gaze on life's broad, ruffled sea to which we quickly go;
But ere we start we'll drink the health of Alma Mater O!
Oh, Alma Mater O! Oh, Alma Mater O!
But ere we start we'll drink the health of Alma Mater O!

No more for us yon tuneful bell shall ring for chapel prayers,
No more to examination we'll mount yon attic stairs;
Our recitations all are passed—Alumnuses, you know——
We'll swell the praises long and loud of Alma Mater O!

We go to taste the joys of life, like bubbles on its tide,
Now glittering in its sunbeams and dancing in their pride;
But bubble-like they'll break and burst, and leave us sad, you
know,
There's none so sweet as memory of Alma Mater O!

Hither we came with hearts of joy, with joy we now will part,
And give to each the parting grasp which speaks a brother's
heart,
United firm in pleasing words, which can no breaking know,
For sons of York can ne'er forget their Alma Mater O!

Then brush the tear-drop from your eye, and happy let us be,
For joy alone shall fill the hearts of those as blest as we.
One cheerful chorus, ringing loud, we'll give before we go—

The memory of college days and Alma Mater O!
Oh, Alma Mater O! Oh, Alma Mater O!
Hurrah! Hurrah! for college days and Alma Mater O!

Next A.V. P. of '68 threw off a little Latin *jeu d'esprit* which does credit to the Latin of the day even though it were to be sung to the tune of the "King of the Cannibal Islands." Then again the "pony" song appears, and a rattling good class song of '68, and another of '69. There are several evidently original songs which are not signed. Here is one of them that the boys of 1910 could sing:

SHEEPSKIN.

Air—"A Little More Cider, Too."

When first I saw a "sheepskin,"
In Prex's hand I spied it;
I'd given my hat and boots, I would,
If I could have been beside it;
But now th' examination's passed,
I "skinned" and "fizzled" through;
And so in spite of scrapes and flunks,
I'll have a sheepskin, too.

Chorus.

I'll have a sheepskin, too,
I'll have a sheepskin, too;
The race is run,
The prize is won,
I'll have a sheepskin, too.

Green boughs are waving o'er us,
Green grass beneath our feet;
The ring is round, and on the ground
We sit a class complete.

But when these boughs shall shed their leaves,
This grass be turned to hay,
We jolly souls who now are here
Will all be far away. (*repeat twice.*)
In white degrees,
We'll take our ease,
And be Alumni, too.

I'll tell you what, my classmates,
My mind it is made up:
I'm coming back three years from this,
To take that silver cup.
I'll bring along the "requisite,"
A little white-haired lad,
With "bib and fixings" all complete,
And I shall be his "dad." (*repeat twice.*)
And you shall see
How this "A.B."
Will look when he's a dad.

The closing part of the book is devoted to the "Burial Songs" sung when the Free Academy was buried and the College of the City of New York was born. C. O. K., '67, or Charles Kimball, M.D., J. R. S., '68, now known in more stately form as Professor John R. Sim, and G. A. B., '68, the ever-tuneful Baker, these three specially revel in the new-born babe. The King was dead—long live the King.

FUNERAL DIRGE.

We've laid her in the silent tomb,
And placed the sod above her head;

The Department of Philosophy.

Tread softly now, in sorrow bow:
The Free Academy is dead.

For seventeen years while ling'ring here
Her work she did, nor scorned to tread
In lowly paths; but now—alas!
The Free Academy is dead.

And when in future years we meet
With those whom now we often see,
We 'll pledge in silence and with tears
The New York Free Academy.

C. O. K. '67.

CHRISTENING SONG.

Shout the glad tidings! exult till the morn!
The Academy's buried, the College is born!

Students, the story be joyfully telling,
And shout it aloud with music and mirth:
In glory and honor all others excelling
New York City's College now reigns upon earth.

Shout the glad tidings! exult till the morn!
The Academy 's buried, the College is born!

Tell how we waited in sad expectation,
And let the whole world know the sorrowful tale,
How patient we lingered, while Senators faltered,
Till our joyous bright hopes were near ready to fail.

Shout the glad tidings! exult till the morn!
The Academy 's buried, the College is born!

But now in the grave Academia's lying;
And the new-born infant before the world's eye
Shall ever seem stronger, more bright and more glorious,
As the swift-flashing current of time doth roll by.

G. A. B., '68.

CHORUS—THERE IS A TIME.

Air—"Old Hundred."

There is a time for joy to reign,
For sorrow also there 's the same;
Then here let no one either shun,
But harmonize them both in one.

Your sorrow show by digging deep,
By eyes bloodshot for want of sleep;
But then let joy your bosoms swell,
To think she 's gone where good folks dwell.

J. R. S., '68.

This song-book shows a remarkable progress. It was largely original and owed little to other colleges. It indicated a brilliant class of men and a fecundity of rhyme that was far above the average of college verse. One thing is noticeable—a tinge of melancholy permeates the book. The rather foolish humor of a later day is wanting. It is elevated in character and is an index to the after life of the men that brought it forth. They are earnest men to-day—they were earnest then.

From 1866 to 1877 is a long stride. What original work was done in those years appeared in the various college publications, the *Budget*, the *Echo*, the *Collegian*, or in manuscript form was handed from one to the other.

In 1877 George E. Hardy, '78, and E. E. Oudin, '78, approached the writer of this on the subject of a new song-book. Whatever the reason, the writer did not officially participate, but was interested in the publication. The little paper-covered book now before me has the owner's name, "Le Gras," on the cover. I had not seen a copy for twenty-five years. It is a creditable production, though not so elaborately presented as the book of '68. George E. Hardy, as is well known, was afterwards Professor of English at the College. Eugene Oudin went on the stage, and the magnificent baritone of his boyhood days developed into the superb tenor of the McCall opera troupe.

It opens with the class song of '78, very appropriately, to the air of "Joe Hardy." Our old friend the "Life Preserver" now appears signed "Anon." The fact that it was published in 1866 signed "Free Academy" has slipped apart from college knowledge. I would we knew who that gallant soul was, whose song looked just as good in '77 as it had in '66. Peace to him.

The class song of '77, by E. H., '77, is good, and a "Vive L'Amour" for '78 is very stirring. The "Song of the Birds" again appears and it shows how strong its hold was on the boys of those fifteen years.

For the first time the "Son of a Gambolier"[1] appears, and with it Henry E. Jenkins, '75, makes his first appearance.

[1] Some years ago the editor met on shipboard in mid-Atlantic a young officer in the Worcestershire regiment. Apropos of something or other, the editor one day whistled the "Son of a Gambolier." "What's that?" said the officer boy. The editor explained. "Oh, no!" said the Englishman, "that's been the regimental march of the Worcestershire since"—— the editor forgets the prehistoric date.

SON OF A GAMBOLIER.

Once I was a nobby youth,
The girls all called me sweet;
Some said I was too good to live
And pretty enough to eat.
But now I 'm old and seedy grown,
And poverty holds me fast,
The girls all turn their noses up
Whenever I go past.

Chorus.

Come join my humble ditty,
From Tippery town I steer;
Like every honest fellow,
I drink my lager beer;
Like every honest fellow,
I take my whiskey clear;
I 'm a rambling rake of poverty
And the son of a Gambolier.
I 'm the son of a—son of a—
Son of a Gambolier!
I 'm the son of a—son of a—
Son of a—son of a—son of a Gambolier!
Like every honest fellow,
I take my whiskey clear;
I 'm a rollicking rake of poverty,
And the son of a Gambolier.

If I had a barrel of whiskey,
And sugar, three hundred pound,
The college bell to put it in
And the clapper to stir it 'round,
I'd drink to the health of Old New York,
And spread it far and near;

The French Department.

I 'm a rambling rake of poverty,
And the son of a Gambolier.
Chorus.

H. E. J., '75.

The class song of '80 foretells what they 've succeeded in doing, and again appears "The Janitor's Song" from the book of '66.

THE JANITOR'S SONG.

Air—"Song of the Shirt."

With features sallow and grim,
With visage sadly forlorn,
The Janitor sat in the Janitor's room,
Weary, and sleepy, and worn.
'T is a fact! fact! fact!
He sat with a visage long;
And still as he sat, with a voice half cracked,
He sang this Janitor's song:

"Sweep! sweep! sweep!
In dirt, in smoke, and in dust,
And sweep! sweep! sweep!
Till I throw down my broom in disgust.
Stairs, and chapel, and halls,
Halls, and chapel, and stairs,
Till my drowsy head on my shoulder falls,
And sleep brings release from my cares.

"From the very first crack of the gong,
From the earliest gleam of daylight,
Day after day and all day long,
Far into the weary night,

It 's sweep! sweep! sweep!
  Till my broom doth a pillow seem;
Till over its handle I fall asleep,
  And sweep away in my dream.

"O students of high degree,
  (I scorn to address a low fellow)
O Seniors most reverend, potent, and grave,
  (In the words of my Uncle Othello)
My story 's a sad one indeed,
  Notwithstanding your laughter and sport;
My life is naught but a broken reed,
  And my broom is my only support."

With features sallow and grim,
  With visage sadly forlorn,
The Janitor sat in the Janitor's room,
  Weary, and sleepy, and worn.
It 's a fact! fact! fact!
  He sat with a visage forlorn,
And still as he sat, with a voice half cracked,
  He sang the Janitor's song.

Next comes one which is sung to this day and yet was the result of an accident. It was the night before the Senior examination in Higher Mathematics. A poor student had worked for hours endeavoring to make up what he had omitted to do during the term. Just before daylight, worn and weary, his brain filled with the nomenclature at least if with nothing else of the science, he scribbled a few stanzas in contempt of what he was doing.

A few days later, when called on for a song, he

handed this out. It touched a tender chord in each sad breast, was adopted as a class song, and was sung by the class of '75 at its introduction to the alumni.

FAREWELL, YE COTANGENT!

Farewell ye cotangent, cosecant, cosine!
All the joys of Ecliptics we now must resign;
In the sphere of the wide world we 're going to soar,
And the old Equinoctial shall know us no more.

Chorus.

Right ascensions, declinations, zenith distances too,
With polar co-ordinates we 're entirely through;
Our hard work with Compton is over and done,
And we don't care a —— for the spots on the sun.

Heliocentric, geocentric, and annual parallax,
Have stuffed our brains full with their horrible fax (facts);
But fill up your glasses and all drink away,
And keep up your drinking for a mean solar day.
Chorus.

Occultations, eclipses, and transits as well
Have cast o'er our poor brains their magical spell;
But now we 've made a transit, and from college are free,
And we leave every planet to its own majesty.
Chorus.

The moon is no longer an object to us,
For the transit of Venus we don't care a cuss:
Our fingers we snap in the face of the stars,
And we heed not Jew-peter, nor Venus, nor Mars.
Chorus.

H. E. J., '75.

The "Graduation Song" of Colonel Gardiner" 59,

again appears. This also seems to have hit the boys from '59 to '77. So here it is:

GRADUATION SONG.

Air—"Litoria."

Once more our College Halls we throng,
Swee de la wee dum bum,
To echo our sad parting song,
Swee de la wee dum bum;
And greet the mates we think most dear,
Swee de la wee chu hi ra sah,
With hearty grasp and friendly cheer,
Swee de la wee dum bum.

Chorus.

Litoria, Litoria, swee de la we chu hi ra sah,
Litoria, Litoria, swee de la we dum bum.

Five years of pleasant toil and strife
Have filled the sum of student life,
Which soon on life's tempestuous sea
Will live alone in memory.

Then sound each voice in heartfelt strain,
We 're linked by fond affection's chain,
Which in the years of swift-winged fate
Shall turn our thoughts to Seventy-eight.

And when in after years we meet,
At York, sage Learning's chosen seat,
Sweet mem'ries to our hearts will come
Of days once passed in College Home.

A. B. G., '59.

The book winds up appropriately with the firmly established if not particularly poetical

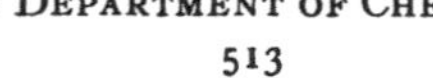

THE DEPARTMENT OF CHEMISTRY.

HERE 'S TO N. Y. COLLEGE.

Here 's to New York College,
Drink it down, drink it down!
Here 's to New York College,
Drink it down, drink it down!
Here's to New York College,
For it 's there we get our knowledge,
Drink it down, drink it down,
Drink it down, down, down.

Balm of Gilead, Gilead,
Balm of Gilead, Gilead,
Balm of Gilead, way
Down on the Bingo farm.

We won't go there any more,
We won't go there any more,
We won't go there any more,
Way down on the Bingo farm.

Bingo, Bingo,
Bingo, Bingo,
Bingo, Bingo,
Way down on the Bingo Farm.
B–I–N–G–O.
We won't go there any more.
We won't, etc.

In 1881 the editors of the *Mercury*, then just founded, published two editions of *Songs Which Every Student Knows, or Ought To.* The little gray pamphlets contain nothing which does not appear in earlier song-books.

The next song-book we can find is called the *C. C.*

N. Y. Song-Book and is dated 1886. It was compiled and edited by Lewis M. F. Haase and Charles K. Johansen.

This is almost a pamphlet, and opens with what the last song-book closed with "Here 's to N. Y. College." It contains but little original work—one "Polly Wolly Doodle," signed J., and a song to C. C. N. Y. by T. Baumeister, '87."

There 's the "Parting Ode of '84" by Julius Mayer, '84, and the "Parting Ode of 85" by George B. McAuliffe. Larremore's "C. C. N. Y." again appears, but the author is lost in the shuffle and it appears as anonymous. The class ode of '88 is by F. C. D., '88, but the remainder of the books is made up of old-time choruses.

The last book we have been able to see was also called the *C. C. N. Y. Song-Book.* It was published in 1889 by E. G. Fischlowitz, William Abraham, and E. G. Alsdorf of the class of '89. It opens with a dignified and impressive song by D. A. H., '90, which should be preserved:

SONG OF THE COLORS.

Our country's stripes and stars,
Its azure sky and bars,
These we adore.
This theme sublime and grand,
Rings now from strand to strand,
Re-echoes o'er the land,
"Flag of the free!"

There, joining hand and hand,
Savage and white man stand—
Flag of our State.
Emblem of law and peace,
Justice and right for each,
In home and school then teach,
Thy godly word.

Back o'er thy early years,
Founded 'mid hopes and fears,
Proudly we gaze.
At thy great work to-day,
Our nation looks and says,
"Shine on, ye purple rays,
In future days."

Join then this triune there,
Together float in air,
Our flags on high.
Liberty, wisdom, law,
Be watchwords as of yore,
Guide thee forevermore,
C. C. N. Y.

T. Baumeister's "C. C. N. Y." again appears, but the book is mainly a brief compilation of old college choruses. A few selections found in the earlier books are presented; the authors, however, are seemingly lost. There 's a "Graduation Song," but it 's the one written by Asa Bird Gardiner of '59. The "pony" song of the earlier books appears unfathered and Henry E. Jenkins, '75, is represented by the "Steady on the Bobtail," but his memory is forgotten and the verses are nameless.

These are all the song-books we have been able to find, but many of the best songs of the College have been written for publication in the various periodicals that have risen and fallen until the *Mercury* has now established itself securely. Such temporary publicity as these journals offered the aspiring lyrist was usually of briefest character; but the following song by Emile A. Huber of '77 is too good to be lost:

SONG OF '77.

By Emile Andrew Huber, Class Poet.

To the tune of "So leb' denn wohl, du altes Haus."

There comes a murmur from the sea;
It strangely calls for you and me.
Our turn has come—we hear it tell;
Farewell, you yet that wait,—farewell.

Our turn has come, we must away;
To where, for what—no man can say.
We leave the port, we make the main;
And, scattering, may not meet again.

But be we strong, and be we stout
To dare the dark and scorn the doubt.
High let a mighty hope upswell,
And cheerly ring the last farewell.

Then fare you well, old guardian hall,
And fare you well, my comrades all;
For weal or woe, for fair or fell,
God speed us all—farewell—farewell.

Here is a very bright little bit which appeared

The Department of Drawing.

anonymously in the *Mercury* at the time when under direction of Professor Doremus, the city authorities covered the obelisk in the park with paraffine to preserve it from the weather:

THE LAMENT OF THE OBELISK.

I am crumbling, Egypt, crumbling
  In this climate of the free,
And I grumble as I crumble,
  That they severed you and me.

And my tenderest thoughts go outward
  To those centuries the while
That I stood in perfect beauty
  And adorned the wending Nile.

Gentle breezes kissed my forehead,
  Fragrant waters laved my feet,
And I held the graven secrets
  With a vigilance complete.

But these sacrilegious moderns
  Saw the product of thy skill,
And their curious disposition
  Nerved a never-conquered will.

I was brought across the ocean
  And erected here to be—
Oh, the shame of my condition:—
  Just a curiosity.

I am crumbling, Egypt, crumbling,
  Of my shame, accept this sign—
And they 're painting me, O Egypt,
  With some horrid paraffine.

Wilbur Larremore, '75, and above all Lewis Sayre Burchard, '77, have been prolific contributors to the College poetical life. Burchard's work has been largely for alumni gatherings. The Fabregou dinner, the Compton jubilee, and alumni meetings have been enlivened by his witty and brilliant fancies.

This is a little "Marching Song" that ought to be sung by all the boys. The air is taken from a hymn much sung in the public schools in former years and perhaps to-day, and based upon the refrain "Venite Adoremus" of a mediæval Latin hymn, "Adeste Fideles."

SERENADE MARCHING SONG.

Refrain.

Venite ad Doremus
    Et Vinum!
Omnes nunc cantemus
    On a bum.

Eboraci Collegio
    Bibendum!
Gilead-Gileadi
    Balsamum! *Refrain.*

In arbore sederunt
    Nigræ tres
Et "Caw, caw, caw!" clamarunt
    Cornices. *Refrain.*

Non panem unquam damus
    Cum una
Maritimi piscis
    Pilula. *Refrain.*

Prop' insulas Canary
  Postremum
Tristissime fumavi
  Cigarum. *Refrain.*

O veni, hospes, imple
  Pateras;
Noct' hac gaudeamus,
  Sobri' cras. *Refrain.*

Ad urbe Tipperari
  Gressus sum;
Filii gambolieri
  Filius sum. *Refrain.*

In ripa canis; rama
  In aqua.
Feminæ, valete!
  Upida! *Refrain.*

L. S. B., '77.

Of the following efforts of Burchard's, the Fabregou verses and the Kiplingesque lines about Compton are not songs, but they are printed here because we love the professors. "A Jubilee Song for '53" and "The Compton Jubilee" should be sung while the College stands and the boys have throats.

LINES READ AT THE FABREGOU DINNER, MAY 27, 1904.

(The "Ancients" of the Class of '77 had Professor Fabregou for only one hour in their entire College course.)

I sit upon the Boulevards
  And hear the flaneurs "parley-voo,"

And pass a few remarks myself—
(I've had an hour with Fabregou.)

The *maître d'hôtel* with bow *superbe*
Hands me *un magnifique* "menoo";
I pick *bifstek* without mistake—
(I've had an hour with Fabregou.)

I walk upon the Norman strand
And gaze in "eyes of Breton blue";
In course of time I hold her hand—
Thanks to that hour with Fabregou!

On Fourvière's cathedral'd height
I breathe these words: "*Je suis à vous!*"
And other things as pertinent—
Grace à cette heure de Fabregou!

"*L'heure verte*" we know—the shading trees,
The *frappéd* absinthe's opal'd hue,
The chat beguiling reveries,
And memories drifting over seas
Back to that hour with Fabregou.

But best this golden hour, dear friend,
When, rallying here for love of you,
While tables ring from end to end,
In tears and cheers old comrades spend
This last great hour with Fabregou.

THE TALE OF THE JUBILOOTIONER.

(AFTER TIPPLING.)

(A Variation on Kipling's "Soldier an' Sailor Too," *The Seven Seas.*)

A-walking away from the Arion Club the night of the Jubilee,
I passed a jovial elderly gent a-cheering for '53.

THE DEPARTMENT OF MATHEMATICS.

He was sailing along both sides of the road, and I said to him, "Who are you?"
Says he: "I 'm a Jubilootioner, and to-night 's the Jubiloo!
"I 'm one of the Class of '53—there was n't no '52.
"There 's nothin' alive that 's older 'n us;—we 're Noah's original crew.
"We 're what you call semi-Centurions, and to-night 's the Jubiloo!

"We 've been floatin' around this small round earth a matter of fifty years;
"There 's me, and John Hardy (you've heard of *him?*), The Banta, and Jimmy Steers;
"And the Little Professor, in honor of whom they're giving this Jubiloo;—
"(For he 's our Compton, our competent Compton, scholar and gentleman too.)
"*He 's* the semi-Centuriest one o' the bunch—the cause of the whole Hurroo.
"There 's nothing too good for *him*, I say—we gave 'im the grand bazoo.
"He 's our hyperest, superest graduate—scholar and gentleman too.

"I saw him a-sittin' in Chellborg's once, in front of a large round bun,
"A-stowin' in lunch at half past five, as if it were half past one.
"He'd been foolin' 'round after hours a bit, a-pullin' some engineers through.
"(Oh! that's our Compton, our competent Compton—always something to do.)
"He can't leave off when he once begins—(and *that 's* where he differs from you!)
"His daily job runs from yesterday till day-after-tomorrer at two.
"He 's a kind o' perpetsh 'l-tuitioner, puttin' post-graduates through.

"I called at the President's Office once, when I heard that they'd
made him Prex—
"'A committee of one from '53 to convey the boys' respects;
"Said they: 'You'll find him around the place; he ain't much
here on view;
"(For he's our Compton, concomitant Compton—Professor and
President too.)
"'He may be up in the North-East tower a-peekin' his telescope
through;
"'Or down in the Workshop showing mechanicals how to fashion
a screw.'
"He's a sort of a super-Professident—Professor and President too.

"He's a good pedestriosopher, and can do his forty mile;
"And a pianisticophysicist, and plays Chopin in style;
"Anon he's off to report an eclipse, or a transit of Venus to view—
"For he's our Compton, our computating Compton—(him and
his logari'ms too!)
"He'll give you, in mathematical terms, the cause of the rain-
bow's hue;—
"It's a wave-length's somethin' or other squared that makes it
yellow or blue.
"He's a telesco-microscopical chap—and full of calculi too.

"I took a vacation with him one year—a sort of a woodland
tramp—
"There was me, and Steers, and Charley Holt;—and he 'took
us into camp.'
"He caught all the trout and made the camp and paddled the
whole canoe,
"For he was our Compton, our camp-locating Compton—a sage
and a hatchet-man too.
"The trees had lamp-post signs for him; with guides he'd 'ave
nothing to do;

The Department of English.

"And I thought, if he died, in the woods so wide, how the deuce could we ever get through?
"He's an Adirondackicographer—guide and philosopher too.

"No matter what subject you tackle him on, from tennis to literatoor,
"When he ain't a professional up to the hilt, he's an A–1 amatoor;
"He can *hablar* in Spanish, and *sprechen* in *Deutsch*, and of course he can 'parley-voo';
"For he's our Compton, our comprehensive Compton, an old and a young man too.
"He handled a Cuban cocoanut ranch, and pulled the whole shootin' match through;—
"(Just then he was Compton, non-combatant Compton—he *had* to keep out of the stew.)
"And he's climbed an Alpine summit or so, when he'd nothing else to do;
"He's a multiple-poly-ability-man—there's *nothin'* that feller can't do!

"But when the College, for all her knowledge, was sadly in want of a site,
"Non-combatant Compton turned combatant Compton, and sailed right into the fight;
"He proved our centre of gravity moved to Convent Avenoo;—
"For he was our Compton, Committee-man Compton, puttin' the Buildin' Bill through.
"And whether it's on St. Nicholas Heights or Lexin'ton Avenoo,
"If ever there's work for a loyal son of our Mother Dear to do,
"You can count on our Compton, our competent Compton—for Captain, Mate, or Crew."

A JUBILEE SONG FOR '53.

Air :—"Jolly Dogs."

Some four and fifty years ago the old Academee
Set up in biz with a noble band, the Class of '53.

Chorus.

For the '50's were so jolly, oh! so jolly, oh! so jolly, oh!
The '50's were so jolly, oh! for the Class of '53.
They Bohned,—they cribbed,—
They flunked, ha! ha! they flunked, ha! ha!
They Bohned,—they cribbed,—
O! just like you and me.
Jubilee! Jubila! (3 times)
La, la, la, la, la, la, la, etc.
SLAP! BANG! here they are again, here they are again, here they are again.
SLAP! BANG! here they are again.
Hurrah for '53!

When Compton was an undergrad., a kid of 5 foot 3,
He scooped most everything in sight, but the Valedictoree.

Chorus.

For he always seemed so stoojus, oh! so stoojus, oh!—so stoojus, oh!
For *he really was* so stoojus, oh! in good old '53.
No Bohns!—No cribs!—no flunks!—OH! NO! no flunks—OH! NO!
All 10's—no 9's—for little A. G. C.
Jubilee! Jubila! (3 times)
La, la, la, etc.
FRESH! SOPH! Bully little man! Bully little man! Bully little man!

Chellborg's.
Fifty years of pie and coffee.

STRAIGHT THROUGH! Bully little man,
Of the Class of '53.

So when his teachers turned him out, up spoke a bold Trustee:
"We'll enter him for a tutorship to train for the Facultee."

Chorus.

And the Tutor tutored very well, so very well, so very well,
And the Tutor tutored very well
In Ancient Historee.
He taught———so much—
They made him Prof, they made him Prof—
He taught———so much,
In the good old Facultee.
Jubilee! Jubila! (3 times)
La, la, la, etc.
TOOT! PROF! Bully little Prof! Bully little Prof! Bully little Prof!
TOOT! PROF! Bully little Prof!
In the good old Facultee.

Now after fifty glorious years of high astronomee,
They put him in the Prex's chair to round up Naughty Three.

Chorus.

And he takes it all so easy, oh! so easy, oh! so easy, oh!
He takes it all so easy, oh! wherever he may be.
And now—for a change—we call him Prex:—we call him Prex,
And now—by Jove! a fine little Prex is he!
Jubilee! Jubila! (3 times)
La, la, la, etc.
PREX! PROF! Both of 'em at once; both of 'em at once; both of 'em at once.

PREX! PROF! Both of 'em at once.
And a tip top "both" is he!

Stand up, stand up, ye silvertops o' the Class of '53,
And hear us, ere we say Good Night, hurrah for Prexy C.!

Chorus.

May he always be so jolly, oh! so jolly, oh! so jolly, oh!
May he always be so jolly, oh! wherever he may be.
Three cheers! Three cheers! Hurrah, hurrah! Hurrah, hurrah!
Three cheers! Three cheers! Hurrah for Prexy C.!
Jubilee! Jubila! (3 times)
La, la, la, etc.
SLAP! BANG! Hit 'er up again! Hit 'er up again! Hit 'er up again!
SLAP! BANG! Hit 'er up again!
Hurrah for A. G. C.!

THE COMPTON JUBILEE.

Air: "Marching through Georgia."

When we went to College, boys, a sandy little man
Taught us that the universe was built on Bartlett's plan;
All our heads could ever hold left off where his began:
Compton, our Compton forever!

Chorus:

Hurrah! Hurrah! From eighteen fifty-three,
Hurrah! Hurrah! 'Way down to "Naughty-three,"
For fifty years of solid work we sing the Jubilee
Of Compton, our Compton forever!

He taught us how the waves of sound came booming through the air;
He taught us all the coy delights that lurk in "¶ r^2";

Alfred G. Compton.

Acting President of the College, 1902–1903.

He never threw no tens around, but always marked us fair,
Did Compton, our Compton forever!

Chorus:

Hurrah! (hip) Hurrah! (hip) The old Academee!
Hurrah! (hip) Hurrah! (hip) The good old Facultee!
Doremus, Woolf, and Werner dear, and likewise Dochartee
And Compton, our Compton forever!

We seen him work the panel-game, explaining of the skies;
We seen him at the bakery, consuming cakes and pies;
He was a wise Professor once—they made him superwise,—
Compton, our Compton forever!

Chorus:

Hurrah! Hurrah! Hurrah! for Prexy C.!
Hurrah! Hurrah! The pride of '53!
He taught the boys for fifty years, so now it's Jubilee
For Compton, our Compton forever!

We'll have a new Commander soon to lead us in the fight,
When Alma Mater takes her stand on yonder castled height;
But fifty years he's been in front—we'll cheer for him to night
For Compton, our Compton forever!

Chorus:

Hurrah! (hip) Hurrah! (hip) Hurrah! for A. G. C.!
Hurrah! (hip) Hurrah! (hip) We shout his Jubilee!
There's fifty years of solid work been done for you and me
By Compton, our Compton forever.

This covers the song work of C. C. N. Y. as revealed by its published works. It is to be hoped that some one will compile and edit what has been produced since 1890, and with what is known from the past one good big creditable song book could be made for the use of future generations of C. C. N. Y.

Adspice

The College of the Present

The College of the Present

John Huston Finley, President of the College

"THERE is an instinctive sense," says Emerson in his essay on *Politics*, "that the highest end of government is the culture of men, that if men can be educated, the institutions will share their improvement and the moral sentiment will write the law of the land." That instinctive sense has found splendid expression in the State universities, and notably in this the first of municipal colleges. Whatever the shortcomings of democratic government in States or cities may be, there is reason for abiding hope so long as the citizens of these States or cities give sincere, intelligent, and generous support to institutions for the culture of men.

And this—the culture of men—is distinctly the object of our College; it is not to make doctors and lawyers, nor even teachers, writers, and scientists; it is first of all to give young men, through guidance and discipline, access to the riches of the race's experience, not for the mere earning of a livelihood but for the ennobling of life, and then to beget or strengthen in them the will to bring that enriched life to the bettering of the life of the community, the State.

I have often made this summation of its functions: to teach men the truth, to teach them how to tell it, and then develop in them the desire always to speak it; because there are many men who cannot tell the truth for one at least of three reasons: either they do not know it, or knowing it do not wish to tell it, or knowing it and wishing to tell it know not how. So I have written under our old, fine motto, another: "Vir, Veritas, Vox,"—the man, the truth, and the voice to speak it.

But in what is this our College peculiar, distinctive, among the colleges, in its aim, character, or scope?

First, it is the only great urban institution of pure collegiate type in this country. The American college has, as a rule, been planted and nourished in the quiet of the country, or has, in its growth, been surrounded by village, town, or small city. But with the development of the great cities has come the need of the urban college, since thousands of young men and women would be deprived of all chance of a higher education, except for such provision. The country college is no less needed now than in the past, but for the reason that the future of this democracy is increasingly dependent upon the great urban populations, it is of increasing importance that these should be informed of that spirit and intelligence which it is

John H. Finley

the mission of the college to help bring. There is now a university in every great city, but our College is unique in that it is the only urban institution of purely collegiate character and aim—and it is one of the largest of the class of colleges.

Second, it is the only higher educational institution supported entirely by a city. Many States with a population varying from a few hundred thousand to four millions provide a collegiate (and even professional) training wholly or partly at the public expense, but New York City is the first of all the cities to make such provision, a provision more generous than is made by any other city of the world, though it is exceeded by many of our States of smaller population.

Third, it sends out a larger proportion of its graduates to teach in the public school than any other college of liberal arts and sciences. This gives it a peculiarly important function in the city's life, for there is no higher service that it can perform for the city than thoroughly to train in body, mind, and spirit the men who are to be in turn the teachers of the city's youth.

Fourth, it maintains its own preparatory department and so has under its immediate supervision the training of most of the students who enter the College. This plan has great advantages in that there is no waste or loss of time. The College is one of the few institutions which make it possible for the student to proceed without serious break in his course from the gate of the elementary school to his degree. Whatever disadvantage there is, comes from the association of college and preparatory students in such physical relationship that they must be under one discipline. The growth of the collegiate department will in time make their dissociation practicable. It is to be noted with gratification that the high schools of the city, under the new plan of promotions recently adopted, will enable the student in these schools to conform more nearly to the requirements of the College, and there is reason to expect that the College will in the near future come into closer and more efficient relationship with all the post-elementary schools supported by the city.

These conditions peculiar to the College give it a unique place among the colleges of America. It is a temperate statement that no college has a work at its hands more vital than has this College. Standing at the place where Europe is "stepping up into America," as Mr. Bryce put it on the day when he visited the College, it has a peculiar task and one upon whose efficient doing the maintenance of the ideals of this people in some good measure depends.

But I may not look forward, as I may not recount the unheralded, unostentatious service of those into whose labors we have entered, those men who have met one of the cardinal requirements of the ideal teacher in their "readiness to be forgotten." I must keep to the present.

Annex at Number 209 East Twenty-third Street.

The men's colleges of the day are under great pressure from the demands of the material, the commercial, the so-called practical; but this College is stoutly maintaining its cultural ideals. It gives such electives in the later years of the courses as will let young men go in the direction of certain professions; it has one building devoted to the mechanical arts; it has also the best equipped chemical, physical, and biological laboratories; but the courses in liberal arts and in the foundations of science are dominant. The College, appreciating the temptations, the obtrusiveness of the nearer—the economic—environment, is ever emphasizing the importance of the wider, the environment of the race's highest and farthest progress.

And there are no special students, no special courses. The result is that there is a body of sturdy students who make their college work their chief occupation, though many of them are under such economic conditions as to be obliged to contribute to their own support while studying. There is little dawdling or trifling or dissipating. The day's work is exacting; the sections are kept at such a size that the teacher may know all his pupils and personally guide them; the general mien of the students is serious, perhaps too serious; the teachers make teaching their main productive work. The total requirement is probably not exceeded by any other college. While the College now prescribes substantially the same conditions for admission as other colleges, it requires four years of residence and eighteen credit hours per week through those four years as compared with fifteen in many.

The College has lacked the benefits of campus life. Even daily or frequent assemblies of the entire student body have not been physically possible. But with the removal to the new buildings, some of the advantages of the country, dormitory college will be had. A campus of some size, high above the city, with parks about; a concourse for the gathering of small groups of students, a commons, a gymnasium, and a great hall for daily assemblies will give the students and teachers some of the opportunities for the development of a community life now wanting, and the cultivation of a stronger, more ardent college spirit.

The best word that can be said for our democracy is that which describes the provision which is made for the education and especially the higher education of its youth. There is no nobler conceit of our civilization than that which has expression in our College —an institution through which one generation seeks to make its experiences the disciplines of the next, its best but unrealized hopes the achievements of those who come after. The responsibility that falls to such a body of teachers is great beyond measure, but the opportunity is commensurate with the responsibility. It is a sacred office and task into which they have come. There is no higher ministry. And it is especially fitting that the House of this ministry is set

THE TURRETS AND SPIRES.
An unusual view of the college looking north and west.

on the Heights, above the city, not only that the people may look up to it out of their labors, but that those who teach and study there may ever keep the hopes and the needs of this great city in their eyes and their thoughts. My word is "*Adspice.*"

Prospice

The College of the Future

The College of the Future

Edward Morse Shepard, '69

AND now, the future of this College of the City, of this Cherishing Mother of our own—what is her future to be? Who can tell? Lest you think I dream I hardly dare put into words the full vision which I see, and see clearly and surely, during years which are to come. In her future, the organized City of the future will itself have a great part—the City with its ever and vastly increasing wealth, its steadily improving ideals of public affairs and duties of citizenship overcoming the corruptions and dangers of that wealth, its larger and larger place of power in the American nation, its larger and larger loyalty to education as a crowning civic service and glory. Yes, the City, democratic in the strict equality of the rights and privileges of its citizens, and imperial only in the range and magnitude of its useful beneficences, will help make the future of the College. A second and a still greater share will belong to the spirit of the citizenship of the New York that is to be, to its fiery and avid zeal for the personal strength and might brought by intellectual discipline, by well ordered and seemly knowledge. That zeal already rules the multifarious strains—national, racial, social, religious—which, in this fusing alembic of the metropolis, are now deeply modifying, and, we hope, enriching, the English-speaking stock upon the foundation of which American life is built. Yes, the very characteristics of the race of America's future, that race to be more truly American than any race America has yet known, that race which, in the making of it, is seen at New York as nowhere else, will gratefully support and mould the College of the future. And thirdly, and nobler even than the share in that future due to the City itself or to the intellectual thirst of its coming people, will be the share which moral integrity and patriotism shall have in future scholarship. For they, I profoundly believe, will be the dominating authority over the affairs of our City and our land. There can be with us—and that is well—no sectarian instruction; but all the more for that, it will be a great duty of our part in the future scholarship of America to end the divorcement of the wits from the morals of men. Yes, this College of ours will abide secure in the hearts and convictions of the coming New York because her profoundest teaching shall be that Righteousness exalteth a Nation.

When, sixty years ago, the College was founded, her students came from a city of 450,000 people; to-day they come from a city of 4,150,000 people—

The New College

561

almost ten times as many. Her students to-day, four thousand in number, are more than ten times as many as they were when, in 1853, her first class graduated. Who dares say what will be the population of the city sixty years hence. Long, very long, before the class of 1967 prepare their Commencement, our academic students—even if there were no other reason—must, because the spacious and sightly buildings now almost finished and the terraced site on which they stand will not hold them, go to separate high schools which we may hope will find in the College their true and efficient guardian and guide. Long before the time shall be ripe for President Finley's *emeritus* presidency, the Freshman, Sophomore, Junior, and Senior classes of the College will outnumber any single body of college students in our country or in the world. But it is not her numbers which will then be her glory; rather will numbers represent the noble privilege of her burdens—the wonderful scope of her influence and her duty. Though the College is not to be an university, we mean that no university shall better or more powerfully help and direct American life than shall our College. In that future day we mean that nowhere—the world over—shall what makes up a liberal education, general but not technical, be better taught to the extent to which the young man must learn it if he would turn to the special mastery of any career for which intellectual discipline is necessary. That education will include the languages and literatures of ancient and modern civilizations with all their humanities and gracious inspiration, the rigorous reasonings of mathematics and its beautiful and world-ruling applications, the sciences of mankind and of the earth beneath and the heavens above, the share which the arts of beauty ought to have in the life of the educated citizen, the histories of the living past with lessons to the living present, the fields of government and laws and the economies of man's subsistence, and the reasonings of divine philosophy herself. Within years which some now living will see, St. Nicholas Heights will not hold the students of our College; buildings as great must, for her crowding ranks, be added to those which have now been reared at so much pains and cost. The students of the College as they leave her Senior classes, or sooner perhaps, under compulsion of *res angusta domi*, forego the crowning witness of the bachelor's degree, will overflow into the life of the city, of the State, and of the Nation, so that the American people beyond the Greater New York, no less than the Americans within its borders, shall call her blessed.

If all this, O Brother Alumni, be rhapsody, is it not the rhapsody of truth? If the feet of the alumnus stand truly and firmly on the ground, ought not his head to strike the stars? If we do not overpass in the present of our work and achievements what is wise and sound and within the knowledge and accomplishment of common life, is it not helpful to realize—

though but dimly—the career which, if her children and her friends be faithful to her, as surely they will be, the Almighty offers this College of our service and devotion.

THE END

www.ingramcontent.com/pod-product-compliance
Lightning Source LLC
LaVergne TN
LVHW011249110826
845149LV00001B/80
9781418189068